All About® Reading

The program that takes the struggle out of reading

Level 2

Color Edition

by Marie Rippel

Printed in the United States of America

Color Edition
v.3.2.0

All About® Learning Press, Inc.
615 Commerce Loop
Eagle River, WI 54521

ISBN 978-1-935197-80-5

Editor: Renée M. LaTulippe
Contributors: Samantha Johnson, Renée M. LaTulippe
Graphics: Shanna Behrens, Donna Goeddaeus, Emily F. Johnson, Dave LaTulippe
Cover Illustrations and Design: Dave LaTulippe

The *All About Reading* Level 2 Teacher's Manual is part of the *All About® Reading* program.

For more books in this series, go to www.AllAboutReading.com.

Contents

1 Preparing for Level 2

2 Complete Step-by-Step Lesson Plans

3 Appendices

1

Preparing for Level 2

Let Us Show You!

If you prefer, you can skip the reading in Part 1 (pages 11-32) and let us show you instead! For a complete overview of how to prepare for *All About Reading*, check out our short videos.

Just follow these three easy steps.

Grab a cup of coffee or tea.

Access www.aalp.tv/reading-level-2 on your phone, tablet, or computer.

Let us show you how to get set up for success!

You will only need to do this once, and then you and your student will be all set for the best teaching and learning experience you've ever had!

After watching the videos, rejoin us on page 35 of this Teacher's Manual to start teaching the first lesson.

Gather the Materials

In addition to this Teacher's Manual, you will need the following items:

1. Student Packet

The Student Packet contains:

- *Leap into Reading* activity book
- Phonogram Cards and Word Cards
- Syllable tags
- Stickers for the Progress Chart

2. Letter Tiles Kit or Letter Tiles App

You can use either the physical letter tiles or the Letter Tiles app. See page 27 for guidance in choosing which option to use.

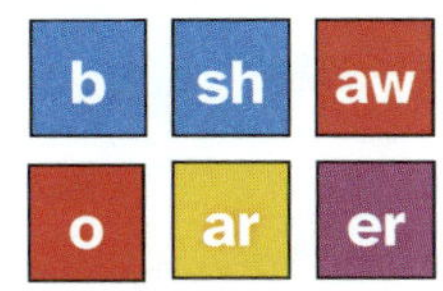

3. Reading Review Box with Divider Cards

The review box is the perfect size to organize your student's flashcards.

4. Readers

- *What Am I?*
- *Queen Bee*

(This Teacher's Manual must be used with the Third Edition or Color Edition of the readers.)

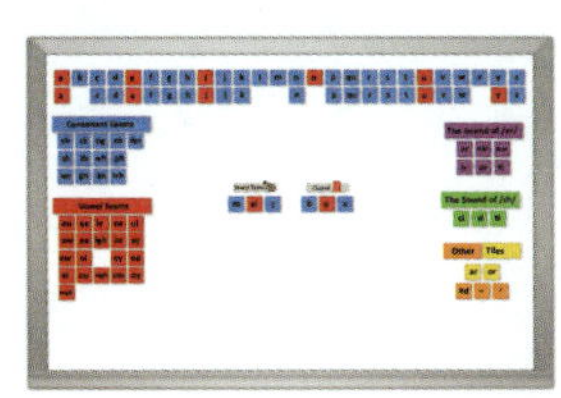

5. Magnetic White Board (Optional)

If you choose to use the physical letter tiles, a 2' x 3' magnetic whiteboard is highly recommended.

6. Common Craft Materials

- Scissors
- Stapler

What You Should Know about This Program

First of all, you can do this! *All About Reading* is a scripted, open-and-go program developed for busy parents, teachers, and tutors who want to teach reading in the most effective way possible. This program doesn't require long periods of study, you don't have to develop your own lesson plans, and you don't have to stress over what to teach next—because everything is laid out for you, step by step. You'll get solid grounding in how to teach reading without being overwhelmed.

Your student will be actively involved in the learning process. This is a truly multisensory program; your student will learn through sight, sound, and touch. Everything is taught in context and your student will apply what he has learned right away. Your student will be engaged in thinking, processing, comparing, and learning.

Students who use the *All About Reading* method tend to feel a sense of excitement in learning. And they should! They are learning how to think, explore, and grow in their abilities. They feel successful as they see continual progress.

There are no gaps in this program. Your student will be taught everything he or she needs to know about reading, so no guessing is required. Each new concept builds upon the previous one, and no steps are skipped.

There are five key components of reading—and our program teaches all of them thoroughly. These five components are:

1. Phonological Awareness
2. Phonics and Decoding
3. Fluency
4. Vocabulary
5. Comprehension

***All About Reading* is a mastery-based program.** As such, the levels don't correspond to grade levels. In mastery-based learning, students master one concept before moving on to a more advanced concept, regardless of age or grade level.

Most importantly, *All About Reading* is committed to results. The *All About Reading* program has a very focused mission: to enable you to teach your student to read while guaranteeing retention and enjoyment. Our approach to reading focuses on enabling students to become confident, fluent readers who can absorb and retain new information.

If you ever have a question as you are teaching, please feel free to contact us at support@allaboutlearningpress.com or 715-477-1976. We're here to help!

Is Your Student in the Right Level?

Be sure your student is comfortable with these concepts before beginning *All About Reading* Level 2.

- ☐ Your student should understand how to sound out words using the blending procedure demonstrated in Appendix C of this Teacher's Manual.

- ☐ Your student should be able to read words with final blends. To test, have your student read the following words.

tent	**bunch**	**dent**	**lost**	**sent**
next	**film**	**help**	**champ**	**milk**

- ☐ Your student should be able to read words with initial blends. To test, have your student read the following words.

stem	**flat**	**brush**	**twin**	**stop**
flap	**drip**	**crab**	**grip**	**fresh**

- ☐ Your student should be able to differentiate between vowels and consonants and understand that every syllable contains at least one vowel. To test, have your student tell you whether each letter below is a vowel or a consonant.

b **a** **e** **t** **h** **r** **o**

- ☐ Your student should have a basic understanding of compound words. To test, have your student read the following words.

sandbox **windmill** **sunset** **cobweb** **chopstick**

Now have your student identify the two smaller words in each compound word.

- ☐ Your student should be able to count syllables. To test, say the following words and have your student tell you the number of syllables in each word. (Note: Your student does not read these words. You will say the words aloud.)

hilltop **duck** **yesterday** **crash** **elephant** **bathtub**

- ☐ Your student should understand the concept of Open and Closed syllable types. To test, have your student read each of the following words and tell you whether it is an Open syllable or a Closed syllable.

me **met** **she** **shed** **we** **wet**

- ☐ Your student should have a basic understanding of plurals. To test, have your student read the following plural words.

stems	**wings**	**wishes**	**acts**
boxes	**chills**	**checks**	**messes**

- [ ] Your student should have mastered the sounds of Phonograms 1-32. These Phonogram Cards can be found in your Level 2 Student Packet. Be sure your student knows all the sounds on each card. Some phonograms have just one sound (h says /h/), while others have two or more sounds (c says /k/ and /s/). For example, if you hold up the Phonogram Card for the letter s, your student should say "/s/–/z/." If you hold up the Phonogram Card for the letter a, your student should say "/ă/–/ā/–/ah/."

- [ ] Your student should be able to read sentences containing one-syllable words with Closed syllables (such as *land*) and Open syllables (such as *she*). To test, have your student read the following sentences.

  Jump from step to step.
  Lend me a hand.
  We can go back up the hill.
  He sang a song with Pam.

How did your student do?

- If your student could easily complete each of these activities, begin with Level 2.
- If just one area was difficult, you can remediate in that specific area.
- If your student needs help in two or more areas, start with Level 1 to build a strong foundation for reading.

Preview the Teacher's Manual

As you flip through the Teacher's Manual, you'll notice that all the lessons are laid out for you, step by step. You'll also notice that there are two types of lessons.

"New concept" lessons. In these lessons, your student will learn new phonograms and new words. You can see an example of a typical "new concept" lesson in Lesson 2 on page 45.

"Read a story" lessons. In these lessons, your student will practice the new concepts taught in the previous lesson by reading a story. Vocabulary and comprehension strategies are emphasized. You can see an example of a typical "read a story" lesson in Lesson 3 on page 51.

The lessons consist of five parts:

1. **Before You Begin.** This cream-colored box contains an overview of the lesson and is meant only for you, the teacher. It never takes more than a few minutes to read it, after which you will be well equipped to teach the lesson confidently.

2. **Review.** Beginning with Lesson 2, you'll give your student a quick review of previously taught concepts. You will need your student's Reading Review Box for this part of the lesson.

3. **New Teaching.** This is the hands-on portion of the lesson. Your student will work with the letter tiles and activity sheets while completing comprehension, vocabulary, and fluency exercises.

4. **Read-Aloud Time.** This section is a friendly reminder to fit in twenty minutes of read-aloud time every day.

5. **Track Your Progress.** At the end of each lesson, you'll record your student's progress on the Progress Chart.

If you are working with a younger student, you may only complete part of a lesson at a time. That's okay! Simply mark your place in the lesson plan. The next day, start your lesson with a quick review and then pick up where you left off.

Don't feel like you must push through an entire lesson in one sitting if your student isn't ready. Do what is best for your student.

Preview the Activity Book

The *Leap into Reading* activity book contains:

- Progress Chart
- Read-Aloud Record
- Activity Sheets
- Warm-Up Sheets
- Practice Sheets
- Certificate of Achievement

The lesson plans in the Teacher's Manual will tell you which pages you need for each lesson. The pages in the activity book are perforated for easy removal.

Let's take a quick look at each part of the activity book.

Progress Chart

The Progress Chart can be found on page 5 of the activity book.

This chart is a motivating part of the lessons for many students because it is a visual reminder of the progress they have made toward reading independently.

Remove the chart on the perforation and decide where to place it. Choose a prominent place like a bulletin board, the refrigerator, the back of a door, or another easily accessible area.

After each lesson has been completed, have your student color in or place a sticker over the next leaf on the chart.

Read-Aloud Record

The Read-Aloud Record can be found on page 7 of the activity book.

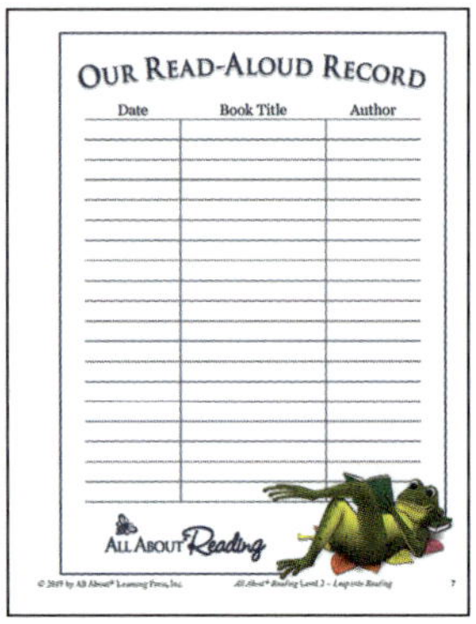

This chart is simply a place to record the books that you read aloud to your student. Toward the end of each lesson, you will be prompted to read to your student for twenty minutes. The daily read-aloud time may seem like a simple part of the reading lessons, but it's actually one of the most important components.

While your student is listening to good books, he'll also be

- gaining important background knowledge on a wide variety of subjects;
- developing a larger vocabulary; and
- hearing a variety of language patterns.

Your student's reading comprehension will be much higher because you've given him these huge benefits through daily read-aloud time.

This list is more for your use than for your student's. Not only is it a reminder of the many books that you enjoyed with your student, it is also great for accountability. If you skip read-aloud time, it will be obvious because of the short list! Aim for a long and varied list of books by the end of Level 2.

Here are some things to think about as you plan ahead for read-aloud time:

- **Figure out the best time of day for your read-aloud time.**
  You might find it easiest to connect read-aloud time to something else that you already do every day. It often works well to schedule it after lunch, recess, or a specific class. If you are a parent, bedtime is a natural time for enjoying books together.

- **Gather a variety of books, both fiction and nonfiction.**
  To keep interest high, look for books related to your student's specific interests and hobbies. You can also stimulate new interests by choosing read-alouds on topics that are completely new to your student.

- **Decide how you will minimize distractions.**
  At home, turn off the TV, computer, and telephone. Clear away competing toys and games. If you have a wiggly student, you can help him concentrate on the story by allowing him to play quietly while you read. Some students will be fine just holding a toy, while others might prefer to build with blocks, knead clay, or color quietly. For some students, it is easier to stay in one place and pay attention to what you are reading if they don't have to remain perfectly still.

Activity Sheets

The activity sheets are very motivating for most kids. They provide a variety of ways to practice the new concepts taught in the lessons. Flashcards and word banks have their place, but it is nice to break out of the "serious" learning and have a little fun applying it!

Take a look at the activity called "Party Monsters Go Shopping" on page 15 of the activity book. When you get to Lesson 1, the lesson plan will prompt you to cut out the monster cards and place them in a pile with the words facing down. Your student will select a monster card, read the word on the back, and decide if the word is a Closed or Open syllable, the two syllable types taught in Level 1. If it's a Closed syllable, she'll put the monster by the closed door. If it's an Open syllable, she'll put the monster by the open door.

If you are working with an older student who doesn't need the additional practice for a certain concept, or who doesn't want to do "kid" activities, feel free to skip that particular activity sheet. But you may find that even adult learners enjoy the mental break that the activity sheets provide.

For the activity sheets, you will need only scissors, a stapler, and a pencil.

Warm-Up Sheets

You can find an example of a Warm-Up Sheet on page 33 of the activity book.

Words Taught in Previous Lesson

trust stunt are you
stomp twist grasp

Phrases

trust me
the best
you are up
swing with the song

stomp with the drums
grasp his hand
you can win

The Warm-Up Sheets are used just before reading a new story and contain words and phrases your student is about to encounter. Although all the words in the stories are completely decodable, these warm-up exercises give your student a little extra practice so he doesn't start reading "cold." Just as warming up our muscles before exercising is beneficial, warming up the brain before jumping right into a story helps your student be more successful.

The illustrations on the Warm-Up Sheets are used during short pre-reading vocabulary discussions.

Practice Sheets

Take a look at the first Practice Sheet on page 19 of the activity book.

New Words

are	you	blend	slept
plump	frost	plant	grunt
trust	shrimp	crust	stomp
blast	stand	blond	crunch
clump	craft	swept	print
spend	branch	grasp	twist
stump	stunt	crept	crisp
grand	spent	stamp	swift

Phrases

has slept	a plump frog
big blast	crisp shrimp
wet frost	swept up
trust him	the cat slept
on a branch	red plant
blond man	stomp and twist

The Practice Sheets give your student practice reading words that reflect newly learned concepts. Most of the Practice Sheets contain four sections: New Words, Phrases, Sentences, and Challenge Words.

The Phrases section includes several phrases of two to five words each. The Sentences section includes short phrases like *The plump cat* and longer sentences like *The plump cat had shrimp.*

This type of practice is called *phrased reading*. Phrasing is important for fluency; fluent readers are able to phrase, or break text into meaningful chunks.

If your student does not need practice with phrasing, feel free to skip the shorter phrases and have your student read just the full sentences.

Over time, the Practice Sheets will help your student move from sounding out words letter by letter to instant recognition of words. This change usually happens gradually, so don't expect perfection at first.

Here are some tips to help you get the most benefit out of the Practice Sheets:

1. **Place the sheet directly in front of your student.**
2. **Read across the page from left to right** to reinforce proper eye movements. Don't read down the columns.
3. **Stop before your student fatigues.** You might not complete the Practice Sheet all in one day, depending on your student's age and attention span.
4. **Would your student benefit from reviewing the Practice Sheet several times?** If so, repeat the exercise several days in a row.
5. **On the other hand, don't overwhelm your student with *too* much practice.** It is important to find the right balance for your individual student. Some students desperately need the practice provided, while others (especially younger students) are better served by reading every other line or every third line.

Preview the Readers

All About Reading Level 2 includes two readers that are 100% decodable.

What Am I?
First used in
Lesson 3

Queen Bee
First used in
Lesson 32

Your student will read one story approximately every other lesson.

The first time a student reads a story is called a "cold reading." The student may read choppily, one word at a time. This is normal because the student is working very hard at decoding many of the individual words. Don't expect smooth reading during the cold reading.

Most students benefit from repeated readings—that is, reading the story a second or even third time. You'll find that during the repeated reading, your student will read more fluently and with better understanding. Since every student's needs will vary, these repeated readings are not scheduled in the lesson plans. Be sure to make time for them!

The Teacher's Manual provides comprehension questions and activity sheets for each story. If you feel your student would benefit from further activities, refer to Appendix J: List of Comprehension Activities.

If your student is having difficulty reading the stories, refer to Appendix N: If Your Student Struggles with the Stories.

Prepare Your Reading Review Box

The Reading Review Box organizes your flashcards so review time can be productive for your student. Every lesson starts with review. Whether you use our custom Reading Review Box or your own index card box, follow the instructions below to set it up.

1. **Place the divider cards in your box.** The divider cards are numbered 1-6 so you can be sure to get them in the correct order. Foam spacers are also provided to allow the cards to stand upright. As you need more room for cards, simply remove a foam spacer.

> If you used *All About Reading* Level 1, your instructions for this first section are a bit different since you already have cards in the Reading Review Box. Simply remove all cards from behind the Mastered dividers. Put a rubber band around them or place in a labeled baggie and store separately.

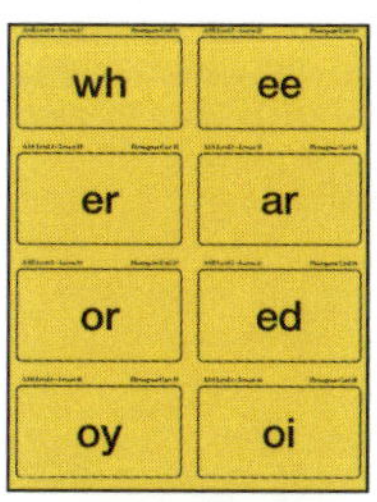

2. **Locate the yellow Phonogram Cards** in the Student Packet. Separate the perforated cards and place them behind the yellow tabbed divider called *Phonogram Cards–Future Lessons.*

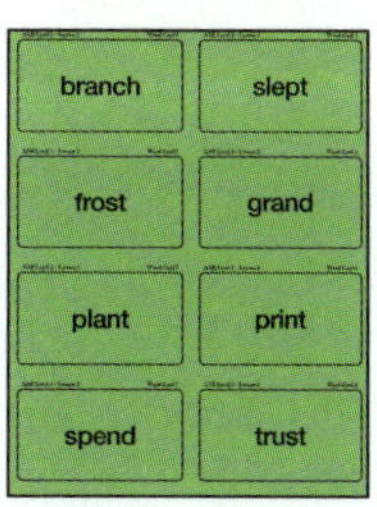

3. **Locate the green Word Cards** in the Student Packet. Separate the perforated cards and place them behind the green tabbed divider called *Word Cards–Future Lessons.*

4. **Preview the Leap Word Cards.** Take a look at Word Card 10. See the frog?

   We use the frog graphic to indicate high-frequency words that either don't follow the normal rules or that contain phonograms that your student hasn't practiced yet. Your student will be "leaping ahead" to learn these words as sight words.

There are thirty-two Leap Words in Level 2, and the first two are taught in Lesson 2. Several techniques will be used to help your student remember these Leap Words:

- The frog graphic acts as a visual reminder to your student that the word is being treated as a sight word.
- Leap Word Cards are kept behind the Review divider in your student's Reading Review Box until your student has achieved instant recognition of the word.
- Leap Words frequently appear on the Practice Sheets.
- Leap Words are used frequently in the readers.
- If a Leap Word causes your student trouble, have your student use a light-colored crayon to circle the part of the word that doesn't say what the student expects it to say. Help your student see that Leap Words generally have just one or two letters that are troublesome, while the rest of the letters say their regular sounds and follow normal patterns.

For the complete list of Leap Words taught in Level 2, see Appendix P.

Set Up the Letter Tiles

Letter tiles are used in every "new concept" lesson to help your student quickly and easily grasp new concepts.

You have the option to use either the Letter Tiles app or the physical letter tiles. Here are some considerations to help you decide between the two formats.

With the Letter Tiles app:

- It's easy to capitalize words.
- You can hear the sounds of the phonograms as you teach.
- No more worries about lost letter tiles.
- Lessons are easy to teach "on the go."
- It's easy to switch between students. Simply select your current lesson in *All About Reading* or *All About Spelling* and you're ready to begin.

The Letter Tiles app has been our most requested product of all time, but the physical letter tiles have devoted fans as well.

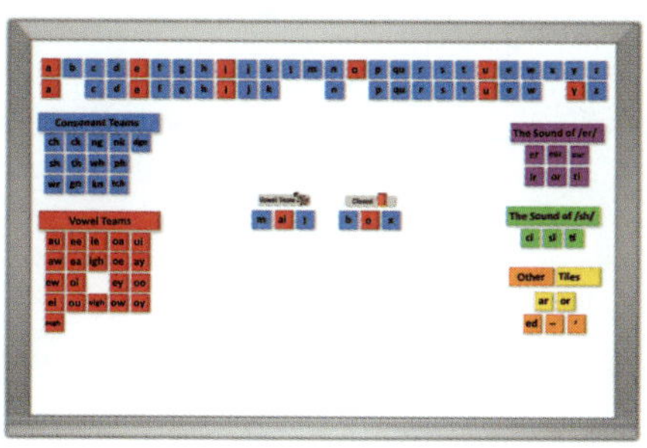

With the physical letter tiles:

- No tablet is required to complete the lessons.
- Larger tiles are easy to read.
- Timeless and traditional educational tool.

Can't decide which tool to use? Consider which one would be most engaging for your student based on his current preferences. For example, does your student prefer colored pencils, or does she like video games? Is your student used to using technology for learning, or is he more comfortable with traditional methods of learning? Does she prefer e-books or paper books?

And don't forget to consider *your* preferences as well. Do you like the larger format of the magnetic white board and physical tiles? Or do you like the more compact nature of the app?

You really can't go wrong with either the app or the physical letter tiles since they both make reading concepts more concrete for your student. Choose one (or both) methods for working with letter tiles.

If You Choose the Letter Tiles App

Visit www.allaboutlearningpress.com/letter-tiles-app to purchase the app for your tablet.

Short tutorial videos are available in the app menu to show you everything you need to know about using the app in your lessons.

If You Choose the Physical Letter Tiles

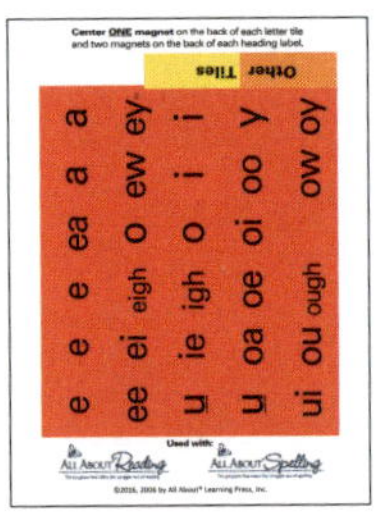

Take out the laminated Letter Tiles sheets. Separate the letter tiles and labels on the perforations.

Apply the magnets to the back of the letter tiles. Stick one magnet on the back of each letter tile and two magnets on the back of each label. (Skip this step if you will be using the letter tiles on a tabletop instead of a magnetic white board.)

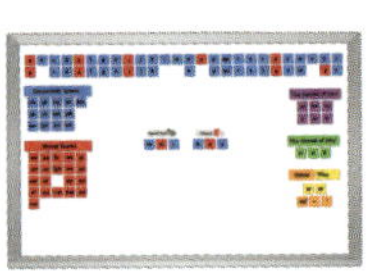

Set aside the following letter tiles for the first lesson. You'll organize them on the next page.

- two sets of letters a to z
- letter tiles ch, ck, ng, nk, sh, th, third s, hyphen
- labels: Consonant Teams, Other Tiles

(If you used Level 1, you already have these letter tiles on your magnetic white board.)

Prepare two small plastic baggies. Label one bag Level 2 and the other bag Levels 3-4. Place the following tiles and labels in your Level 2 baggie:

- wh, ee, er, ar, or, ed, oy, oi, aw, au, ow, ou
- apostrophe tile
- labels: Vowel Teams, Sound of /er/

Put the remaining tiles and labels, including the blank ones, in the Levels 3-4 baggie. Store the baggie in your *All About Reading* tote bag or another safe place.

Set Up Your Magnetic White Board

You'll be using the letter tiles in every lesson. Set up the letter tiles on your magnetic white board as shown below.

a b c d e f g h i j k l m n o p qu r s t u v w x y z
a b c d e f g h i j k l m n o p qu r s t u v w x y z
s

Consonant Teams
ch ck ng
nk sh th

Space for Word Building

Prepare the Syllable Tags

1. **Take out the laminated Syllable Tags sheet.** Separate the syllable tags on the perforations.

2. **Apply the magnets to the back of the syllable tags.** Stick two magnets on the back of each syllable tag. Note that the magnets go on the side with the word on it, not the picture. Store the syllable tags on your magnetic white board for use in the lessons.

Answers to Common Questions about Letter Tiles

What do the different colors mean?

b Blue tiles are consonants and consonant teams.

u Red tiles are vowels and vowel teams.

er Purple tiles are for the sound of /er/.

or Yellow tiles are for Bossy R combinations that don't say /er/.

ci Green tiles are for alternate spellings of /sh/: ti, ci, si.

ed Orange tiles are for miscellaneous symbols and letters.

You'll learn about each category when you get to it in the lessons.

Why are there two different y's?

- Y can be a consonant or a vowel, depending on the word.
- When it is a consonant, it says /y/.
- When it is a vowel, it can say /ĭ/, /ī/, or /ē/.

Why are q and u together on a tile?

Since q is always followed by a u in English words, they are placed together on a single tile.

What will happen with the other letter tiles that are left in my Level 2 baggie?

- Starting in Lesson 19, we will gradually add these letter tiles to the board.
- Keep the baggie in a safe place (such as your reading tote bag) until the tiles are needed.

What if I don't have a magnetic white board?

A magnetic white board makes it easier and faster to set up for your reading lessons, but if you don't have a magnetic white board, you can set up the letter tiles right on your table.

What do all these funny marks and symbols mean?

As a shorthand way to represent the sounds of letters in this Teacher's Manual, we use slashes. For example, /m/ stands for the spoken sound *mmm* as in *monkey*.

You will also see two other sound symbols:

- A straight line above a letter, as in /ā/, represents the long vowel sound. This symbol is called a *macron*.
- A "smile" above a letter, as in /ă/, represents the short vowel sound. This symbol is called a *breve*.

For a complete list of letter sounds and key words, please see Appendix B.

Preview the Letter Sounds

Your student will learn the sounds of letters and letter combinations, called *phonograms*. For example, phonogram t says /t/ as in *tent*. Phonogram sh says /sh/ as in *ship*.

The lesson plans will prompt you to preview the sounds of new phonograms before you teach them to your student. There are three ways you can preview the sounds:

1. **Phonogram Sounds app.** This free app can be used on your computer, tablet, or phone. Go to www.allaboutlearningpress.com/phonogram-sounds-app to download. Simply tap the phonogram to hear the sound.

2. **Letter Tiles app.** If you own the Letter Tiles app, "long hold" on a letter tile to hear the sound(s). (As discussed on page 27, this app has many other features as well, including moveable letter tiles.)

3. **Chart in Appendix B.** Key words are given for each phonogram.

Using the method you prefer, take a moment to preview phonograms wh and ee, which are the first two phonograms you will be teaching in Level 2.

How Much Time Should I Spend on Reading?

Lessons are designed so that you can work at your student's pace. Following are general guidelines.

Spend 20 minutes per day teaching reading.

We recommend spending about 20 minutes per day, five days a week, on reading instruction, but you can adjust this if necessary for early readers or for older remedial students. Short daily lessons are much more effective than longer, less frequent lessons.

It can be helpful to set a timer. When 20 minutes are up, mark the spot in the lesson where you stopped. When you begin teaching the next day, briefly review some of the daily review cards and then begin in the Teacher's Manual wherever you left off previously.

Lessons often take more than one day to complete.

Please know that the lessons in *All About Reading* are **not** meant to be completed in one day.

In fact, some lessons may take a week or more to finish. A number of variables including your student's age, attention span, prior experience, the difficulty of the concept being taught, and the length of the stories all play a part in how quickly a lesson can be completed.

In addition to the lessons, read aloud to your student for 20 minutes per day.

Reading aloud to your student is one of the most important things you can do to promote future reading ability. In fact, it is so important that we've added a reminder at the end of every lesson.

Reading aloud for 20 minutes a day may not seem like a lot, but the cumulative effect cannot be overstated. By reading aloud for just 20 minutes a day over a five-year period, your student will have the advantage of 600 hours of read-alouds. That equates to huge gains in vocabulary, comprehension, and background information.

When you combine 20 minutes of direct reading instruction with 20 minutes of read-aloud time, you are providing your student with the very best opportunity for long-term reading success.

2
Complete Step-by-Step Lesson Plans

Hi there, new friend!
I'm Herman, and I'm so hoppy to meet you.
I'll be working on Level 2 with you! We can pretend
the lessons are lily pads and splash from one to the next.
Besides bouncing, I'm also really good at giving pep
talks, so I hope you'll like studying with me.
See you at the end of Lesson 1!
We're in for a swamp-ful of fun!

Lesson 1 Closed and Open Syllables

Objective

This lesson reviews concepts taught in Level 1 and teaches the Closed and Open syllable types.

You Will Need

- ☐ *Leap into Reading* pages 9-20
- ☐ Phonogram Cards 1-32
- ☐ Closed and Open syllable tags
- ☐ Progress Chart

Before You Begin

If you are new to the *All About Reading* program, have your student take the Placement Test for Level 2 on page 15.

At the beginning of each lesson, you will find a cream-colored Before You Begin section like this one. Review these instructions before you begin the lesson.

The actual lesson plan you will teach to your student begins *after* the Before You Begin section.

We'll start the lessons in Level 2 with a review of the concepts taught in Level 1. **Depending on your student's age and attention span, you may wish to divide this review lesson into two or more sessions.**

If your student finished Level 1 within the last few days and you don't feel that review is needed, you may choose to skip the Review sections and start immediately with the New Teaching section on page 40.

Review Closed and Open Syllables

Although Closed and Open syllables were introduced in Level 1, today will be the first time that syllable tags are used. We'll use syllable tags throughout Level 2 to help your student recognize syllable types, which in turn will help her decode words with greater accuracy.

> Very soon, your student will be learning to read longer multisyllable words, so recognizing syllable types will become doubly important. The foundation we are building at this early stage will allow your student to quickly and confidently decode words like *insect*, *beyond*, and *music* simply by applying her knowledge of Open and Closed syllable types.

Before You Begin
(continued)

A **Closed syllable** ends in a consonant and has a short vowel sound, as in the word *bat*. On the syllable tag, the closed door represents a Closed syllable because the final consonant "closes in" the vowel.

An **Open syllable** ends in a vowel. The vowel has a long vowel sound, as in the word *me*. On the syllable tag, the open door represents an Open syllable because there is nothing after the vowel; there is just "open space."

> To save space in the Teacher's Manual, syllable tags are shown with text only, like this:
>
> **Closed Syllable** **Name Game Syllable**
>
> When you're working with your student, however, you'll use the syllable tags with the graphics that came in the Student Packet.
>
> 
>

Why is knowing the syllable types so beneficial? Let's say your student is reading a story and she comes across the word *craft*. She doesn't instantly recognize the word because she has never read it before. Although the word is unfamiliar, she isn't flustered because she has a method for determining whether the letter a̲ says its long or short sound. She sees that the a̲ is followed by a consonant, which means that it is in a Closed syllable, so the vowel most likely says its short sound. She is able to decode the word *craft* independently and continue reading the story.

For an overview of the remaining syllable types and why they are helpful for decoding, see Appendix D.

Review

Review Phonogram Cards 1-32

Review Phonogram Cards 1-32, which were taught in Level 1. Show the front of the card to your student and have him say the sound(s).

Review
(continued)

If your student could instantly recite all the sounds of the phonograms, file these thirty-two flashcards behind the **Phonogram Cards Mastered** divider in your student's Reading Review Box. If there was any hesitation on the sounds, file those cards behind the **Phonogram Cards Review** divider. Those cards will be reviewed at the beginning of the next lesson.

Review Words from Level 1

"In this first activity, we'll review words that you already know. See how accurately you can read these words."

> **Don't Forget!**
> If you are working with an older student, feel free to skip any of the activity sheets that your student wouldn't enjoy. You can review the words from Level 1 using flashcards, if you prefer.

Feed the Anteater

Remove pages 9-13 from the *Leap into Reading* activity book.

Cut two slits on page 10 as indicated by the dotted lines. Cut apart the word strips. Tape the ends of several strips together to make one long strip. Repeat with the remaining strips.

Take one of the word strips and weave it through the slits. A word and an ant will appear on the anthill, as shown below.

Review
(continued)

Pull the slip up from the back so that one word is revealed at a time. Have your student read the word aloud and then pull the slip to reveal the next word.

Continue until the anteater has "eaten" all the words on the word strips.

Review Plural Words

Build the word *wings* with letter tiles.

Cover the s with your finger.

"We say one *wing*."

"And we say two *wings*."

"*Wings* is **plural** because it means **more than one**."

Build the word *dishes*.

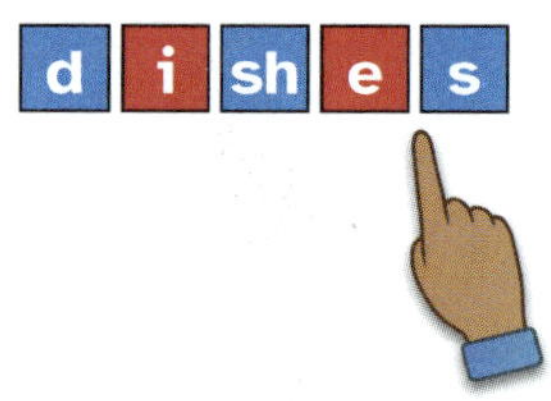

Point to e-s. "Words can be made plural by adding s or e-s."

"I'm going to say a word, and then you'll say the plural version of that word."

"One *drum*, two ______." If necessary, prompt your student to say *drums*.

"One *box*, two ______." *Boxes.*

"One *desk*, two ______." *Desks.*

Review Vowels

"What are the vowels?" *The vowels are a, e, i, o, u, and sometimes y.*

"What is a consonant?" *Any letter that isn't a vowel.*

Review
(continued)

Move the letter tiles a, e, i, o, and u into the workspace.

a e i o u

Point to the a tile. a

"Tell me the sounds of the letter a." */ă/–/ā/–/ah/.*

"Tell me the first sound of the letter a." */ă/.*

"Good. A vowel's first sound is its short sound."

"I will point to a vowel and you will tell me its **short** sound."

a */ă/.*
e */ĕ/.*
i */ĭ/.*
o */ŏ/.*
u */ŭ/.*

"Now tell me the **long** sound of each vowel." Point to each vowel.

a */ā/.*
e */ē/.*
i */ī/.*
o */ō/.*
u */ū/.*

Review the First and Second Syllable Types: Closed and Open Syllables

Build the word *well* with letter tiles. w e l l

"What does this word say?" *Well.*

Point to the e.

"What does this vowel say?" */ĕ/.*

Review
(continued)

"Is there anything after the e?" *Yes, l-l.*

"Good. We say that the e is closed in by the l-l. This is a Closed syllable."

"Is the vowel in this word short or long?" *Short.*

"Right. When a vowel is in a Closed syllable, it usually says its short sound."

Remove the two l's. w e

"What does this new word say?" *We.*

"Is there anything after the e now?" *No.*

"There is 'open space' after the vowel, so we call this an Open syllable."

"When a vowel is in an Open syllable, it usually says its long sound."

Point to the e. "What does the e say in this word?" */ē/.*

New Teaching

Introduce Closed and Open Syllable Tags

Move the Closed and Open syllable tags into the workspace.

"This **closed door** represents a **Closed** syllable."

"This **open door** represents an **Open** syllable."

Build the following words. Have your student place the correct tag above the syllable.

Open Syllable	Closed Syllable	Open Syllable
h e	b a t	s o
Closed Syllable	**Closed Syllable**	**Open Syllable**
c r a sh	s p o t	m e

New Teaching
(continued)

Complete Activity Sheet

"Now let's help some friendly monsters get supplies for a party!"

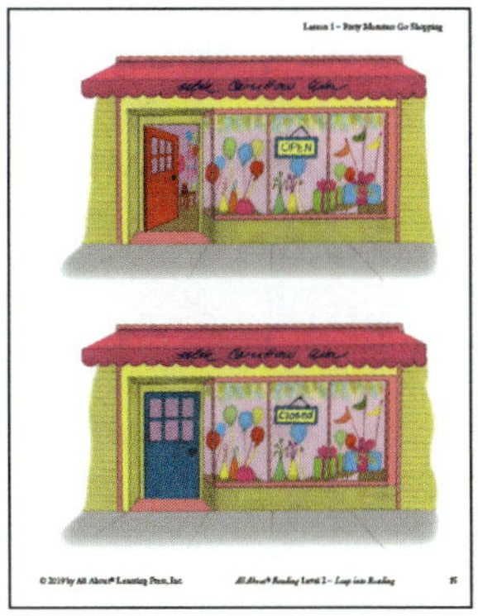

Party Monsters Go Shopping
Remove pages 15-18 from the activity book.

Place page 15 in front of your student. Cut out the monster cards on page 17 and place them in a pile with the words facing down.

"These Party Monsters are planning a party and need to buy some supplies at the store. Let's see if the store is open or closed when the monsters get there."

Have your student select the monster cards one at a time and read the word on the back. If the word is a Closed syllable, she should put the monster by the closed door. If the word is an Open syllable, put the monster by the open door.

Once all the monster cards have been sorted, have your student count how many monsters were at the store when it was open and how many were at the store when it was closed.

Answer Key
Open: go, we, no, me, be, he, she, so
Closed: met, hem, got, web, bed, tin, sob

Practice Fluency

Review Words

plum	puff	wish	quack
finch	be	quiz	blank
thrill	himself	she	said
he	bobcats	such	shred
rang	so	them	buzz
class	of	text	swing
eggshell	go	crack	fishes
pets	chopsticks	was	sniff
for	fox	codfish	shrank

Phrases

pink gum	tan handbag
ten wishes	the last duck
go west	a bad dog
glass of milk	box lunch
his long song	red quilt
on the shelf	six wet frogs

Turn to pages 19-20 in the activity book.

Have your student read from the Practice Sheets to review words, phrases, and sentences from Level 1.

New Teaching
(continued)

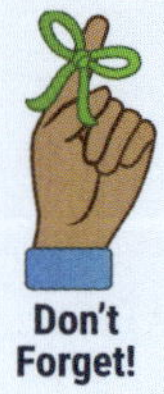

For tips on using the Practice Sheets, refer to Appendix K.

Read-Aloud Time

Read a Story or Poem

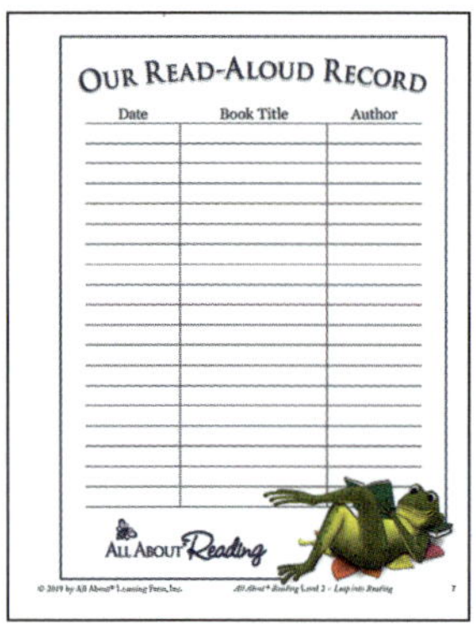
Our Read-Aloud Record

Date	Book Title	Author

Read aloud to your student for twenty minutes. You can keep track of your read-alouds on the Read-Aloud Record found on page 7 of the activity book.

Track Your Progress

Mark the Progress Chart

If you haven't already done so, remove page 5 from the activity book.

After each lesson has been completed, have your student color in or place a sticker over that lesson number on the Progress Chart.

The ants
in that anteater activity were
sticky-tongue delicious! (Oh, and
the review words weren't bad either).

Speaking of delicious ... I wonder if those
Party Monsters were going to get
some good snacks? No party is complete
without french flies, you know!

If you're ready for Lesson 2,
I'll hop along with you.
Let's bounce!

Lesson 2 Blends at the Beginning and End

Objective

This lesson teaches words containing consonant blends at the beginning and end.

You Will Need

- ☐ *Leap into Reading* pages 21-29
- ☐ Word Cards 1-11

Before You Begin

Preview Blends at the Beginning and End

In Level 1, your student learned words with consonant blends either at the beginning, as in *plan*, or at the end, as in *lump*. A consonant blend consists of two sounds that are said together quickly. For example, the word *stop* has a consonant blend at the beginning. The /s/ and /t/ sounds are said in rapid succession, but each consonant keeps its own sound.

> A consonant blend is different from a consonant team (also known as a digraph). In a consonant team, two or more letters work together to make one sound, such as sh and th, while the letters in a blend retain their own individual sounds.

In this lesson, your student will learn words containing blends at both the beginning and end. Read the following examples and listen for the blends.

bland **slump** **grunt** **trust** **cramp**

Words with consonant blends will be decoded using the same procedure your student used in Level 1. This procedure is described in detail in Appendix C: Blending Procedure.

Review

Phonogram Cards

Review the Phonogram Cards that are behind the Review divider in your student's Reading Review Box. Show each card to your student and have him say the sound(s). If necessary, remind your student of the sound(s).

> If your student knows the Phonogram Card without prompting and you feel that the card has been mastered, place the card behind the **Phonograms Mastered** divider. If the card has not yet been mastered, place it back behind the **Phonograms Review** divider.

Previous Concepts

Build the following words with letter tiles. Have your student label the words with the proper syllable tags and then read the words.

Closed Syllable	Open Syllable
d r o p	n o

New Teaching

Play "Change the Word"

Build the word *plan*. p l a n

"What is this word?" *Plan.*

"I'm going to add a tile to this word." Add a t to form the word *plant.*

p l a n t

"What does this new word say?" Encourage your student to sound out the new word, *plant.*

Build the word *plum.* p l u m

"Sound out this word." *Student sounds out the word* plum.

New Teaching
(continued)

Add a p to form the word *plump*.

"What does this new word say?" *Student sounds out the word* plump.

Continue this activity using several of the words below.

Add a letter tile to the end of the following words.

bran	→	**branch***	**scan**	→	**scant**
bran	→	**brand**	**slum**	→	**slump**
clam	→	**clamp**	**Stan**	→	**stand**
cram	→	**cramp**	**stun**	→	**stunt**
prim	→	**primp**			

Add a letter tile to the beginning of the following words.

land	→	**bland**	**runt**	→	**grunt**
last	→	**blast**	**lamp**	→	**clamp**
lend	→	**blend**	**lump**	→	**clump**
limp	→	**blimp**	**rust**	→	**trust**
ranch*	→	**branch***	**rump**	→	**grump**
risk	→	**brisk**	**wept**	→	**swept**

*Use the ch tile for the words *branch* and *ranch*.

Complete Activity Sheet

"Let's help these pups find their favorite things."

It's a Dog's Life
Remove pages 21-26 from the *Leap into Reading* activity book.

Cut out the dog cards and the object cards. Place the dog cards in a pile with the words facing down. Spread the object cards on the table with the words facing down.

Your student should select a dog card and then locate the two cards whose objects match the object on the dog card. For example, if your student selects the dog card with the image of a puppy and a bone, he will locate the cards with the image of a bone. He will then turn over all three cards and read the rhyming words.

Continue playing until all the dog cards have been matched with the appropriate object cards.

New Teaching
(continued)

Practice Reading Words

Have your student practice reading the words on Word Cards 1-9.

File the Word Cards behind the Review divider in the Reading Review Box.

Teach Two Leap Words: *you* and *are*

Show Word Card 10 to your student.

"This word is *you*, as in *Did you ask?* The y says /y/ and the o and u work together to say /o͞o/. You haven't learned the sounds of ou yet, but this is a common word that you will see often."

"What is this word?" *You.*

> The words *craft/kraft* and *you/ewe* are homophones (two words that sound alike but are spelled differently). A sentence has been added to the Word Cards for *craft* and *you* and all cards containing homophones in future lessons. Your student does not need to read these sentences, but they are there in case you wish to discuss the correct word usage.

Show Word Card 11 to your student.

"This word is *are*, as in *My shoes are brown*. The a and the r work together

New Teaching
(continued)

to say /ar/, and the e isn't pronounced—it's a Silent E. You haven't learned about ar and Silent E yet, but this is a common word that you will see often."

"What is this word?" *Are.*

Review these Leap Words several times today.

File the flashcards behind the **Word Cards Review** divider in your student's Reading Review Box. The cards will be reviewed at the beginning of the next lesson.

Practice Fluency

New Words

are	you	blend	slept
plump	frost	plant	grunt
trust	shrimp	crust	stomp
blast	stand	blond	crunch
clump	craft	swept	print
spend	branch	grasp	twist
stump	stunt	crept	crisp
grand	spent	stamp	swift

Phrases

has slept	a plump frog
big blast	crisp shrimp
wet frost	swept up
trust him	the cat slept
on a branch	red plant
blond man	stomp and twist

Turn to pages 27-29 in the activity book.

Have your student read from the Practice Sheets.

Most of the Practice Sheets contain a section called Challenge Words. Skip this section if you are working with younger students. Use the section with older students who need an additional challenge.

Read-Aloud Time

Read a Story or Poem

Read aloud to your student for twenty minutes.

Track Your Progress

Mark the Progress Chart

Have your student mark Lesson 2 on the Progress Chart.

Ohhhh ...
I like these consonant blends.
We can make a lot of fun words with them.
My favorite words with blends are
croak and swamp. What are yours?

You know what else blends well together?
Mosquitoes and dragonflies. Mmmm ... time to
whip up a nice batch of bug stew! I'll bring you
some for the next lesson.
Don't forget your spoon!

Lesson 3 Read "Twist and Stomp"

Objective

In this lesson, students read a short story and use pantomime to act out actions from the story.

You Will Need

- ☐ *Leap into Reading* pages 31-33
- ☐ optional: sticky notes
- ☐ *What Am I?* book

Before You Begin

Preview the Story-Related Lessons

You've reached the first story-related lesson in Level 2! That means that your student will read a short story today. This is a great chance to practice newly learned decoding skills and learn comprehension strategies.

And of course we want to set your student up for success! To help her get the most out of this lesson, your student will do several warm-up activities before reading the story:

- **Completing an activity sheet** that introduces a new literary concept.
- **Reading a Warm-Up Sheet** to refresh her memory about words that have been explicitly taught in previous lessons.
- **Learning new vocabulary and activating prior knowledge** about story-specific topics through interesting pre-reading discussion.

During and after the story, we ask open-ended questions because we want students to relate to and put thought into what they're reading. We want them to contribute their ideas, test their predictions, and comprehend in a meaningful way. To encourage an active reading process, our reading comprehension strategies also focus on visualizing, questioning, summarizing, making predictions, and drawing conclusions.

Post-reading activities include discussing the main character or conflict, story sequencing, imagining alternate endings, and relating the story to your student's life. A complete list of reading comprehension activities can be found in Appendix J.

Together, these pre- and post-reading activities move your student toward the goal of reading with comprehension.

Before You Begin
(continued)

After completing the warm-up activities in this lesson, your student will read "Twist and Stomp" in the *What Am I?* book. All the words in the story are decodable using previously taught concepts.

Review

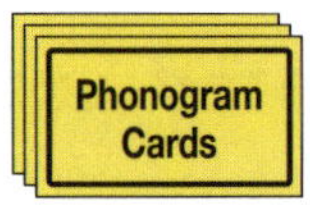

Review the Phonogram Cards that are behind the Review divider in your student's Reading Review Box. Show each card to your student and have him say the sound(s). If necessary, remind your student of the sound(s).

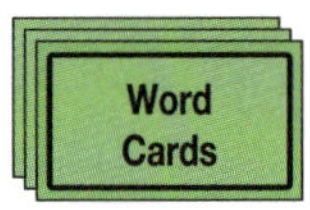

Shuffle and review the Word Cards that are behind the Review divider in your student's Reading Review Box. If your student has difficulty reading a word, build the word with letter tiles and have your student sound it out using the blending procedure shown in Appendix C.

Remember: as your student masters the flashcards, move them behind the appropriate **Mastered** dividers.

How do you know when your student has mastered a card? Here are the signs:

- Your student responds quickly and easily when you hold up the card.
- You have no doubt that your student knows the card thoroughly.

New Teaching

Complete Activity Sheet

"There are many different ways you can move. Show me how you can wave." *Student waves.*

"Show me how you can jump." *Student jumps.*

"Good. Let's act out more ways of moving."

New Teaching
(continued)

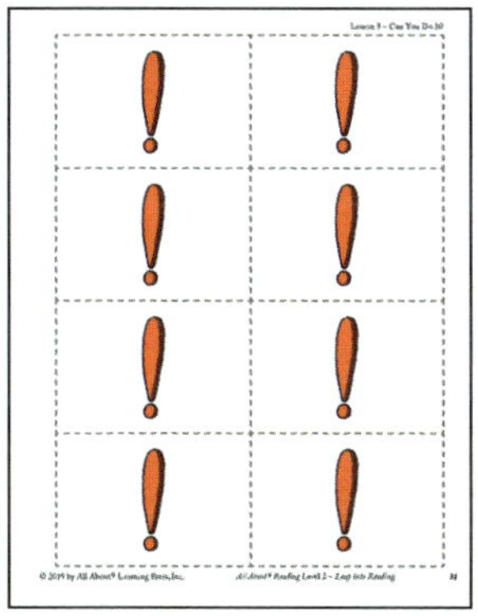

Can You Do It?

Remove pages 31-32 from the *Leap into Reading* activity book.

Cut out the cards and arrange them on the table with the words facing up.

Read each card with your student so you are both familiar with the words. Then mix the cards and place them in a pile with the words facing down. Have your student choose a card and act it out in pantomime. Try to guess which card your student is acting out.

Continue until your student has acted out all the cards.

Read the Warm-Up Sheet for "Twist and Stomp"

Turn to page 33 in the activity book.

Have your student practice reading words and phrases that will be encountered in "Twist and Stomp."

> If your student is reading words with blends very easily, you can skip this Warm-Up Sheet.

Teach Vocabulary and Activate Prior Knowledge

Point out the illustration of the stunt on the Warm-Up Sheet. "A *stunt* is a daring trick, like doing flips on a snowboard. In the movies, a person who performs daring stunts is called a *stuntman* or *stuntwoman*."

"Have you ever seen someone do a stunt? What did the person do? Was it scary or funny?"

"In today's story, a lot of animals perform stunts in a contest. Let's see who wins."

New Teaching
(continued)

Read "Twist and Stomp"

During the story, you will stop your student in several places to model important comprehension strategies. You'll model for your student how to stop to think about unfamiliar words or ideas. You'll also model the beginning stages of making predictions by thinking ahead to what might happen next.

If you wish, you can place a small sticky note at the bottom of pages 13 and 21 of the reader so you remember to stop after reading those pages.

"Turn to page 9 in your reader and read 'Twist and Stomp' aloud." Discuss your student's ideas for the questions below as you come to them.

After page 13: "Whose stunts do you like better, the pigs' or the dogs'? Why?"

After page 21: "Why does the animals' pyramid fall down? Look at the illustration for clues."

After reading: "Do you think that Fox's team wins the stunt competition? If not, which team do you think wins the competition, the pigs or the dogs? Why?"

Read-Aloud Time

Read a Story or Poem

Read aloud to your student for twenty minutes.

Read-Aloud Tip!

Increase a Short Attention Span

Since young children have short attention spans, start small with your read-alouds. Begin by choosing shorter books or books with less text. As your student's attention span increases, gradually add in a mix of longer, more complex stories.

Track Your Progress

Mark the Progress Chart

Have your student mark Lesson 3 on the Progress Chart.

Lesson 4 Y Can Say /ī/

Objective

This lesson teaches words containing the sound of /ī/ spelled y.

You Will Need

- ☐ *Leap into Reading* pages 35-41
- ☐ Word Cards 12-21

Before You Begin

Review Phonogram Y

In this lesson, your student will learn to read words in which y says its third sound, /ī/. As a quick review, here are the four sounds of y:

- /y/ as in *yarn* (emphasized in Level 1, Lesson 4)
- /ĭ/ as in *gym* (emphasized in Level 4, Lesson 55)
- /ī/ as in *my* (emphasized in this lesson)
- /ē/ as in *happy* (emphasized in Level 3, Lesson 6)

The letter y says /ī/ when it comes at the end of one-syllable words. Many of these are high-utility words that your student will encounter frequently. Read the following examples and listen for the /ī/ sound.

my	**try**	**by**	**fly**
cry	**dry**	**sky**	**shy**

> The letter y is unusual because it can represent either a consonant sound or a vowel sound.
>
> Y represents a consonant sound in approximately sixty words including *yarn*, *yellow*, and *beyond*. Much more often, in thousands of words, y is a vowel, and it has the same three sounds that i has: /ĭ/–/ī/–/ē/. Y is also part of the vowel teams ay, oy, and ey.

For this lesson, we'll use the red y letter tile since we'll be emphasizing the vowel sound of /ī/. When we use the y letter tile to represent the sound of /ī/, we only say the sound /ī/. To facilitate blending, we don't say all four sounds. Later, if your student comes across a word and isn't sure which sound to use for the letter y, he should try all the sounds in sequence until he finds the right one.

Refer to the Letter Tiles app or Phonogram Sounds app for a demonstration of the y phonogram sounds.

Review

Phonogram Cards

Review the Phonogram Cards that are behind the Review divider in your student's Reading Review Box. Show each card to your student and have him say the sound(s). If necessary, remind your student of the sound(s).

Word Cards

Shuffle and review the Word Cards that are behind the Review divider in your student's Reading Review Box. If your student has difficulty reading a word, build the word with letter tiles and have your student sound it out using the blending procedure shown in Appendix C.

Previous Concepts

Build the following words with letter tiles. Have your student label the words with the proper syllable tags and then read the words.

Closed Syllable	Open Syllable
s l e p t	w e

New Teaching

Teach that Y Can Say /ī/

Move the red and blue y tiles into the workspace. y y

"As you know, y can be a consonant or a vowel. Point to the consonant y." *Student points to the blue tile.*

Build the word *yell.* y e l l

"When y is at the beginning of a word, it is always a consonant."

Point to the red y tile. "When y is a vowel, it can say /ĭ/, /ī/, or /ē/."

Build the word *cry.* c r y

"This word is *cry*. How many syllables are in the word *cry*?" *One.*

"Good. At the end of one-syllable words, the letter y says /ī/."

New Teaching
(continued)

"Is *cry* an Open or Closed syllable?" Help your student see that it is an Open syllable because it ends with a vowel.

"Label this word with the syllable tag."

Leave the word *cry* in the workspace.

Play "Change the Word"

"I'm going to change the first letter of this word."

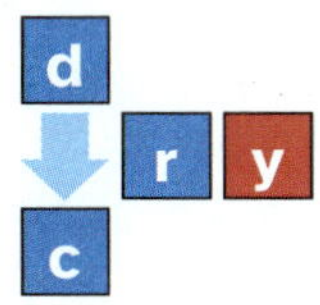

"What does this new word say?" Encourage your student to sound out the new word, *dry*.

Continue to change one or two tiles at a time to form the following words. Each time, have your student sound out the new word.

dry → pry → fry → try → fly → sly → sky → my → by → shy*

*Use the sh tile for the word *shy*.

Complete Activity Sheet

"Let's sort some yaks and flies."

Sound Sorting for Phonogram Y

Remove pages 35-38 from the *Leap into Reading* activity book.

Cut out the word cards, mix them up, and place them in a pile.

Have your student choose the cards one by one and read the words aloud. He will then decide whether the word has a /y/ sound (as in *yak*) or an /ī/ sound (as in *fly*) and place the card in the appropriate column.

When all cards have been placed, the student may flip them over to check his work.

New Teaching
(continued)

__Answer Key__
/y/: yam, yak, yum, yes, yet, yell, yuck
/ī/: by, dry, fly, my, shy, spy, try

Practice Reading Words

Have your student practice reading the words on Word Cards 12-19.

File the Word Cards behind the Review divider in the Reading Review Box.

Teach Two Leap Words: *from* and *your*

Show Word Card 20 to your student.

"This word is *from*, as in *I am from Utah*. What does the o̲ say in this word?" */ŭ/.*

"Right. In this word, the o̲ says its fourth sound instead of the more common short sound."

"You haven't learned other words in which o̲ says /ŭ/ yet, so this frog will remind you to stop and remember this special Leap Word."

"What is this word?" *From.*

New Teaching
(continued)

Show Word Card 21 to your student.

"This word is *your*, as in *This is your cat.* It is another common word that doesn't follow the rules that you have learned so far. In this word, the o, u, and r work together to say /or/."

"What is this word?" *Your.*

Review these Leap Words several times today and then file them behind the Review divider in the Reading Review Box.

Practice Fluency

New Words

cry	shy	myself	by
fly	spy	from	try
your	dry	my	sky
fry			

Phrases

by myself	did you cry?	did not try
is not dry	fry a fish	fly fast
can cry	in the sky	you can
a bad spy	a shy man	step by step
my dog	your yak	a black fly

Turn to pages 39-41 in the activity book.

Have your student read from the Practice Sheets.

Your beginning student isn't expected to read through the Practice Sheets in one sitting.

Many students will still be at the stage of sounding out many of the words, and that can be tiring mental work. Stop before your student fatigues. You can always continue tomorrow.

Read-Aloud Time

Read a Story or Poem

Read aloud to your student for twenty minutes.

Track Your Progress

Mark the Progress Chart

Have your student mark Lesson 4 on the Progress Chart.

Lesson 5 Read "The Grump"

Objective

In this lesson, students read a short story and practice meaningful expression.

You Will Need

- ☐ *Leap into Reading* pages 43-45
- ☐ *What Am I?* book

Before You Begin

Preview Reading with Meaningful Expression

When we talk, we use a lot of expression to communicate how we feel. If we're angry, we might frown and speak loudly. If we're happy, we might smile and speak in a cheerful voice.

Likewise, when we read, we can use expression to show how the characters feel. Today's activity sheet encourages students to pay attention to expression as they read.

Review

Review the Phonogram Cards that are behind the Review divider in your student's Reading Review Box. Show each card to your student and have him say the sound(s). If necessary, remind your student of the sound(s).

You might like to have some fun with today's Phonogram Card review by playing the game "Phonogram Go Fish." For instructions, look for this icon in Appendix L.

Shuffle and review the Word Cards that are behind the Review divider in your student's Reading Review Box. If your student has difficulty reading a word, build the word with letter tiles and have your student sound it out using the blending procedure shown in Appendix C.

New Teaching

Read the Warm-Up Sheet for "The Grump"

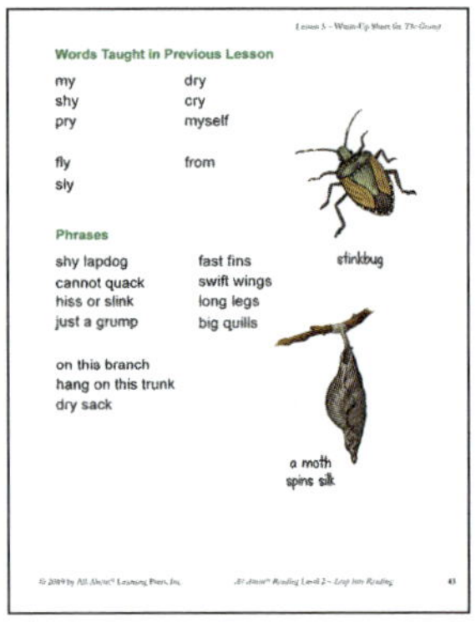

Words Taught in Previous Lesson

my dry
shy cry
pry myself

fly from
sly

Phrases

shy lapdog fast fins
cannot quack swift wings
hiss or slink long legs
just a grump big quills

on this branch
hang on this trunk
dry sack

stinkbug

a moth
spins silk

Turn to page 43 in the *Leap into Reading* activity book.

Have your student practice reading words and phrases that will be encountered in "The Grump."

Teach Vocabulary and Activate Prior Knowledge

Point out the illustration of a stinkbug on the Warm-Up Sheet. "There are many kinds of insects, and this particular insect is called a *stinkbug*. Why do you think it is called a stinkbug?"

"A stinkbug gives off a bad smell if it is touched. And they taste really nasty to predators, too. If a bird or animal accidentally bites into a stinkbug, they spit it out."

Point out the illustration of the cocoon on the Warm-Up Sheet. "Have you ever watched a caterpillar make a *cocoon*? Moth caterpillars make cocoons to protect themselves from predators while they are changing into moths. They spin the silk for their cocoons using a special gland in their mouths."

"This next story is about a caterpillar who feels grumpy. He's in a crabby mood. Let's find out if he's still crabby at the end of the story."

Read "The Grump"

"Turn to page 23 in your reader and read 'The Grump' aloud." Discuss your student's ideas for the questions below as you come to them.

After page 29: "What do you think *prick* means? The porcupine has quills, which can poke or stab something, so *prick* means...?"

After page 31: "What do you think will happen while the caterpillar takes a nap?"

New Teaching
(continued)

Complete Activity Sheet

"Are you ready to act like the Grump?"

Be a Grump

Remove page 45 from the activity book. Point to the first illustration of the stinkbug.

"Today you're going to practice reading with meaningful expression. Read each of these quotes in the way that you imagine the Grump would say it, with full expression." Continue until your student has read all the quotations. Discuss the appropriate expression needed for each quote.

If desired, you can continue the activity by asking your student to demonstrate different ways of saying the same quote. For example, your student could read "I can fly! I am *not* a grump!" in a delighted, happy voice and then read the quote again with a sad and melancholy voice. Or your student could read "I wish I had big quills to prick" with a very sad voice followed by a secretive, whispery voice.

Read-Aloud Time

Read a Story or Poem

Read aloud to your student for twenty minutes.

Read-Aloud Tip!

Why Read Aloud?

Reading aloud to your student is one of life's great joys, to be sure. But it's also one of the most important things you can do to promote your student's future reading ability. Reading aloud to children...

- creates a lifetime interest in reading
- extends their attention spans
- aids in language development
- strengthens their power of imagination
- builds reading comprehension
- creates a special one-on-one bond

Track Your Progress

Mark the Progress Chart

Have your student mark Lesson 5 on the Progress Chart.

Lesson 6 Syllable Division Rules for Compound Words and Two Consonant Tiles

Objective

This lesson reviews the concept of compound words and teaches the first two syllable division rules.

You Will Need

- ☐ *Leap into Reading* pages 47-54
- ☐ Word Cards 22-30
- ☐ Syllable Division Rules chart

Before You Begin

Locate the Syllable Division Rules Chart

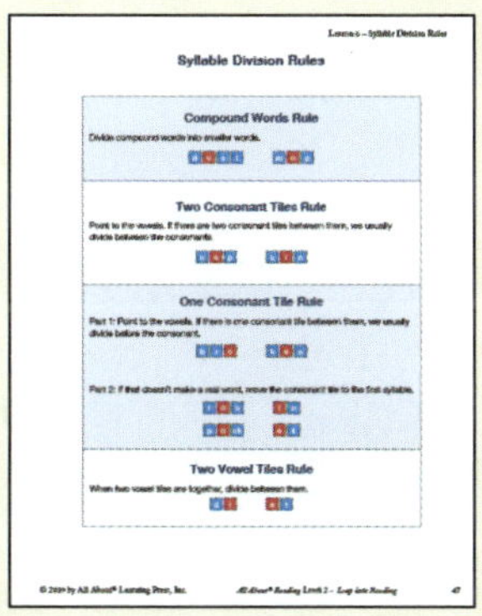

Turn to pages 47-48 in the activity book. The Syllable Division Rules chart will be used in future lessons so you may want to bookmark it, tuck it into the back of the Teacher's Manual, or attach it to a bulletin board for future reference.

Today's lesson will cover the first two syllable division rules. For a listing of all the syllable division rules and when they are first introduced, see Appendix E.

Preview the Syllable Division Rule for Compound Words

In Level 1, your student learned that compound words are special words made up of two smaller words, such as *suntan*. Today's lesson reviews that concept and then introduces the first syllable division rule: Compound words are divided between the two smaller words.

s u n   t a n

Preview the Syllable Division Rule for Two Consonant Tiles

Since most words in the English language have more than one syllable, we need to give your student a strategy for decoding multisyllable words. Your student already knows how to decode short Closed syllable words, such as *nap* and *kin*, so now we are going to transfer this skill to reading multisyllable words.

Before You Begin
(continued)

For words containing two consonant tiles between the vowels, as in *napkin*, we divide between the consonants.

> This syllable pattern is sometimes referred to as the VCCV pattern (vowel-consonant-consonant-vowel pattern).

Here's how we'll do this:

1. Build a word. Point to the two vowel tiles.

2. Determine how many consonant tiles are between the vowels. (There are two.)

3. When there are two consonant tiles between the vowels, we usually divide the word between the two consonants.

Now, using previous knowledge of Closed syllables, it's easy to read the word.

> **Tip!**
>
> Resist the temptation to create a shortcut by locating just the two consonant tiles and dividing between them instead of first locating the two vowels. This may seem more efficient at first glance, but locating the vowels first is an important habit that we'll build upon in Lessons 10 and 12.

As the rule states, we *usually* divide between the two consonants. There are a few exceptions to this rule, such as *secret, apron,* and *declare*, where we divide *before* the two consonants instead of between them. Since there are very few of these words, we will teach them on an as-needed basis.

Preview the Schwa Sound

A *schwa* is a muffled vowel sound frequently found in unaccented syllables. In dictionaries, the schwa is symbolized with an upside-down e: /ə/. Listen for the schwa sound in the second syllables of these words: *cotton, signal, item.* The schwa is the most common and most frequently heard vowel sound in the English language.

Before You Begin
(continued)

In our lessons, we don't use the term *schwa* with students. Instead, we give them strategies to read words containing schwas. For more information on schwas, see "How to Handle the Schwa Sound" in Appendix H.

Review

Phonogram Cards

Review the Phonogram Cards that are behind the Review divider in your student's Reading Review Box. Show each card to your student and have him say the sound(s). If necessary, remind your student of the sound(s).

Liven up today's Phonogram Card review with the game "Phonogram Ball." For instructions, look for this icon in Appendix L.

Word Cards

Shuffle and review the Word Cards that are behind the Review divider in your student's Reading Review Box. If your student has difficulty reading a word, build the word with letter tiles and have your student sound it out using the blending procedure shown in Appendix C.

Previous Concepts

Build the following words with letter tiles. Have your student label the words with the proper syllable tags and then read the words.

Open Syllable	Closed Syllable
s l y	t w i s t

Teach Syllable Division Rule: Compound Words

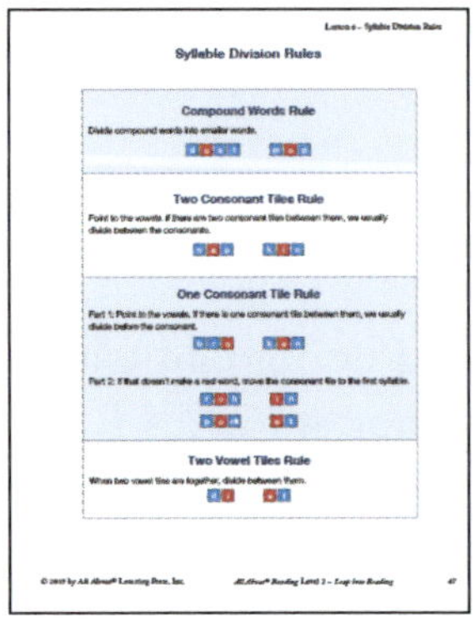
Syllable Division Rules

Compound Words Rule

Two Consonant Tiles Rule

One Consonant Tile Rule

Two Vowel Tiles Rule

Take out the Syllable Division Rules chart, found on pages 47-48 in the *Leap into Reading* activity book. Set it aside.

Build the word *anthill.*

a n t h i l l

"This is a compound word. As you know, a compound word has two smaller words in it. What are the two smaller words in this word?" *Ant, hill.*

"Compound words can be divided into their two smaller words. This is the **Compound Words** rule." Point to the rule on the Syllable Division Rules chart and read it with your student.

"Now that you know the Compound Words rule, divide *anthill* into two syllables." *Student divides the word between* ant *and* hill.

a n t   h i l l

Using letter tiles, have your student practice dividing the following words into syllables.

suntan **dishcloth** **bathtub** **cobweb**

"Now you are ready to learn the second rule for dividing words into syllables."

Teach Syllable Division Rule: Two Consonant Tiles

Build the word *insect.* i n s e c t

"The easiest way to read longer words is to divide them into syllables and then read each syllable."

"First, we locate the vowels." Point to the i and the e.

New Teaching
(continued)

"How many consonant tiles do you see between the two vowels?" *Two.*

Point to the n and the s. "When there are two consonant tiles between the vowels, we divide between the consonants, like this."

"Now it is easy to read the word. What does the first syllable say?" *In.*

"What does the second syllable say?" *Sect.*

Push the two syllables back together. "What is the word?" *Insect.*

Point to the Two Consonant Tiles rule on the Syllable Division Rules chart.

"This is the **Two Consonant Tiles** rule." Read the rule with your student.

Using letter tiles, have your student practice dividing the following words into syllables.

contest **invent** **upset** **muffin** **napkin**

Play "Guess What I'm Saying"

> When your student first learns to sound out two-syllable words, he may pause between the syllables. This exercise will give your student practice in combining two syllables into a single word.

"I will say two syllables, and you will guess what word I am saying: *pic...nic.*" *Student says* picnic *at normal conversational speed.*

Repeat this activity using the following words. Be sure to pause between the syllables as you say them.

pup...pet **pil...grim** **rab...bit** **hap...pen** **mag...net**

New Teaching
(continued)

Introduce the Concept of Muffled Speech Sounds

Build the word *problem*. p r o b l e m

"Divide this word into syllables." *Student divides the word between the b and the l.*

p r o b   l e m

"Read each syllable." *Prob-lem.*

"What does this word say?" *Problem.*

Point to the e. "When we say the word quickly, the sound of the e gets muffled. The word sounds like /prob-lum/ in normal speech."

"When you sound out a two-syllable word like this, you can get very close to the correct pronunciation. Sound out each syllable and then say the syllables together like a normal word, just like you did a minute ago."

Complete Activity Sheet

"I hope you're feeling strong, because we have a bunch of logs to split now."

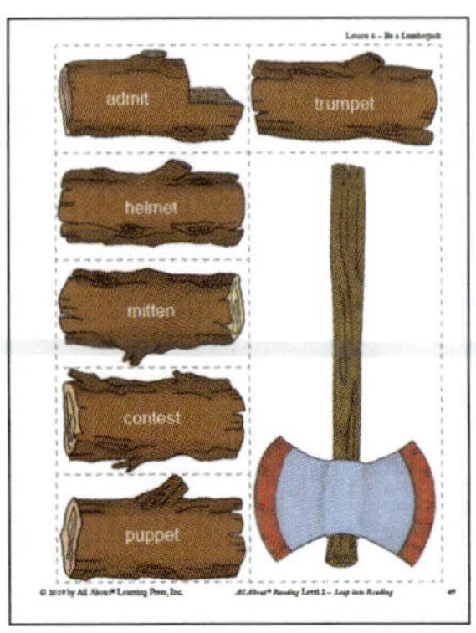

Be a Lumberjack
Remove pages 49-51 from the activity book.

Cut out the logs and the ax. Have your student pretend to chop each multisyllable word with the ax, dividing the word on the log between the two syllables.

The student should read each portion of the word separately and then read the entire word.

Answer Key

ad–mit	trum–pet	hel–met	mit–ten
con–test	pup–pet	in–vent	Den–nis
nut–meg	cac–tus	bas–ket	in–sult
chip–munk	pic–nic	mag–net	muf–fin

New Teaching
(continued)

Practice Reading Words

Have your student practice reading the words on Word Cards 22-29.

File the Word Cards behind the Review divider in the Reading Review Box.

Teach a Leap Word: *have*

Show Word Card 30 to your student.

"This word is *have*, as in *I have six fish.* The e̲ isn't pronounced; it's a Silent E."

Cover the e̲ with your finger. "What would this word say without the e̲?" *Have.*

"Right! When we read this word, we don't pronounce the e̲."

Review this Leap Word several times today and then file it behind the Review divider in the Reading Review Box.

New Teaching
(continued)

Practice Fluency

New Words

chipmunk	mitten	admit	until
upset	have	picnic	invent
muffin	trumpet	puppet	happen
insect	plastic	problem	contest
Dennis	basket	sudden	helmet
napkin	Ellen	kitten	cactus
rabbit	magnet	hello	

Phrases

the sad kitten	my red mitten
big insect	had a picnic
not upset	a dry muffin
did not happen	win a contest
brass trumpet	plastic bag
have a problem	

Turn to pages 53-54 in the activity book.

Have your student read from the Practice Sheets.

Hello is the last word in the New Words section. It follows the same syllable division rule as the other two-syllable words in this section, but it is the only word on the page that ends with an open syllable.

When you get to the Challenge Words, you may notice that the last two rows contain homographs (words that are spelled the same but have different pronunciations and meanings). You don't need to teach the term *homograph* to your student at this point, but just be aware that the verb form of these words is pronounced differently than the noun form. For example:

noun: They took the *suspect* into custody. (SUS-pect)
verb: I *suspect* that you ate garlic. (sus-PECT)

Be prepared to accept either pronunciation at this time.

How Much Time?
How much time should you spend on the Practice Sheets? Only you can be the judge of that since the answer is different for every student. Some students may not need all the practice provided here. Other students may benefit from rereading the sheets multiple times over a period of a week.

The goal is to keep making progress, not to achieve perfection.

Read-Aloud Time

Read a Story or Poem

Read aloud to your student for twenty minutes.

Track Your Progress

Mark the Progress Chart

Have your student mark Lesson 6 on the Progress Chart.

Compound words are
so cool! And I just had my best idea yet:
I'm going to change my name to a compound
word. From now on, you can call me ...
WEBFOOT
King of the Swamp

Not bad, eh? Now I have to find a crown.
Your turn–what's your new compound
word name?

Lesson 7 Read "The Bantam Spy Club"

Objective

In this lesson, students learn about unaccented syllables, read a short story, and analyze the text for important details.

You Will Need

- ☐ *Leap into Reading* pages 55-58
- ☐ pencil
- ☐ *What Am I?* book

Before You Begin

Preview the Six Question Words

After reading today's story, your student will complete a "spy journal" activity that focuses on the six question words: *who, what, when, where, why*, and *how*. Using question words is a great way to help develop your student's reading comprehension skills and to make her think more deeply about what she hears and reads in daily life.

Review Box Tip

Remember, as your student masters the flashcards, move them behind the appropriate **Mastered** dividers.

How do you know when your student has mastered a card? Here are the signs:

- Your student responds quickly and easily when you hold up the card.
- You have no doubt that your student knows the card thoroughly.

Review

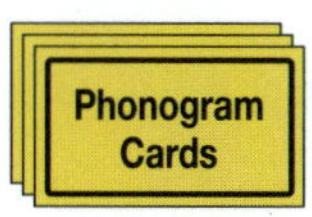

Review the Phonogram Cards that are behind the Review divider in your student's Reading Review Box. Show each card to your student and have him say the sound(s). If necessary, remind your student of the sound(s).

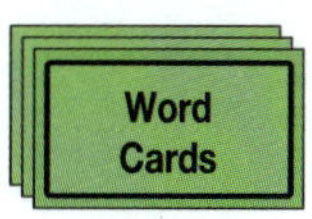

Shuffle and review the Word Cards that are behind the Review divider in your student's Reading Review Box. If your student has difficulty reading a word, build the word with letter tiles and have your student sound it out using the blending procedure shown in Appendix C.

Use a favorite family board game to review Word Cards. For instructions, look for this icon in Appendix M.

New Teaching

Teach the Words *Bantam* and *Chicken*

Build the word *bantam*. b a n t a m

"Here is a word that you may not be familiar with, but that you can still sound out. Divide it into syllables." *Student divides the word between the n and the t.*

"Read each syllable." *Ban-tam.*

"Good! *Bantam.* A bantam is a type of small chicken."

Turn to page 55 in the *Leap into Reading* activity book.

Point to the illustration of the bantam chicken on the Warm-Up Sheet. "Bantam chickens are small and are easy to teach, so some people raise them as pets. Their unusual looks also make them fun to own. This one has a feathered crown, but some have beards or fully feathered heads and feet. They come in a lot of different colors like red, white, brown, black, and gold."

"And that leads us to our next word."

Build the word *chicken*. ch i ck e n

"I'll divide this word into syllables and you see if you can read it."

ch i ck   e n

"Read each syllable." *Chick-en.*

"What is this word?" *Chicken.*

"Good!"

> If you wish, you may explain to your student that the syllable division rule for the word *chicken* hasn't been taught yet, but she is still able to read the word.
>
> If your student encounters this word in text and divides it using the syllable division rule that she is already familiar with, the word will still be decodable: /chĭc/-/kĕn/.

New Teaching
(continued)

Read the Warm-Up Sheet for "The Bantam Spy Club"

Words Taught in Previous Lesson

muskrat	have	wigwam	problem
mascot	intend	upset	napkin

New Decodable Words

bantam chicken

Phrases

Bantam Spy Club
big problem
just for you

the club mascot
grab this spy hat
run back to us

on this napkin
sit still

go to the wigwam
spy pin

Names

Ellen
Dennis

bantam chicken

Turn again to page 55 in the activity book.

Have your student practice reading words and phrases that will be encountered in "The Bantam Spy Club."

Activate Prior Knowledge

"What kinds of things do spies do?"

"Do you think you have to be brave to be a spy?"

"If you were a spy, how would you dress to disguise yourself?"

"Some spies have secret signals, like a special handshake with people they trust. What would your secret signal be?"

"The story you are about to read is about some young spies who need to find their club mascot, which is missing. A mascot is an animal that represents a club. Maybe you can help them!"

Read "The Bantam Spy Club"

"Turn to page 39 in your reader and read 'The Bantam Spy Club' aloud." Discuss your student's ideas for the questions below as you come to them.

> **Don't Forget!**
>
> You may want to place a small sticky note at the bottom of pages 41, 43, and 47 so you remember to stop after reading those pages.

After page 41: "Do the kids look upset? How does your face look when you are upset?"

New Teaching
(continued)

After page 43: "Ellen asks you five questions. Why do you think she asks you so many questions?" *Possible answer: She wants to see if I would be a good spy and help them get the Bantam Chicken back.*

After page 47: "Why do you think it says *Run as fast as you can*?"

Complete Activity Sheet

"Now let's fill out your spy information booklet."

My Spy Pad

Remove pages 57-58 from the activity book.

Cut out the pages on the dotted lines as indicated and arrange them in order. Staple the booklet together as shown on the cover. Have your student turn to page 1 and write her name on the line. Have her turn to each successive page as you dictate the following questions.

Page 2: Question for WHAT: "What was stolen: the Bantam Chicken or the smelly socks?" *Student circles her response.*

Page 3: Question for WHO: "Who stole the Bantam Chicken: the Muskrat Club or the Bantam Spy Club?" *Student circles her response.*

Page 4: Question for WHERE: "Where was the plan written: in a book or on a napkin?" *Student circles her response.*

Page 5: Question for WHEN: "When did you run: when you saw a dog, or when Dennis flapped and quacked?" *Student circles her response.*

Page 6: Question for HOW: "How did you carry the Bantam Chicken: in your hat or on your bike?" *Student circles her response.*

Page 7: Question for WHY: "Why did you get a spy pin?" *Student marks a box in response.*

Read-Aloud Time

Read a Story or Poem

Read aloud to your student for twenty minutes.

Read-Aloud Tip!

Reading to Kids Who Can't Sit Still

If you have a wriggler, you know how hard it is to keep her attention during read-aloud time. Here are some strategies for making sure your active student is getting the most out of reading time.

- Read after physical activity so your student gets all her energy out.
- Look for interactive books with flaps, sounds, tabs, or things to count.
- Listen to audio books in the car.
- Find books that appeal to your student's unique interests.
- Eliminate distractions like phones, television, and computer games.
- Keep your student's hands busy with quiet toys and activities like playdough, building blocks, lacing cards, or coloring books.

Track Your Progress

Mark the Progress Chart

Have your student mark Lesson 7 on the Progress Chart.

Lesson 8 Three-Letter Blends

Objective

This lesson teaches words containing three-letter blends.

You Will Need

- ☐ *Leap into Reading* pages 59-69
- ☐ Word Cards 31-40

Before You Begin

How We Teach Three-Letter Blends

Blends are two or three consonants grouped together. Your student learned two-letter blends in Level 1, and in this lesson we will concentrate on three-letter blends. Just as in a two-letter blend, each letter in a three-letter blend keeps its own sound.

While there are dozens of two-letter blends, there are only four common initial three-letter blends and they all start with s:

- s-c-r as in *scrap*
- s-p-l as in *split*
- s-p-r as in *spring*
- s-t-r as in *strong*

When your student sounds out a word containing a blend, each letter should be pronounced during the blending process. With practice, your student will recognize these three-letter blends and be able to blend them quickly while reading, as we do in everyday speech.

Some phonics programs teach blends as a unit. For example, the blends pr and str would be taught as their own sounds on letter tiles or flashcards. But that method requires much more memory work because the student would have to memorize dozens of blends. It is much simpler to have the student learn the basic phonograms and blend them to sound out words.

> There are a few words that have three-letter blends at the end of the word, including *unkempt, excerpt, prompt, tempt, contempt,* and *exempt*. None of these words are common in the beginning reader's vocabulary, so we won't cover them in this lesson. The strategy that your student learns in this lesson will apply to blends in any position in a word.

Review

It's time to review the cards behind the Mastered dividers to ensure they stay fresh in your student's mind.

Shuffle the cards behind both Mastered dividers and choose a selection for review.

Previous Concepts

Build the following words with letter tiles. Have your student divide the words where necessary, label with syllable tags, and read. *Sudden* is divided using the Two Consonant Tiles rule.

New Teaching

Play "Change the Word"

Build the word *slit*. s l i t

"What is this word?" *Slit.*

"I can change *slit* to *split* by adding a p̲." s p l i t

"Touch each letter in the word and say its sound." */s/–/p/–/l/–/ĭ/–/t/.*

"Good! Now blend all the letters to form a word." *Split.*

"I will change the vowel."

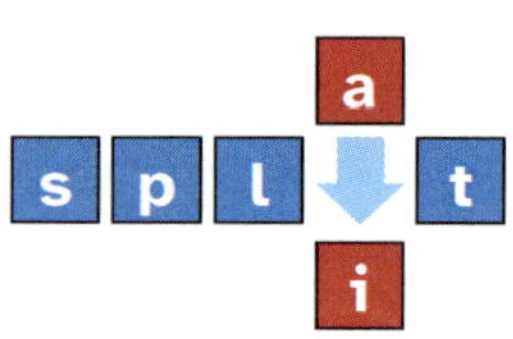

"What does this new word say?" *Splat.*

New Teaching
(continued)

Continue to change one tile at a time to form the following words. Each time, have your student sound out the new word.

splat → splash* → slash* → stash*

sting → string → strip → strap → scrap

*Use the <u>sh</u> tile for the words *splash, slash,* and *stash.*

Complete Activity Sheet

"Now let's take these blends out for a test drive."

<u>Word Flippers for Three-Letter Blends</u>

Remove pages 59-65 from the *Leap into Reading* activity book.

There are four Word Flippers in this lesson. Each page will create one flipper.

Refer to Appendix I for assembly instructions.

Have your student turn the pages and read the words that are formed.

Practice Reading Words

Have your student practice reading the words on Word Cards 31-39.

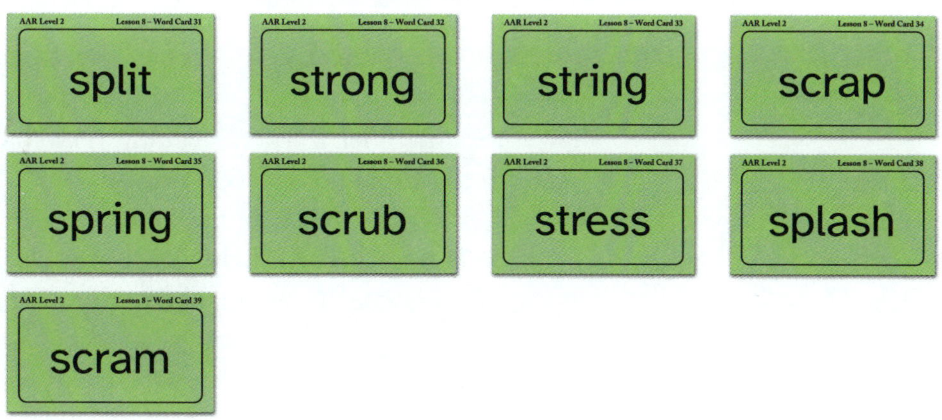

File the Word Cards behind the Review divider in the Reading Review Box.

New Teaching
(continued)

Teach a Leap Word: *her*

Show Word Card 40 to your student.

"This word is *her*, as in *Her dress is red*. The e and the r work together to make the sound /er/. This is a sound we haven't studied yet, so this is a Leap Word."

Review this Leap Word several times today and then file it behind the Review divider in the Reading Review Box.

Practice Fluency

New Words

scrap	scram	strong	splat
her	strap	split	stress
strip	scrub	string	spring
splash	strict		

Phrases

scrub it well	splash in the pond
a strong branch	do a jig
go splat	her string
is not strict	strip of grass
scrap of cloth	a lot of stress
thin strap	split the log

Turn to pages 67-69 in the activity book.

Have your student read from the Practice Sheets.

To engage your student in the fluency exercises, try the activity "Roll the Dice." For instructions, look for this icon in Appendix K.

For many older learners needing remedial work, extra practice with the Practice Sheets is critical.

For younger learners whose eye muscles are still developing, you should choose a reasonable number of lines to practice. Every situation is different, and you need to do what is best for your student.

For more tips on using the Practice Sheets, see Appendix K.

Read-Aloud Time

Read a Story or Poem

Read aloud to your student for twenty minutes.

Track Your Progress

Mark the Progress Chart

Have your student mark Lesson 8 on the Progress Chart.

Hi, there!
You'll have to speak up because
every frog in the swamp is reviewing
flashcards, and boy, is it noisy here!
Have you been reviewing yours?

Those were some fun words we learned today.
In fact, I think I'll use some now ...

spring ...
sprong ...
sproing ...
SPLASH!

(See you soon!)

Lesson 9 Read "An Elf in the Swiss Alps"

Objective

In this lesson, students read a short story and practice skimming for information.

You Will Need

- ☐ *Leap into Reading* pages 71-75
- ☐ *What Am I?* book
- ☐ world map or globe
- ☐ photos of the Swiss Alps

Before You Begin

Preview Skimming

Part of being a fluent and flexible reader is knowing how to skim text. *Skimming* is a reading technique in which the reader moves quickly through the text to get a general idea of the material. Today your student will practice skimming after reading the story.

Prepare Extra Materials

The story in this lesson is set in the Swiss Alps in Switzerland. Since we'll be discussing setting, have a map or globe handy to locate Switzerland before reading the story. It would be ideal if you could also locate photos of the Swiss Alps to show your student.

Review

Review the Phonogram Cards that are behind the Review divider in your student's Reading Review Box. Show each card to your student and have him say the sound(s). If necessary, remind your student of the sound(s).

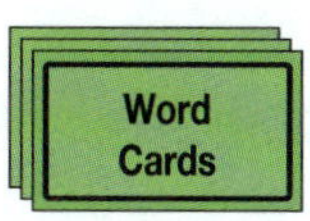

Shuffle and review the Word Cards that are behind the Review divider in your student's Reading Review Box. If your student has difficulty reading a word, build the word with letter tiles and have your student sound it out using the blending procedure shown in Appendix C.

Have some fun with today's Word Card review by playing the game "Word Card Slapjack." For instructions, look for this icon in Appendix M.

New Teaching

Teach the Word *Ostrich*

Build the word *ostrich*. o s t r i ch

"I'll divide this word into syllables and you see if you can read it."

o s   t r i ch

"What does this word say?" *Ostrich.*

Turn to page 75 in the *Leap into Reading* activity book.

Point out the illustration of the ostrich on the Warm-Up Sheet. "The *ostrich* is the largest bird on earth. A grown ostrich is six to nine feet tall, which is taller than most people. An ostrich can't fly, but it can run very fast on its long legs. Ostriches are so strong that people can even ride them!"

> If you wish, you may explain to your student that the syllable division rule for the word *ostrich* hasn't been taught yet, but he should still be able to read the word.
>
> The Three Consonant Tiles rule will be taught in Level 3.

Complete Activity Sheet

"Today's story is set in the Swiss Alps. Let's discover some facts about this place before we read the story."

Facts About the Swiss Alps
Remove pages 71-73 from the *Leap into Reading* activity book.

Cut out the cards on page 73. Place the cards on the table with the illustrations facing up.

"The Swiss Alps are a large mountain range in Europe that spans seven countries: France, Italy, Switzerland, Liechtenstein, Germany, Austria,

New Teaching
(continued)

and Slovenia. Here are some things that can be found in the Swiss Alps."

One by one, read the following facts to your student.

Card No. 1: One of the tallest peaks in the Alps—the Matterhorn—is nearly 15,000 feet high.

Card No. 2: The alphorn is a long wooden horn that is used to communicate in the Alps.

Card No. 3: The large St. Bernard dog is known for its talent as a rescue dog in the Alps.

Card No. 4: The Brown Swiss cow is native to the Alps and produces lots of milk.

Card No. 5: Edelweiss is a white, star-like flower that is found in the Alps.

Card No. 6: The ibex, a type of goat, lives in the mountains of the Swiss Alps.

Your student may then stack the cards, staple them into a small booklet, and paste the booklet to the sheet with the illustration of the Swiss Alps.

Read the Warm-Up Sheet for "An Elf in the Swiss Alps"

Words Taught in Previous Lesson

strong spring her do
splits splash

New Decodable Word

ostrich

Phrases

to the Swiss Alps
soft mittens
thick socks

strong wind
the flock is content
bunch of fuzz

her long legs
do fun tricks
as the socks dry

snacks on insects
picnic on the bluff
spring into a handstand

jump in the slush
eggnog with nutmeg
munch on grass

Names

Ed Oz the ostrich

Turn again to page 75 in the activity book.

Have your student practice reading words and phrases that will be encountered in "An Elf in the Swiss Alps."

New Teaching
(continued)

Teach Vocabulary and Activate Prior Knowledge

"The setting of this next story is the Swiss Alps in Switzerland. The *setting* of a story is where it takes place." Point out where Switzerland is on a map or globe.

"There is often a lot of snow in the Alps. If you went on a vacation to a place with snow, what are some of the things you could do?"

"What would you wear to stay warm?"

"The story you are about to read is about a boy who goes on vacation to the Swiss Alps and meets a very unusual friend."

Read "An Elf in the Swiss Alps"

> Be sure to have your student read the stories aloud, not silently. Oral reading practice is much more effective in developing fluency than silent reading practice.

"Turn to page 51 in your reader and read 'An Elf in the Swiss Alps' aloud." Discuss your student's ideas for the question below when you come to it.

After page 56: "What do you think a flock of sheep is?"

Practice Skimming for Information

"If you went to the Swiss Alps and met Ed the Elf, which activities would you like to do with him?" Encourage your student to flip through the story and select an interesting activity. Have your student read that page aloud.

Read-Aloud Time

Read a Story or Poem

Read aloud to your student for twenty minutes. During the read-aloud time, briefly discuss the setting of the story.

> **Read-Aloud Tip!**
>
> **Model Good Reading Habits**
>
> During your read-aloud times, model how you sometimes stop and think about what you are reading. You want your student to understand that good readers think about what they are reading and that they should expect the text to make sense. Reading is like a conversation between the author and the reader.

Track Your Progress

Mark the Progress Chart

Have your student mark Lesson 9 on the Progress Chart.

I need a new book for bedtime
in the swamp. Any suggestions?

Most people don't know that frogs are big readers, but we are! I especially like tales of adventures at sea. I love all the people I meet and places I go when I read. Just the other day I met a band of panicking pirates on a sinking ship. Lucky for them that Webfoot, King of the Swamp, was there to save them!

What have you been reading during
Read-Aloud Time?

Lesson 10 Syllable Division Rule for One Consonant Tile, Part 1

Objective

This lesson teaches Part 1 of the One Consonant Tile syllable division rule and words that contain both Open and Closed syllables.

You Will Need

- ☐ *Leap into Reading* pages 77-83
- ☐ Word Cards 41-50
- ☐ Syllable Division Rules chart

Before You Begin

Preview Words Containing Both Open and Closed Syllables

Open syllables, such as *we* and *I*, were first introduced in Level 1 and have been reviewed in every lesson so far in Level 2. Now your student is ready to read multisyllable words that include open syllables. Read the following words and note the open syllables.

ho-tel **pre-tend** **he-ro** **e-ven** **stu-dent**

Preview the Syllable Division Rule for One Consonant Tile, Part 1

Your student has learned how to divide words with two consonant tiles between the vowels, as in the word *insect.*

In this lesson, your student will learn how to divide words with just <u>one</u> consonant tile between the vowels, as in the word *frozen.*

1. Build the word *frozen*. Point to the two vowel tiles.

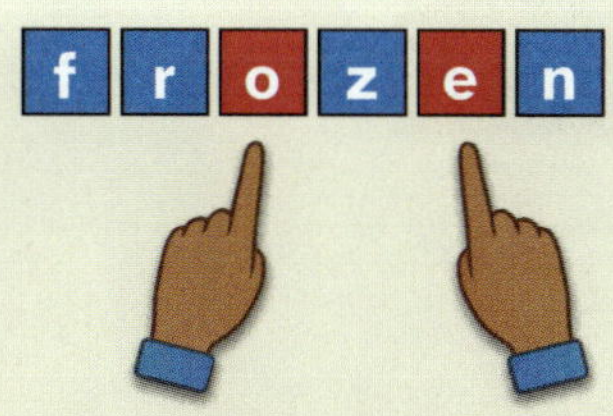

2. Determine how many consonant tiles are between the vowels. (There's just one.)
3. When there is just one consonant tile between the vowels, we usually divide the word so the consonant goes with the second syllable.

Now, using previous knowledge of Open and Closed syllable types, it's easy to read the word.

Before You Begin
(continued)

> The syllable pattern taught in this lesson is sometimes referred to as the VCV pattern (vowel-consonant-vowel pattern).
>
> In Lesson 12, your student will learn Part 2 of this syllable division rule, which states that sometimes the consonant stays with the first syllable, as in the word *finish*.

Review Tips

Review takes only a few minutes a day, yet it is critical to your student's success. But what do you do if you have a lot of Word Cards in your review pile?

Remember that you don't need to review *all* of the Word Cards every day. Instead, just rotate through a selection of ten or so cards each day, or decide to spend the first two or three minutes of your lesson time in review. Then pick up in the Teacher's Manual wherever you left off.

If you feel that there are too many Word Cards behind the review divider and that you shouldn't move on to the next lesson, trust your instincts. Spend more time reviewing the concepts in previous lessons using the letter tiles or activity sheets. You might even consider having a game or activity day in place of your regular lesson. See Appendix L and Appendix M for fun ways to review Phonogram Cards and Word Cards.

Review

Review the Phonogram Cards that are behind the Review divider in your student's Reading Review Box. Show each card to your student and have him say the sound(s). If necessary, remind your student of the sound(s).

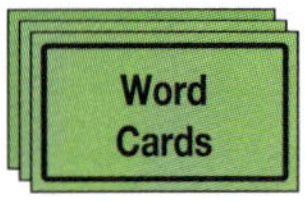

Shuffle and review the Word Cards that are behind the Review divider in your student's Reading Review Box. If your student has difficulty reading a word, build the word with letter tiles and have your student sound it out using the blending procedure shown in Appendix C.

Review
(continued)

Previous Concepts

Build the following words with letter tiles. Have your student divide the words where necessary, label with syllable tags, and read. *Plastic* is divided using the Two Consonant Tiles rule.

plastic

Closed Syllable | Closed Syllable

p l a s | t i c

be

Open Syllable

b e

New Teaching

Teach Syllable Division Rule: One Consonant Tile, Part 1

Build the word *belong*. b e l o ng

"Put your fingers under the vowels."

b e l o ng

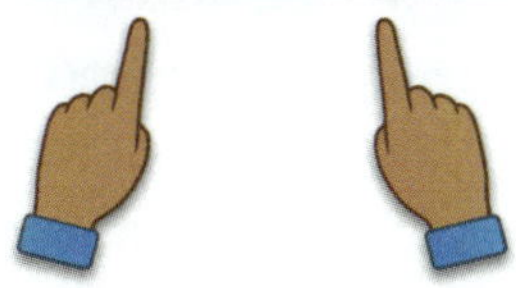

"How many consonant tiles do you see between the vowels?" *One.*

"When there is one consonant tile between two vowels, we usually divide the word before the consonant. Divide this word into syllables." *Student divides the word.*

b e | l o ng

"Most of the time, the consonant goes with the second syllable."

"Is the first syllable Open or Closed?" *Open.*

"Good. Put the **Open** syllable tag over the first syllable. This vowel will make its long sound."

"Is the second syllable open or closed?" *Closed.*

"Good. Put the **Closed** syllable tag over the second syllable. This vowel will make its short sound."

Open Syllable | Closed Syllable

b e | l o ng

New Teaching
(continued)

"Read the first syllable." *Be.*

"Read the second syllable." *Long.*

"Now read the word." *Belong.*

"Great! *Belong* is a real word, so you have divided the word correctly."

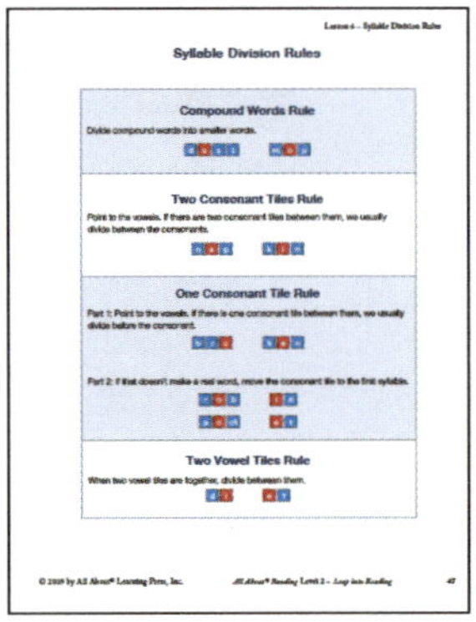

Point to Part 1 of the One Consonant Tile rule on the Syllable Division Rules chart.

"This is Part 1 of the **One Consonant Tile** rule." Read the rule with your student.

Repeat this activity with as many of the following words as necessary until your student can divide the words and read them easily.

hotel **item** **hero** **protect** **basic**

Build the words with letter tiles and have your student follow these steps:

1. Point to the vowels.
2. How many consonants are between the vowels?
3. Divide the word. If there is one consonant, it usually goes with the second syllable.
4. Label both syllables with syllable tags.
5. Read the word. If it sounds like a real word, the student is done.

Play "Guess What I'm Saying"

"I will say two syllables and you will guess what word I am saying: *o...pen.*" *Student says* open *at normal conversational speed.*

Repeat this activity using the following words. Be sure to pause between the syllables as you say them.

ze...ro **be...gin** **ro...bot** **fro...zen** **de...mand**

New Teaching
(continued)

Complete Activity Sheet

"Uh-oh, looks like you need to rescue some kittens!"

Be a Hero

Remove pages 77-80 from the *Leap into Reading* activity book.

Cut out the mother cat and the twelve kitten cards.

Place the kitten cards on the tree with the words facing down.

Have your student choose a card and read the word aloud. If he reads the word correctly, he can rescue the kitten by returning it to the mother cat. If he reads the word incorrectly, return the kitten card to the tree for another try.

Continue until all the kittens have been happily reunited with their mother.

Practice Reading Words

Have your student practice reading the words on Word Cards 41-50.

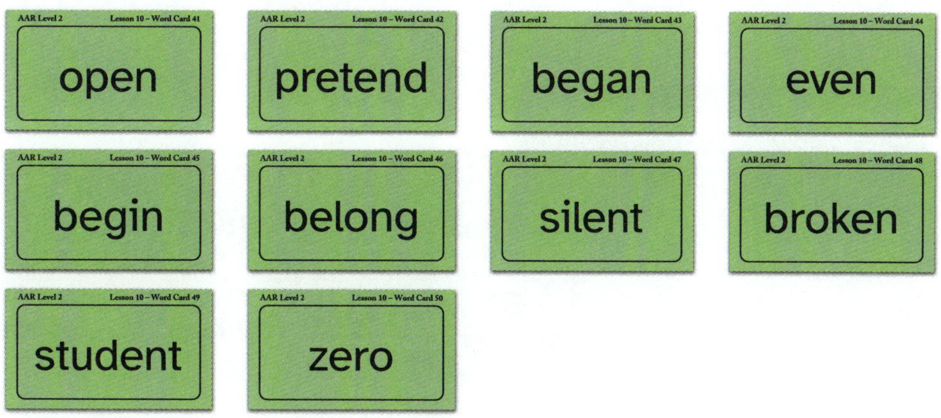

Most students read the word *student* easily, but others may notice that the u in *student* doesn't say its full name. Instead, the /y/ sound is dropped, leaving just the /o͞o/ sound. Although the two sounds of long u will be covered in Lesson 17, you may wish to point this out now if your student asks.

File the Word Cards behind the Review divider in the Reading Review Box.

New Teaching
(continued)

Practice Fluency

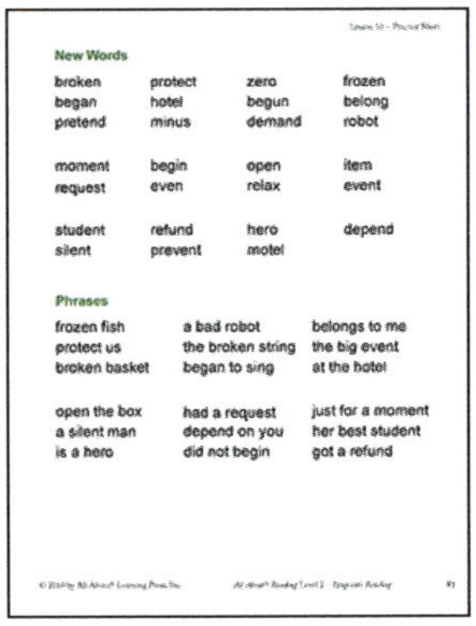

New Words

broken	protect	zero	frozen
began	hotel	begun	belong
pretend	minus	demand	robot
moment	begin	open	item
request	even	relax	event
student	refund	hero	depend
silent	prevent	motel	

Phrases

frozen fish	a bad robot	belongs to me
protect us	the broken string	the big event
broken basket	began to sing	at the hotel
open the box	had a request	just for a moment
a silent man	depend on you	her best student
is a hero	did not begin	got a refund

Turn to pages 81-83 in the activity book.

Have your student read from the Practice Sheets.

Try using sticker dots to break up the Practice Sheet. For instructions, look for this icon in Appendix K.

Read-Aloud Time

Read a Story or Poem

Read aloud to your student for twenty minutes.

Track Your Progress

Mark the Progress Chart

Have your student mark Lesson 10 on the Progress Chart.

Lesson 11 Read "Open Rink"

Objective

In this lesson, students learn about the use of speech bubbles for dialogue and read a short story.

You Will Need

- ☐ *Leap into Reading* pages 85-87
- ☐ *What Am I?* book

Before You Begin

Preview Speech Bubbles and Slang

"Open Rink" is the first story that uses speech bubbles for dialogue. Your student may be familiar with speech bubbles from comic strips. In this lesson, students will practice reading dialogue in speech bubbles before reading the story.

Note also that some slang is used in "Open Rink," such as the phrase "Got it?" to mean "Do you understand?" The story discussion will help students distinguish between proper English and slang.

Warm-Up Sheet Tip

Words Taught in Previous Lesson

open frozen rodent
begin protects hero

Phrases

rink is open
puck and stick
have to go

just a rodent
have a contest
a big event

into the rink
protects the net

have fun
pond is frozen

Names

Chick
Hog
Cat

Yak
Rat
Ram

ref

"Open Rink" is the first story that incorporates multisyllable words containing both Open and Closed syllable types. For some students, this story represents a big step.

To help your student be successful, be sure that he is comfortable reading all the words on the Warm-Up Sheet before continuing on to the story.

Review

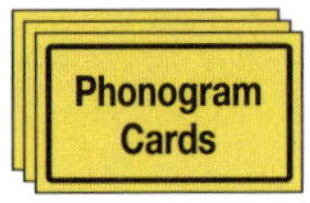

Review the Phonogram Cards that are behind the Review divider in your student's Reading Review Box. Show each card to your student and have him say the sound(s). If necessary, remind your student of the sound(s).

Shuffle and review the Word Cards that are behind the Review divider in your student's Reading Review Box. If your student has difficulty reading a word, build the word with letter tiles and have your student sound it out using the blending procedure shown in Appendix C.

Try spicing up today's Word Card review by playing the game "Swat the Words." For instructions, look for this icon in Appendix M.

New Teaching

Complete Activity Sheet

"Have you ever read a comic book or comic strip? Often in comic books, the words people say are written in speech bubbles. Let's use some speech bubbles to see what these animals have to say."

What Would They Say?

Remove page 85 from the *Leap into Reading* activity book.

Cut out the character cards and the speech bubble cards. Arrange them on the table with the words and illustrations facing up.

Have your student read each speech bubble card aloud, and then have him match it with the appropriate character card. (Some of the cards will work for more than one character.) Or you can encourage your student to make humorous matches of speech bubbles and characters.

Continue until all the characters are matched with a speech bubble card.

New Teaching
(continued)

Read the Warm-Up Sheet for "Open Rink"

Lesson 11 - Warm-Up Sheet for *Open Rink*

Words Taught in Previous Lesson

open frozen rodent
begin protects hero

Phrases

rink is open
puck and stick
have to go

into the rink
protects the net

just a rodent
have a contest
a big event

have fun
pond is frozen

Names

Chick
Hog
Cat

Yak
Rat
Ram

ref

© 2019 by All About® Learning Press, Inc. *All About® Reading Level 2 - Leap into Reading* 87

Turn to page 87 in the activity book.

Have your student practice reading words and phrases that will be encountered in "Open Rink."

Teach Vocabulary and Activate Prior Knowledge

Point to the illustration of the ref on the Warm-Up Sheet. "The word *ref* is short for *referee*. A referee is a person who closely watches a game like basketball or soccer to make sure that the players follow all the rules."

"What is your favorite sport to play? What do you like most about playing it?"

"How do you feel when you win a game? How about when you lose? How do you think the other team feels when it loses?"

"In the story you are about to read, two teams play a great game of hockey. Let's see who wins."

Read "Open Rink"

"Turn to page 65 in your reader and read 'Open Rink' aloud." Discuss your student's ideas for the questions below when you come to them.

After page 67: "What do you think Rat is afraid of?"

After page 79: "Do you think Chick will kick the other animals off the rink?"

New Teaching
(continued)

Discuss Slang

"Sometimes when we speak, we use slang. Slang is a casual way of speaking. It is often found in dialogue in stories. Let's look at 'Open Rink' to find examples of slang."

Turn to page 71, point out the slang terms, and discuss the meaning with your student.

Slang	**Meaning**
"...you scram."	"You will have to leave."
"Got it?"	"Do you understand?"
"Got it."	"Yes, I understand."

Read-Aloud Time

Read a Story or Poem

Read aloud to your student for twenty minutes.

Track Your Progress

Mark the Progress Chart

Have your student mark Lesson 11 on the Progress Chart.

Lesson 12 Syllable Division Rule for One Consonant Tile, Part 2

Objective

This lesson teaches Part 2 of the One Consonant Tile syllable division rule.

You Will Need

- ☐ *Leap into Reading* pages 89-93
- ☐ optional: toothpick or pencil
- ☐ Syllable Division Rules chart
- ☐ Word Cards 51-60

Before You Begin

Preview the Syllable Division Rule for One Consonant Tile, Part 2

In the last lesson, your student learned that when there is just one consonant tile between two vowels, the consonant usually goes with the second syllable, like this:

f r o   z e n

Read the word. If it sounds like a real word—and it is, in this case—your student is done.

For some words, we have to take this one step further. Let's try this with the word *robin*.

1. Build the word *robin*. Point to the two vowel tiles.

2. Determine how many consonant tiles are between the vowels. (There's just one.)
3. Divide the word so the consonant goes with the second syllable.

   r o   b i n

4. This would say /rō-bin/, which doesn't sound like a real word, so the consonant needs to be moved to the first syllable.

   r o b   i n

Robin is a real word, so we know that we've divided the word correctly.

Before You Begin
(continued)

Most VCV words can be decoded by moving the consonant tile to the second syllable, but there are some words in which the consonant tile stays with the first syllable. Examples include *seven, planet,* and *finish.*

Just remember: the consonant *usually* goes with the second syllable, but if that doesn't form a real word, slide the consonant over to the first syllable.

Students typically grasp this idea very quickly using the letter tiles.

Review

Phonogram Cards

Review the Phonogram Cards that are behind the Review divider in your student's Reading Review Box. Show each card to your student and have him say the sound(s). If necessary, remind your student of the sound(s).

Word Cards

Shuffle and review the Word Cards that are behind the Review divider in your student's Reading Review Box. If your student has difficulty reading a word, build the word with letter tiles and have your student sound it out using the blending procedure shown in Appendix C.

Previous Concepts

Build the following word with letter tiles. Have your student divide the word using the One Consonant Tile syllable division rule, label with syllable tags, and read.

depend

New Teaching

Teach Syllable Division Rule: One Consonant Tile, Part 2

Build the word *relax*. r e l a x

"Show me how you would divide this word." *Student locates the vowels, sees one consonant tile between them, and divides the word between the e and the l.*

"Read the word." *Relax.*

"Good. *Relax* is a real word, so you know that you divided this word properly."

Build the word *cabin*. c a b i n

"Show me how you would divide this word." *Student locates the vowels.* At this stage, most students divide the word between the a and the b.

c a   b i n

"Most of the time, the consonant goes with the second syllable. But this time, that doesn't work. This would say /cā-bin/, which isn't a real word. So we know that the consonant needs to stay with the first syllable, like this." Slide the b over to the first syllable.

c a b   i n

"Read this word." *Cabin.*

> If your student has any difficulty reading the word, have him label the syllables with syllable tags and try again.
>
> **Tip!**

Build the word *pocket*. p o ck e t

Point to the ck. "In the word *pocket*, there are two letters on one tile. We usually keep phonograms together. Show me how you would divide this word." *Student locates the vowels and divides the word.*

p o ck   e t

New Teaching
(continued)

> Some students may try to divide *pocket* like this:
>
> p o   ck e t
>
> In that case, have your student read the word aloud so he can see that */pō-cket/* isn't a real word.

"Right. Like in the word *cabin*, the consonant team in the word *pocket* needs to stay with the first syllable. Label this word with syllable tags."

Closed Syllable	Closed Syllable
p o ck	e t

"Good. So the rule is that the consonant or consonant team goes with the second syllable *most* of the time. If that doesn't make a real word, slide the consonant over to the first syllable."

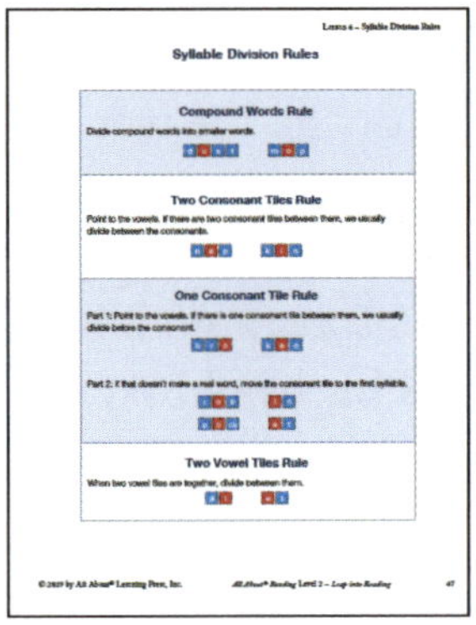
Syllable Division Rules

Compound Words Rule

Two Consonant Tiles Rule

One Consonant Tile Rule

Two Vowel Tiles Rule

Point to Part 2 of the One Consonant Tile rule on the Syllable Division Rules chart.

"This is Part 2 of the **One Consonant Tile** rule." Read the rule with your student.

Repeat this activity with as many of the following words as necessary until your student can divide the words and read them easily. In some of these words, the consonant goes with the second syllable; in others, the consonant needs to be slid over to the first syllable.

habit **humid** **blanket*** **seven** **hero** **minus** **rocket***

*Use the nk and ck tiles for these words.

Answer Key

hab–it	hu–mid	blank–et	sev–en
he–ro	mi–nus	rock–et	

New Teaching
(continued)

Complete Activity Sheet

"Are you ready to use your karate moves to divide some words?"

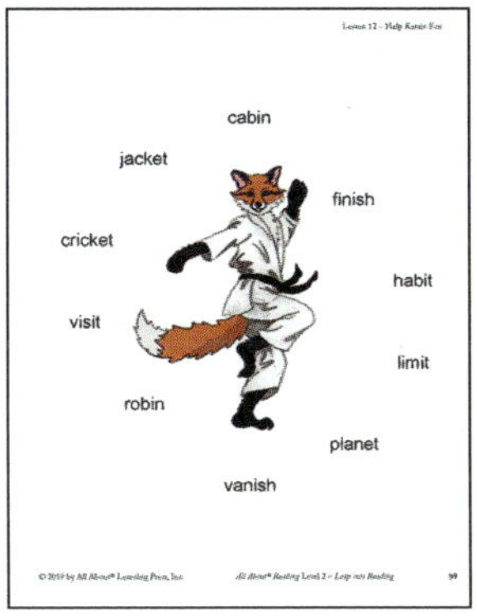

Help Karate Fox

Remove pages 89-90 from the *Leap into Reading* activity book.

"Karate Fox needs help chopping these words into syllables. Can you help him?"

Starting with page 89, have your student use a toothpick as a marker to chop each word into two syllables. Your student should read each part of the word separately and then read the entire word. If your student would prefer not to use a toothpick, he can use a pencil to draw a line dividing the syllables.

Continue with page 90, which offers mixed practice with words introduced in Lessons 10 and 12.

Answer Key

cab–in	fin–ish	hab–it	lim–it	plan–et
van–ish	rob–in	vis–it	crick–et	jack–et
tal–ent	ho–tel	den–im	re–lax	tim–id
spo–ken	be–gin	fro–zen	sev-en	si–lent

Practice Reading Words

Have your student practice reading the words on Word Cards 51-60.

File the Word Cards behind the Review divider in the Reading Review Box.

New Teaching
(continued)

Practice Fluency

New Words

limit	cricket	rocket	finish
jacket	robin	pocket	habit
cabin	radish	seven	blanket
bucket	planet	Helen	

Phrases

no limit	his black jacket
in your pocket	in the cabin
a red radish	fast rocket
log cabin	a thick blanket
bucket of milk	bad habit
the hot planet	seven stamps

Turn to pages 91-93 in the activity book.

Have your student read from the Practice Sheets.

To engage your student in the fluency exercises, try the activity "Buddy Reading." For instructions, look for this icon in Appendix K.

Freeing Up Mental Space for Comprehension

Reading requires two main tasks:

1. Fluently decoding the printed word
2. Comprehending the printed word

For beginning readers, decoding is very difficult because they have to work hard to sound out words to pronounce them. This takes up so much of a beginning reader's attention that your student's mind actually switches between decoding and comprehending a few words at a time. That's why a student's reading can be somewhat choppy when he is initially learning to read. It's all a part of the process!

By consistently working through the fluency exercises, though, your student will learn to decode the printed word more quickly and easily, which will free up the mental space and attention needed for reading comprehension.

Read-Aloud Time

Read a Story or Poem

Read aloud to your student for twenty minutes.

Track Your Progress

Mark the Progress Chart

Have your student mark Lesson 12 on the Progress Chart.

Hi-YA!
Karate Fox was cool!
You probably did a better job than I did
of chopping those words into syllables.
Just between you and me, I'm a little slimy.
Makes it hard to get a good grip on things,
you know?
But I'm a good kicker!
Or should I say KICK-ER?

Lesson 13 Read "Broken Robot"

Objective

In this lesson, students learn about abbreviations and read a short story.

You Will Need

- ☐ *Leap into Reading* pages 95-97
- ☐ *What Am I?* book
- ☐ pencil

Before You Begin

Preview Abbreviations

In today's story, your student will encounter some common abbreviations, or shortened versions of words. Some abbreviations need periods while others don't. Here are some examples of the most common abbreviations.

With periods:

U.S.	**Mrs.**	**Mr.**	**Dr.**	**a.m.**
etc.	**Sr.**	**Rd.**	**e.g.**	**Feb.**

Without periods:

EST	**rpm**	**FBI**	**CEO**	**cm**
CD	**TV**	**NASA**	**NY**	**mph**

Preview Colons

Your student will also be introduced to the colon. This punctuation mark is used most commonly in these two ways:

- **formal correspondence:** *Dear Mrs. Marshall:*
- **to introduce a list of items:** *Bring these three things: bananas, mangoes, and forks.*

Review

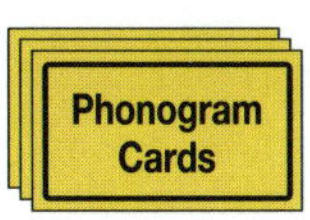

Review the Phonogram Cards that are behind the Review divider in your student's Reading Review Box. Show each card to your student and have him say the sound(s). If necessary, remind your student of the sound(s).

Review
(continued)

Shuffle and review the Word Cards that are behind the Review divider in your student's Reading Review Box. If your student has difficulty reading a word, build the word with letter tiles and have your student sound it out using the blending procedure shown in Appendix C.

New Teaching

Teach Abbreviations

> Your student is not expected to memorize these abbreviations. At this point, we are just introducing the concept.

"An *abbreviation* is a shortened version of a word. In this activity, we'll look at abbreviations that we would use when addressing an envelope."

Address an Envelope
Remove page 95 from the *Leap into Reading* activity book.

Point to the envelope at the top of the page. "In our next story, a boy named Todd writes a letter. Here is the front of the envelope that Todd used."

Point to the line that reads *Zigzag Robot Shop.* "Here is the name and address of the company that Todd wrote to. Who did Todd send this letter to?" *Zigzag Robot Shop.*

Point to the *Rd.* in Todd's return address. "*Rd.* is an abbreviation for the word *road.* When we read *Rd.,* we don't say the abbreviation—we say *road.* So in this case, we would say that Todd lives on Chipmunk Road."

Point to the *ME* in Todd's address. "*ME* is an abbreviation for the state of *Maine.* Todd lives in Maine."

Point to the postmark. "This postmark says that the letter was mailed on Jan. 12, 2025. *Jan.* is an abbreviation for the month of *January.*"

Point to the abbreviation *St.* in the address of the Zigzag Robot Shop. "We see that the Robot Shop is located at 634 Robin Street. See how the word *street* is abbreviated *St.*? We still pronounce the entire word, *street,* even though the abbreviation only says *St.*"

New Teaching
(continued)

Point to the abbreviation *MN*. "*MN* is an abbreviation for the state of *Minnesota*. The robot shop is in Minnesota."

Point to the blank envelope at the bottom of the page. "Let's pretend that you're sending a letter to someone. To whom would you like to write?"

Guide your student in the process of filling in the lines on the envelope. Encourage your student to write his name and address in the upper left corner, using whatever abbreviations are necessary. Then ask your student to fill in the name and address for the recipient of the letter. Discuss any additional abbreviations that are introduced in this process.

Read the Warm-Up Sheet for "Broken Robot"

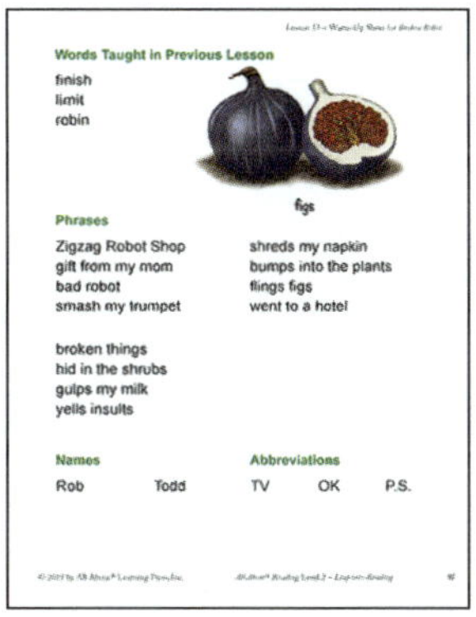

Words Taught in Previous Lesson

finish
limit
robin

figs

Phrases

Zigzag Robot Shop
gift from my mom
bad robot
smash my trumpet

shreds my napkin
bumps into the plants
flings figs
went to a hotel

broken things
hid in the shrubs
gulps my milk
yells insults

Names

Rob Todd

Abbreviations

TV OK P.S.

Turn to page 97 in the activity book.

Have your student practice reading words and phrases that will be encountered in "Broken Robot."

Point out the abbreviations at the bottom of the sheet. Explain that *TV* is an abbreviation for *television*, *OK* is an abbreviation for *okay*, and *P.S.* is an abbreviation for *post script*, which means a bit of writing added at the end of a letter.

Teach Vocabulary and Activate Prior Knowledge

"Today you will read a letter written by a boy named Todd. Todd receives a robot as a gift, but the robot causes a lot of trouble."

Point out the illustration of the figs on the Warm-Up Sheet. "Part of the trouble involves *figs*. Have you ever eaten a fig? Figs are very sweet. In the U.S., figs are usually sold as a dried fruit, but sometimes you can buy them fresh."

"Let's find out what kind of trouble this robot causes."

New Teaching
(continued)

Read "Broken Robot"

"Turn to page 83 in your reader and read 'Broken Robot' aloud." Discuss your student's ideas for the questions below when you come to them.

After page 84: Point to the colon after the words *To the Zigzag Robot Shop*. "This symbol is called a colon. It is often used in the greeting of business letters."

After page 85: "Why do you think Rob the Robot runs into the shrubs and hides?"

After page 87: "Why do you think the hotel staff sent a bill for the broken things?"

After page 90: "Do you think the robot shop will refund Todd's money?"

After reading: "What are some of the bad things that Rob the Robot does?" Have your student skim the text to find answers.

"If you had a robot like Rob, would you want to return him?"

Read-Aloud Time

Read a Story or Poem

Read aloud to your student for twenty minutes.

Read-Aloud Tip!

Stay Awake During Read-Aloud Time!
Does read-aloud time find you fighting fatigue? Here are some parent-tested ways to keep you from drifting into dreamland in the middle of a story.

- Vary your location, especially if your sofa is too comfy. Try outside or at the kitchen table.
- Read early in the day after breakfast or lunch when you are still fresh and wide awake.
- Distract yourself by sipping tea or nibbling popcorn or, even better, by creating funny voices for the characters.
- Read where there is bright, natural light.
- Have an older student read aloud to younger siblings—while you sneak off for a well-deserved doze!

Track Your Progress

Mark the Progress Chart

Have your student mark Lesson 13 on the Progress Chart.

Lesson 14 The First Job of Silent E

Objective

This lesson teaches how Silent E makes a vowel long in vowel-consonant-e words.

You Will Need

- ☐ *Leap into Reading* pages 99-110
- ☐ pencil
- ☐ Jobs of Silent E chart
- ☐ Word Cards 61-70

Before You Begin

Locate the Jobs of Silent E Chart

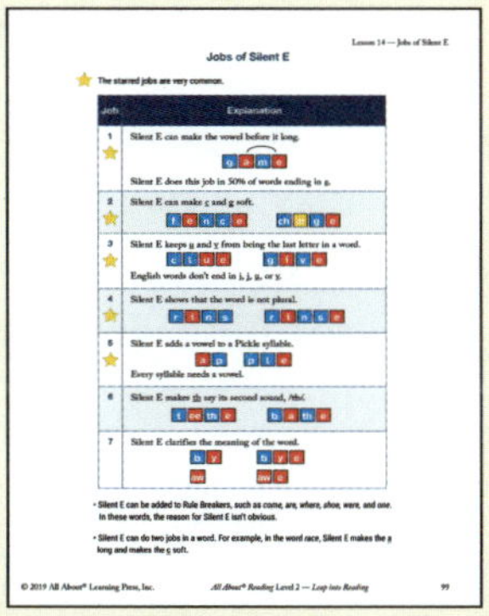

Turn to page 99 in the activity book. The Jobs of Silent E chart will be used in future lessons so you may want to bookmark it, tuck it into the back of the Teacher's Manual, or attach it to a bulletin board for future reference.

Today's lesson will cover the first job of Silent E. For a listing of all the jobs of Silent E and when they are first introduced, see Appendix F.

Preview the First Job of Silent E

When e occurs at the end of a word, it is usually silent and we call it Silent E. Silent E can perform several different jobs. Today's lesson teaches the first and most common job of Silent E: Silent E can make the preceding vowel say its name (or its long vowel sound). Consider the following example of how Silent E affects the preceding vowel.

In the word *hop*, o says its short sound. h o p

When we add Silent E, o says its long sound. h o p e

This pattern is often referred to as the vowel-consonant-e pattern (or VCE pattern).

Review

Review the Phonogram Cards that are behind the Review divider in your student's Reading Review Box. Show each card to your student and have him say the sound(s). If necessary, remind your student of the sound(s).

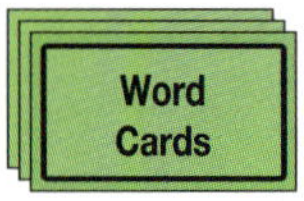

Shuffle and review the Word Cards that are behind the Review divider in your student's Reading Review Box. If your student has difficulty reading a word, build the word with letter tiles and have your student sound it out using the blending procedure shown in Appendix C.

Your student may enjoy practicing Word Cards by typing a selection of them on a computer. This activity is especially good for kids who struggle with handwriting.

New Teaching

Introduce Silent E

Build the word *mad*.

"We can change the word *mad* to *made* by adding e to the end of the word."

Point to the e. "When e is added to the end of a word, it is usually silent. We call it Silent E. It can also make the vowel before it say its long vowel sound, or its name. So in this word, a says /ā/."

Remove the e. "If we take away Silent E, what does this word say?" *Mad.*

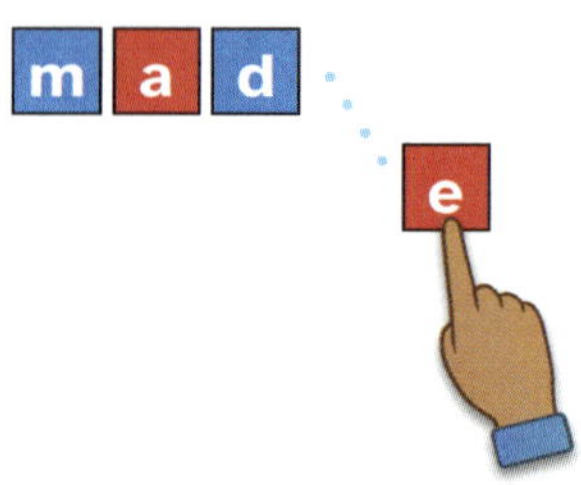

"The a no longer says its name. Instead, it goes back to its short sound."

New Teaching
(continued)

Build the word *hop*. 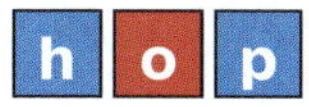

"We can change the word *hop* to *hope* by adding Silent E."

"The job of Silent E in this word is to make the vowel before it long."

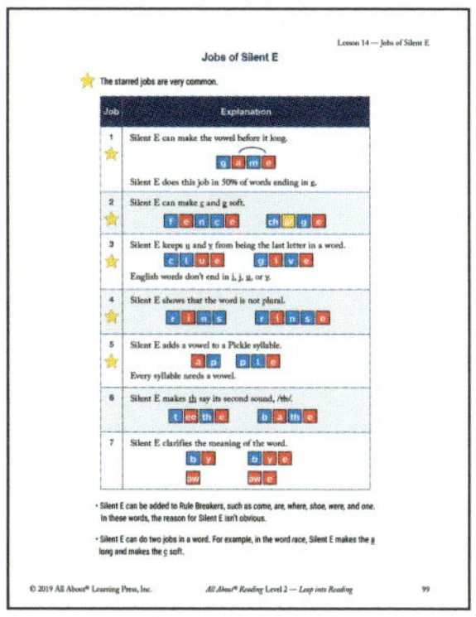

Take out the Jobs of Silent E chart, found on page 99 of the *Leap into Reading* activity book. Point to the first job on the chart and read it with your student. "This is the first and most common job of Silent E. Silent E does other jobs as well, and you will learn about those in later lessons."

Teach Words with Silent E

Build the word *dime*. 

Demonstrate your thought process as you decode the word.

"This word ends in Silent E, so I know that the i will probably be long. I will sound out this word."

Touch under the d and say */d/*.

Touch under the i and say */ī/*.

Touch under the m and say */m/*.

New Teaching
(continued)

Touch under the e. "This is Silent E."

Now go back to the beginning of the word. Slide your finger under the letters d-i-m-e and say *dime* slowly.

Finally, read the word *dime* at a normal pace as we do when we speak.

Using the same procedure for blending, have your student sound out the word *kite*.

Complete Activity Sheets

"Let's help Detective Dog find some Silent E's."

Help Detective Dog

Remove pages 101-105 from the activity book.

Cut out the word cards and place them in a pile.

Have your student select a word card from the pile and read the word aloud. He should then place the card in the empty box next to the Silent E on the sheet with Detective Dog and read the new word that has been created.

This activity gives your student practice with short vowel sounds (as in *kit*) and long vowel sounds (as in *kite*).

New Teaching
(continued)

"Good work! Now let's discover some more Silent E words."

Kit or Kite?
Remove page 107 from the activity book.

Beginning with the first square, have your student read the pair of words aloud. He should then select and circle the word that matches the illustration.

Continue until all the squares have been completed.

Practice Reading Words

Have your student practice reading the words on Word Cards 61-70.

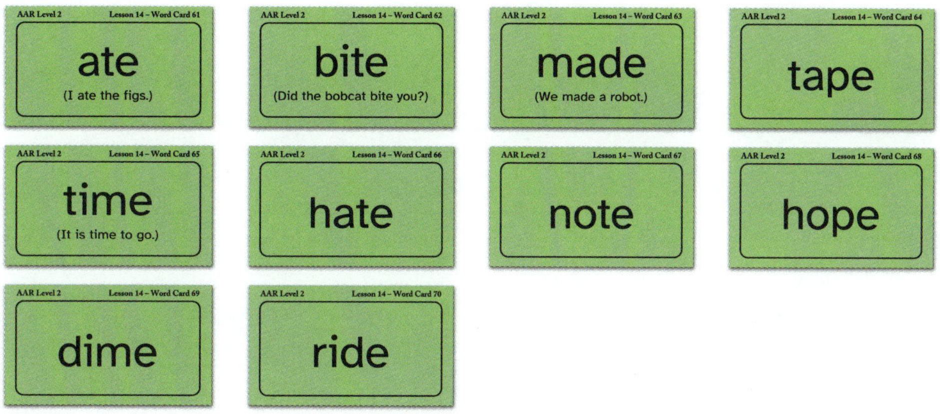

File the Word Cards behind the Review divider of the Reading Review Box.

Practice Fluency

New Words

fine quite Jane rode
ride same pale hate
tape shine ripe dime

ate bite time fade
code dine kite cane

rate pine hide made
note Pete robe hope

Phrases

strip of tape fly a kite ate jam
time to hide made a note quite big
bite a radish shine the glass so pale

rode a yak mad at Jane a ripe fig
not the same hate clams is fine
at this rate has a robe

Turn to pages 109-110 in the activity book.

Have your student read from the Practice Sheets.

Read-Aloud Time

Read a Story or Poem

Read aloud to your student for twenty minutes.

Track Your Progress

Mark the Progress Chart

Have your student mark Lesson 14 on the Progress Chart.

Lesson 15 Name Game Syllables

Objective

This lesson teaches the Name Game syllable type, plus more words in which Silent E makes the preceding vowel long.

You Will Need

- ☐ *Leap into Reading* pages 111-124
- ☐ Word Cards 71-79
- ☐ Name Game syllable tag

Before You Begin

Preview Name Game Syllables

Your student has already learned two syllable types, Closed and Open. Today she will learn the third syllable type, the Name Game syllable.

In the last lesson, your student learned that Silent E can make the preceding vowel say its name, as in the word *game*. This syllable type is often referred to as the vowel-consonant-e (VCE) syllable.

Name Game

We have a name for this syllable that is easier to remember: the Name Game syllable.

Beginning readers who do not recognize this syllable type have a more difficult time decoding vowel-consonant-e words, often trying to decode the word with a short vowel sound instead of a long vowel sound. When your student can instantly recognize a Name Game syllable, she will be able to read Silent E words more easily.

Remember that Silent E can perform jobs other than making the preceding vowel long (see Appendix F), so not every word ending in Silent E is automatically a Name Game syllable.

Preview Words Containing R

In some regions, the letter r may slightly change the vowel sound in words ending in -are, such as *bare, care, dare, fare,* and *rare*. If these words are pronounced in your area with more of a short e sound than a long a sound, or if the pronunciation causes difficulty for your student, you may wish to teach them as Leap Words.

The Practice Sheets and Word Flippers provide extra practice with these words.

Review

Review the Phonogram Cards that are behind the Review divider in your student's Reading Review Box. Show each card to your student and have him say the sound(s). If necessary, remind your student of the sound(s).

Get your student on her feet for the Phonogram Card review with the game "Phonogram Hopscotch." For instructions, look for this icon in Appendix L.

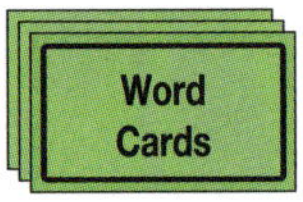

Shuffle and review the Word Cards that are behind the Review divider in your student's Reading Review Box. If your student has difficulty reading a word, build the word with letter tiles and have your student sound it out using the blending procedure shown in Appendix C.

New Teaching

Teach the Third Syllable Type: Name Game

Build the word *cake*.

"What is the job of Silent E in this word?" *To make the a long*, or *to make the a say its name.*

"Right. When Silent E gets in line after the consonant to make the vowel before it long, we have a new syllable type." Move the Name Game syllable tag above the word *cake*.

"Have you ever gone to a party? Have you ever worn a party hat? This tag has a party hat on it because we are pretending that the vowels in the word *cake* are at a party and they are playing a game called the Name Game."

New Teaching
(continued)

Point to the a in *cake*. "Here's how the Name Game works: Silent E asks the vowel what its name is, and the vowel says its name. That's the Name Game."

Point to the e in *cake*. "Silent E is at the end of the word *cake*, and a says its name."

Build the following words with letter tiles. Have your student label each syllable with the proper tag.

Keep the word *bike* in the workspace. Point to Silent E. "Making the vowel long is the most common job of Silent E. But remember, Silent E does other jobs as well, and you will learn about those in later lessons."

Complete Activity Sheets

"The Party Monsters are back! This time they are playing the Name Game."

Party Monsters Play the Name Game

Remove pages 111-112 from the *Leap into Reading* activity book.

Cut out the two syllable type strips and lay them on the table. Cut out the monster cards and place them in a pile with the words facing down.

Have your student select a monster card and read the word on the back. If the word is a Closed syllable, he should put the monster by the closed door. If the word is a Name Game syllable, put the monster by the party hat.

Continue until all the monster cards have been read and sorted.

> **Tip!** Whenever necessary, remind your student that Silent E asks the vowel to say its name. This will prompt your student to use the long vowel sound for the first vowel.

New Teaching
(continued)

<u>Answer Key</u>
Closed: glop, pop, thump, gift, smash, lick
Name Game: hide, joke, cake, chase, wave, five

"Now lets flip through some Name Game syllables!"

<u>Word Flippers for Name Game Syllables</u>
Remove pages 113-119 from the activity book.

There are four Word Flippers in this lesson. Each page will create one flipper.

Refer to Appendix I for assembly instructions. Note that these flippers will be stapled on the left instead of on the right.

Have your student turn the pages and read the words that are formed.

Practice Reading Words

Have your student practice reading the words on Word Cards 71-79.

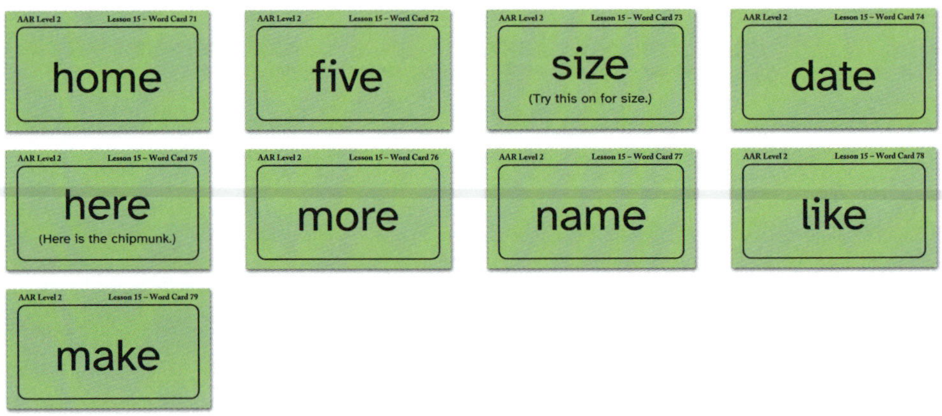

File the Word Cards behind the Review divider in the Reading Review Box.

New Teaching
(continued)

Practice Fluency

New Words

mile	bike	shave	shade
shake	line	here	gave
nine	safe	wore	share
Kate	cave	maze	Mike
home	shape	rope	hive
chase	wake	more	care
wave	size	take	bone
tide	fire	pole	save
bake	dive	late	pile
gate	cake	vine	woke
sale	hole	wide	vote
name	five	Jake	wire
hike	mine	life	joke
tire	lake	wife	pipe
game	side	like	

Turn to pages 121-124 in the activity book.

Have your student read from the Practice Sheets.

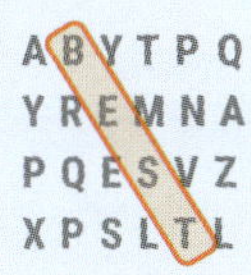

To engage your student in the fluency exercises, make a word search puzzle. For instructions, look for this icon in Appendix K.

Read-Aloud Time

Read a Story or Poem

Read aloud to your student for twenty minutes.

Track Your Progress

Mark the Progress Chart

Have your student mark Lesson 15 on the Progress Chart.

Party time!
Get your pointy hat on,
grab that Silent E,
and let's get out of here.
There are cupcakes in the next story.
Follow me!

Lesson 16 Read "The Bake Sale"

Objective

In this lesson, students read a short story and discuss character motivation.

You Will Need

- ☐ *Leap into Reading* pages 125-127
- ☐ *What Am I?* book

Before You Begin

Preview Character Motivation

Characters in a story often have a goal or something that they want. This goal is the reason, or the *motivation*, behind their actions. This lesson touches lightly on the concept of character motivation. Your student may not fully grasp this concept right away, and that's fine. You might bring it up during any read-aloud time when a character has clear motivation, or you might discuss the motivation behind the actions of people in real life.

Here are a few examples of character motivation from classic stories:

- In *Jack and the Beanstalk*, Jack sells his cow for five magic beans. His motivation is his desire to help himself and his mother.
- In *The Three Little Pigs*, one pig builds a house of brick. His motivation is to protect himself from the Big Bad Wolf.
- In *Cinderella*, the stepsisters give Cinderella many chores to do. Their motivation is to prevent her from going to the ball.

Review

Review the Phonogram Cards that are behind the Review divider in your student's Reading Review Box. Show each card to your student and have him say the sound(s). If necessary, remind your student of the sound(s).

Shuffle and review the Word Cards that are behind the Review divider in your student's Reading Review Box. If your student has difficulty reading a word, build the word with letter tiles and have your student sound it out using the blending procedure shown in Appendix C.

New Teaching

Complete Activity Sheet

"In today's story, the main character wants to earn some money. Before we read the story, let's explore some ways to earn money."

Earn Some Cash!

Remove page 125 from the *Leap into Reading* activity book.

Cut out the cards and arrange them on the table with the illustrations facing up.

Have your student read each card and then discuss the various ways to earn money.

"If you wanted to earn money, which of these jobs would you like to do?" Have your student select one of the cards, or use the blank card to create his own preferred job.

"Is there a job you *wouldn't* want to do? Why not?"

Read the Warm-Up Sheet for "The Bake Sale"

Words Taught in Previous Lesson

more bake sale like cupcake home gave hope ate came time fine

shine bike same take note bite

Phrases

cupcake mix
bake sale
we can bake them
it still runs fine
shine them up
help the dogs

cash from the bake sale
my pen pal
got a sad note

fix-it shop
red bike

$100

Names

Kate Nate Jane Helen Dave Beth Sang

Turn to page 127 in the activity book.

Have your student practice reading words and phrases that will be encountered in "The Bake Sale."

New Teaching
(continued)

Teach Vocabulary and Activate Prior Knowledge

Point out the *$1.00* written under the illustration of the dollar bill on the Warm-Up Sheet. "This is a common way to write *one dollar:* a dollar sign, the number 1, a decimal point, and two zeros. The number after the dollar sign refers to how many dollars, and the zeros after the decimal point refer to how many cents. In this case, there is one whole dollar and no additional cents."

"The girl in the next story holds a bake sale so she can earn the money to buy a new red bicycle. What is something special that you would buy if you earned money at a bake sale?"

"The girl in the story decides not to spend her money on a bicycle after all. Can you guess what she decides to do with the money she earned from her bake sale? You'll have to read the story to find out!"

Read "The Bake Sale"

"Turn to page 93 in your reader and read 'The Bake Sale' aloud." Discuss your student's ideas for the questions below as you come to them.

After page 96: "Look at the sign in the illustration. What would you buy from the bake sale if you had one dollar to spend?"

After reading: "Characters in a story often have a goal or something that they want. This goal is the reason, or the *motivation*, behind their actions. For example, a runner who wants to win a marathon trains every day. The marathon is his motivation, or reason, for training."

"In the story 'The Bake Sale,' what is Kate's motivation for having a bake sale at the beginning of the story? How does her motivation change at the end of the story?" *Kate's motivation in the beginning is to get a red bike; at the end it is to help Beth and the dogs.*

Read-Aloud Time

Read a Story or Poem

Read aloud to your student for twenty minutes.

Read-Aloud Tip!

When Your Student Reads Too Fast

Reading too fast may not seem like a problem to worry about, but there are definite drawbacks to it. Your fast reader may skip or add words, ignore punctuation, mumble, or have a hard time remembering details of the story. Here are some strategies to slow your reader down.

- Model the same passage reading fast with no expression, and then again slowly with expression. Can your student hear the difference?
- See if having a physical reminder, like using a piece of paper as a guide, helps your student slow down.
- Invent a code phrase, like "speedy bunny," to remind your student to slow down.
- If your student ignores punctuation, have her pinch her fingers together when she gets to punctuation at the end of sentences. This is a good physical reminder for her to slow down.

Track Your Progress

Mark the Progress Chart

Have your student mark Lesson 16 on the Progress Chart.

Lesson 17 Long U and the Sound of S between Two Vowels

Objective

This lesson teaches the two sounds of long u and the sound of s between two vowels.

You Will Need

- ☐ *Leap into Reading* pages 129-136
- ☐ Word Cards 80-89

Before You Begin

Review Phonogram U

u In Level 1, your student learned the three sounds of u:

- /ŭ/ as in *up* (emphasized in Level 1, Lesson 12)
- /ū/ as in *unit* (emphasized in this lesson)
- /o͝o/ as in *put* (emphasized in Level 2, Lesson 37)

Note that the letter r changes the sound of the long u slightly, as in the words *cure, pure,* and *lure.*

Preview the Two Sounds of Long U

The name of the letter u (its long sound) starts with a consonant /y/ sound. Listen for the /y/ sound in the following words.

unit **fume** **mule** **cute** **music** **uniform**

In some words, however, the /y/ sound is dropped. Read the following words aloud.

tulip **rule** **tuna** **dude** **June** **rude**

The /y/ sound is naturally dropped from long u when you say these words. Though there is no rule stating whether the /y/ sound should be pronounced before long u, most students will naturally say the correct pronunciation.

Review Phonogram S

s In Level 1, your student learned that the letter s can say /s/ or /z/ when used as a suffix, as in *bats, cans,* and *batches*. In this lesson, your student will learn that s can also say /z/ when it is between two vowels. Read the following examples and listen for the /z/ sound.

these	**music**	**nose**	**use**	**wise**
chose	**hose**	**muse**	**rise**	**pose**

Before You Begin
(continued)

Note that while s often says /z/ between two vowels, this is not always the case. The letter s retains the /s/ sound between two vowels in many words, such as *goose, case,* and *house.*

Refer to the Letter Tiles app or Phonogram Sounds app for a demonstration of the u and s phonogram sounds.

Review

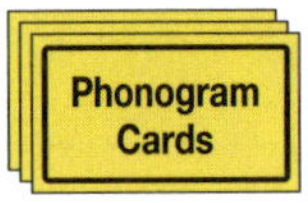

Review the Phonogram Cards that are behind the Review divider in your student's Reading Review Box. Show each card to your student and have him say the sound(s). If necessary, remind your student of the sound(s).

Shuffle and review the Word Cards that are behind the Review divider in your student's Reading Review Box. If your student has difficulty reading a word, build the word with letter tiles and have your student sound it out using the blending procedure shown in Appendix C.

Your student may enjoy reviewing Word Cards with the activity "Tell a Story." For instructions, look for this icon in Appendix M.

Build the following words with letter tiles. Have your student label the words with syllable tags and read.

shade

Name Game Syllable

sh | a | d | e

bent

Closed Syllable

b | e | n | t

New Teaching

Teach the Two Sounds of Long U

> For teaching purposes, it is helpful to exaggerate the sound of long u in the words *cute* and *rude*.

Build the word *cute*. c u t e

"In the word *cute*, what sound does the u make?" */ū/.*

"Do you hear the /y/ part of the /ū/ sound? You can hear it in the word *use*." Have your student read the word and listen for the long u sound.

Build the word *rude* beneath the word *cute*. r u d e

"In many words, though, the full /ū/ sound is not pronounced. Say the word *rude*." *Rude.*

Point to the letter u in the word *rude*. "What sound is the u saying in this word?" */o͞o/.*

"So you can see that long u sometimes says /ū/ while other times it says /o͞o/."

Build the word *rule*. r u l e

"Read this word." *Rule.*

Teach Words with S between Two Vowels

Move the s letter tile into the workspace. s

"What sounds can the letter s make?" */s/–/z/.*

Build the word *nose*. n o s e

New Teaching
(continued)

"Most of the time when s̲ is between two vowels, it says /z/. What does this word say?" *Nose.*

Build the following words with letter tiles to practice.

wise **rose** **chose** **use**

Complete Activity Sheet

"Let's go cherry picking!"

__Cherry Picking__

Remove pages 129-132 from the *Leap into Reading* activity book.

Cut out the cherry cards and basket.

Arrange the word cards on the tree with the cherries facing up. Have your student pick a cherry card, turn it over, and read the word. If she reads the word correctly, she may add the cherry card to her basket. If she reads the word incorrectly, return the card to the tree for another try.

Continue until all the cherries have been picked.

Practice Reading Words

Have your student practice reading the words on Word Cards 80-89.

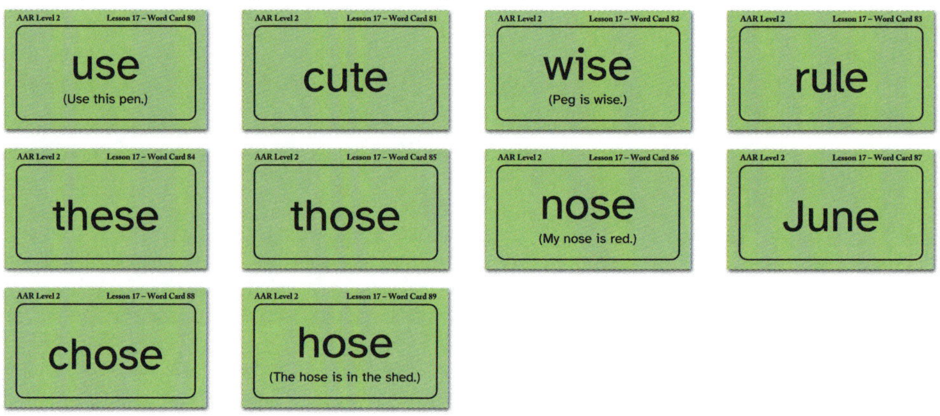

File the Word Cards behind the Review divider in the Reading Review Box.

New Teaching
(continued)

Practice Fluency

New Words

June	rose	use	those
these	cure	rise	cute
hose	rule	wise	chose
rude	nose	pure	

Phrases

a wise man	can cure her
his red nose	those ants
the cute kitten	a pink rose
these muffins	is not rude
use a hose	chose a gift
rise up	has a rule

Turn to pages 133-136 in the activity book.

Have your student read from the Practice Sheets.

To engage your student in the fluency exercises, let her illustrate a selection of words. For instructions, look for this icon in Appendix K.

Read-Aloud Time

Read a Story or Poem

Read aloud to your student for twenty minutes.

Track Your Progress

Mark the Progress Chart

Have your student mark Lesson 17 on the Progress Chart.

Lesson 18 Read "Matt the Musk Ox"

Objective

In this lesson, students read a short story and compare and contrast characters.

You Will Need

- ☐ *Leap into Reading* pages 137-139
- ☐ *What Am I?* book

Before You Begin

Help Your Student Read for Meaning

As your student reads today's story, monitor yourself to see if you interrupt him too often. Instead of immediately correcting your student's misread words, let him finish the sentence so he has a chance to self-correct.

For example, if the student reads *The sheep was flapping on the clothesline,* he will probably self-correct because the sentence obviously doesn't make sense. He will look back to see where his error is and reread the sentence as *The sheet was flapping on the clothesline.*

If he does continue reading without correcting himself, prompt him to notice the error after he has completed the sentence: "Try reading that sentence again" or "You've almost got that—try it one more time." If the error resulted in a sentence that didn't make sense, prompt your student to try again to achieve the correct meaning.

Review

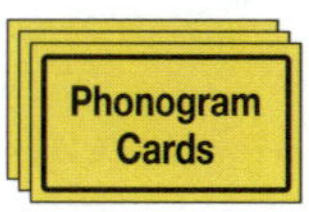

Review the Phonogram Cards that are behind the Review divider in your student's Reading Review Box. Show each card to your student and have him say the sound(s). If necessary, remind your student of the sound(s).

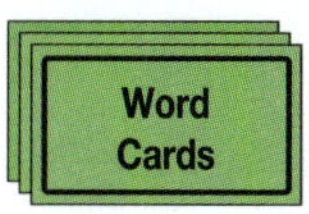

Shuffle and review the Word Cards that are behind the Review divider in your student's Reading Review Box. If your student has difficulty reading a word, build the word with letter tiles and have your student sound it out using the blending procedure shown in Appendix C.

New Teaching

Teach the Word *Selfish*

Build the word *self.* s e l f

"Read this word." *Self.*

"I'm going to add i-sh." s e l f i sh

"Now what word is this?" *Selfish.*

"*Selfish* means *only thinking of oneself.* If a person is selfish, he doesn't think about others and he doesn't share."

> If necessary, your student can use the Two Consonant Tiles syllable division rule to decode this word.
>
> s e l   f i sh
>
> Alternatively, *selfish* can be divided using the Suffix rule, which is taught in Level 3.
>
> s e l f   i sh

Read the Warm-Up Sheet for "Matt the Musk Ox"

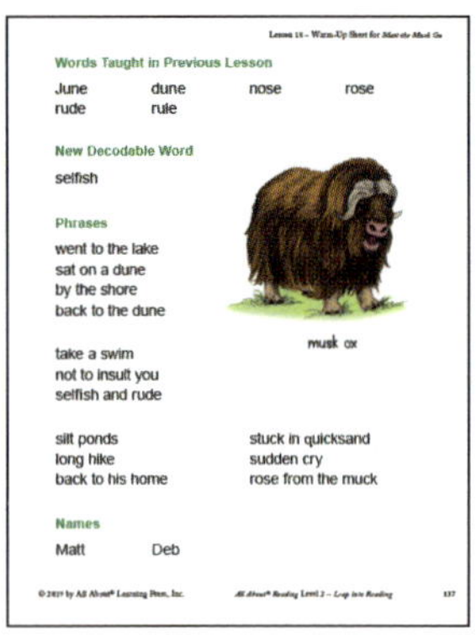
Words Taught in Previous Lesson

June dune nose rose
rude rule

New Decodable Word

selfish

Phrases

went to the lake
sat on a dune
by the shore
back to the dune

take a swim
not to insult you
selfish and rude

silt ponds
long hike
back to his home

stuck in quicksand
sudden cry
rose from the muck

Names

Matt Deb

Turn to page 137 in the *Leap into Reading* activity book.

Have your student practice reading words and phrases that will be encountered in "Matt the Musk Ox."

New Teaching
(continued)

Teach Vocabulary and Activate Prior Knowledge

Point out the illustration of the musk ox on the Warm-Up Sheet. "In our next story, a *musk ox* is one of the main characters. A musk ox is a large, wild animal with thick, shaggy fur and horns that lives in cold, snowy, arctic areas. They have a strong odor that smells bad to people, but it is a good thing for the musk oxen because it helps them attract their mates."

"The setting of today's story is a lake. Next to the lake is a sand dune. A *dune* is a hill of sand that is created either by wind or water flow. A dune can be big or small."

"This story also mentions a *silt pond.* A silt pond is a muddy pond. Would you rather swim in a muddy pond or a clean lake?"

"What do you think might happen if a musk ox met a dog on the way to swim in a lake? Would the musk ox and the dog be friends?"

"Let's see if your prediction comes true."

Read "Matt the Musk Ox"

"Turn to page 105 in your reader and read 'Matt the Musk Ox' aloud." Discuss your student's ideas for the question below when you come to it.

After page 110: "Deb is stuck in quicksand. *Quicksand* is a mixture of water and sand. It can be hard to get out of quicksand because the more you move around, the deeper you sink. How do you think Deb will get out of the quicksand?"

New Teaching
(continued)

Complete Activity Sheet

"Let's see how the characters of Matt and Deb are alike and different."

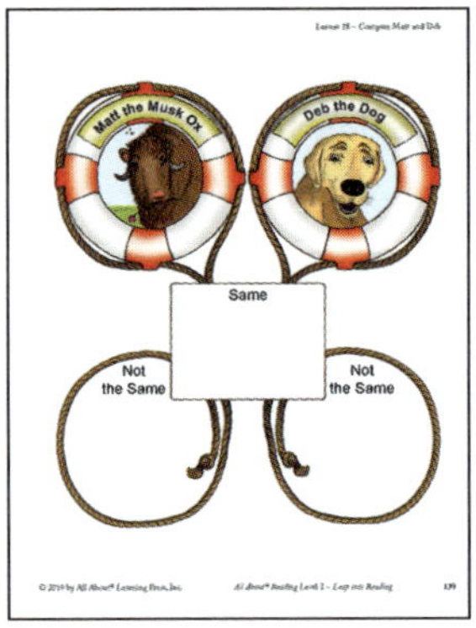

Compare Matt and Deb
Remove page 139 from the activity book.

Guide your student in recording the similarities and differences between the two main characters, Matt and Deb.

Possible Answers
Similarities
Matt and Deb are animals.
Matt and Deb are mammals.
Matt and Deb are furry.
Matt and Deb walk on all fours.
Matt and Deb want to swim in the lake.

Differences

Matt is kind.	Deb is bossy.
Matt is smelly.	Deb is rude.
Matt is strong.	Deb is smug.
Matt is a musk ox.	Deb is a dog.
Matt is brave.	Deb is selfish.
Matt is a hero.	Deb is not a strong swimmer.

Read-Aloud Time

Read a Story or Poem

Read aloud to your student for twenty minutes.

Read-Aloud Tip!

Let Others Do the Work
Make use of audio books. Your student will have the opportunity to hear demonstrations of excellent reading as it is modeled by the narrator. You'll also give your voice a rest!

Track Your Progress

Mark the Progress Chart

Have your student mark Lesson 18 on the Progress Chart.

Lesson 19 WH

Objective

This lesson teaches phonogram wh and words beginning with wh.

You Will Need

- ☐ *Leap into Reading* pages 141-145
- ☐ letter tile wh
- ☐ Phonogram Card 33
- ☐ Word Cards 90-99

Before You Begin

Preview Phonogram WH

Phonogram wh says /hw/ as in *white*. Read the following examples and listen for the /hw/ sound.

white **when** **why** **which** **whale**

In many regions, the difference between wh and w is subtle. The wh is said with more breath. If you hold your hand in front of your mouth, you should be able to feel your breath as you say the /hw/ sound.

When we practice the Phonogram Card for wh, we say "/hw/." If there is no difference between the w and wh phonograms in your region, you can change the wording on Phonogram Card 33 to read "/w/, two-letter /w/." This will help distinguish between w and wh.

The wh tile is stored under the Consonant Teams category.

Refer to the Letter Tiles app or Phonogram Sounds app for a demonstration of the wh phonogram sound. When we use the wh letter tile, we say the sound /hw/. If the phonogram sounds like /w/ in your region, say only the sound /w/. To facilitate blending, we don't say the second part, "two-letter /w/."

Review

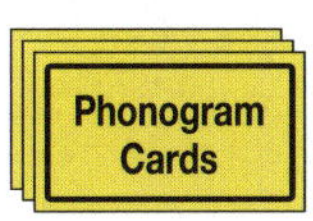

Review the Phonogram Cards that are behind the Review divider in your student's Reading Review Box. Show each card to your student and have him say the sound(s). If necessary, remind your student of the sound(s).

Review
(continued)

Word Cards

Shuffle and review the Word Cards that are behind the Review divider in your student's Reading Review Box. If your student has difficulty reading a word, build the word with letter tiles and have your student sound it out using the blending procedure shown in Appendix C.

Previous Concepts

Build the following word with letter tiles. Have your student divide the word using the One Consonant Tile syllable division rule, label with syllable tags, and read.

before

Open Syllable	Name Game Syllable
b e	f o r e

New Teaching

Teach New Phonogram WH

Hold up the wh Phonogram Card.

AAR Level 2 Lesson 19 – Phonogram Card 33

wh

"W-h says /hw/. Repeat after me: /hw/." Hold up your hand to feel your breath as you say the sound. *Student repeats the sound.*

Mix in several other Phonogram Cards for mixed review and practice until your student can say the sounds accurately.

Move the wh tile into the workspace. wh

Mix in several other letter tiles for mixed review and practice with the new phonogram until your student can say the sound accurately.

Your student may enjoy reviewing this and other phonograms with the "Feed the Monster" activity. For instructions, look for this icon in Appendix L.

New Teaching
(continued)

Store the wh Phonogram Card behind the **Review** divider and review the flashcard at the beginning of the next lesson. Doing so will help you better determine if your student has really mastered the phonogram.

It often seems as if a student has mastered a new card during the reading lesson, but when you revisit that card in a day or two, it becomes obvious that she really hasn't.

It often takes multiple sessions to master a new phonogram.

Blend Sounds with Letter Tiles

Build the word *when*.

"I'll sound out this first word, and then you'll sound out the next word."

Touch under the wh and say */hw/*.

Touch under the e and say */ĕ/*.

Touch under the n and say */n/*.

Now go back to the beginning of the word. Slide your finger under the letters wh-e-n and say *when* slowly.

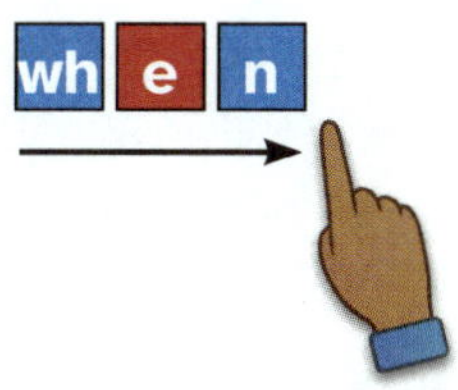

New Teaching
(continued)

Finally, read the word *when* at a normal pace as we do when we speak.

Using the same blending procedure, have your student sound out the word *whip*.

Leave the word *whip* in the workspace.

Play "Change the Word"

"I'm going to change the last part of this word."

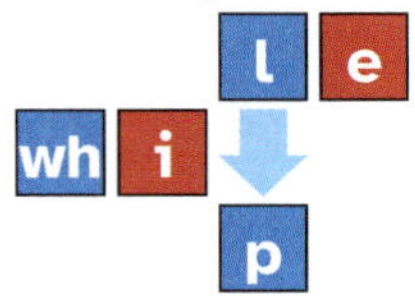

"What does this new word say?" Encourage your student to sound out the new word, *while*.

Continue to change one or two tiles at a time to form the following words. Each time, have your student sound out the new word.

while → white → which* → whim → why → whale

*Use the ch tile for *which*.

Complete Activity Sheet

"Let's feed some whales!"

Feed the Whale

Remove pages 141-142 from the *Leap into Reading* activity book.

Cut out the fish cards and place them in a pile with the words facing down. Cut the dashed line on page 142 to form the whale's mouth.

Have your student select a fish card and read the word on the back. If she reads the word correctly, she can feed the hungry whale by inserting the fish into the whale's mouth. If she reads the word incorrectly, return the fish to the pile for your student to try again.

Continue until the whale has eaten all the fish.

New Teaching
(continued)

Practice Reading Words

Have your student practice reading the words on Word Cards 90-95.

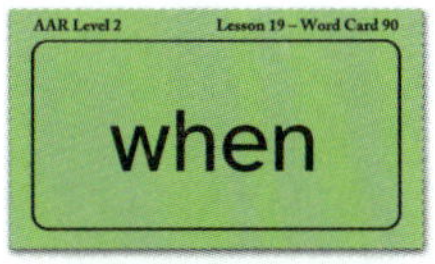

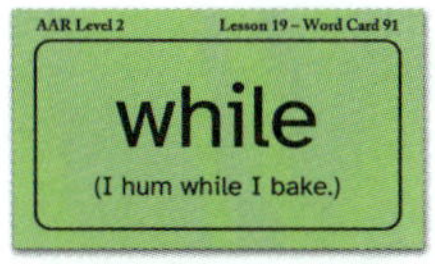

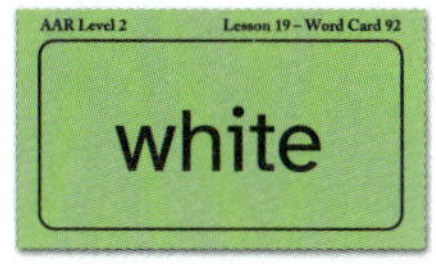

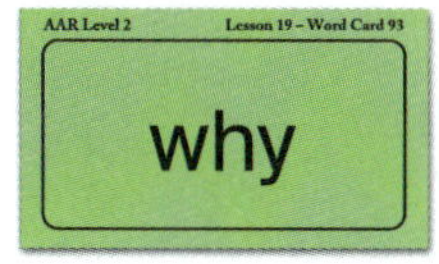

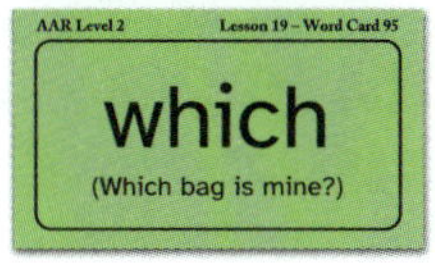

File the Word Cards behind the Review divider in the Reading Review Box.

Teach Four Leap Words: *some, something, come,* and *what*

Show Word Card 96 to your student.

"This word is *some*, as in *Some cats are white*. The letter o says its fourth sound, /ŭ/. The e is silent, but it doesn't make the o say its name. It doesn't follow the rules that you have learned so far, so it is a Leap Word."

Show Word Card 97 to your student.

"This is a compound word. What are the two smaller words?" *Some* and *thing*.

"Good. *Something*, as in *You dropped something*."

Show Word Card 98 to your student.

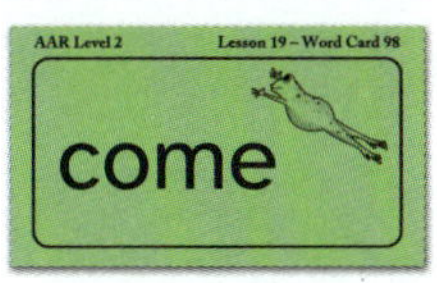

"This word is *come*, as in *Come to my house for dinner*. The letter o says its fourth sound, /ŭ/. The e is silent, but it doesn't make the o say its name. It doesn't follow the rules that you have learned so far, so it is a Leap Word."

New Teaching
(continued)

Show Word Card 99 to your student.

"This word is *what*, as in *What is your name?* The a doesn't say the sound we expect it to, so this is a Leap Word. What does the a say in this word?" */ŭ/.*

Review these Leap Words several times today and then file them behind the Review divider in the Reading Review Box.

Practice Fluency

New Words

what	whack	why	whale
whip	which	some	when
whisk	whine	white	whiff
while	whim	something	come

Phrases

a big whiff	for a while
some jam	when I can
why not	on a whim
which pocket	something big
egg whisk	a sad whine
whack with a bat	white whale
crack the whip	quite a while
	come for lunch

Turn to pages 143-145 in the activity book.

Have your student read from the Practice Sheets.

To engage your student in the fluency exercises, play the game "Swat the Words." For instructions, look for this icon in Appendix K.

Read-Aloud Time

Read a Story or Poem

Read aloud to your student for twenty minutes.

Track Your Progress

Mark the Progress Chart

Have your student mark Lesson 19 on the Progress Chart.

Ooh, I love WH words!
They really spin my lily pad!
Without them, we wouldn't have

whirlybirds,
whortleberries,
whippersnappers,
wheelbarrow rides,
and whatchamacallits!

Well, I'm off to whistle while I work.
Whibbit, whibbit!

Lesson 20 Read "Whale Songs"

Objective

In this lesson, students learn about text features, read a short story, identify the main character, and discuss the characters.

You Will Need

- [ ] *Leap into Reading* pages 147-149
- [ ] *What Am I?* book

Before You Begin

Preview Text Features

In today's activity, your student will create a small reference booklet that highlights the use of subheadings, captions, bold print, and a glossary.

You can help your student gain skills in locating important information by using other reference books with him, such as cookbooks, atlases, and encyclopedias. Point out features such as the table of contents, icons, and charts.

Review

Review the Phonogram Cards that are behind the Review divider in your student's Reading Review Box. Show each card to your student and have him say the sound(s). If necessary, remind your student of the sound(s).

Shuffle and review the Word Cards that are behind the Review divider in your student's Reading Review Box. If your student has difficulty reading a word, build the word with letter tiles and have your student sound it out using the blending procedure shown in Appendix C.

> **Don't Forget!** Are you remembering to shuffle the Word Cards before reviewing them? Make sure your student practices words with a variety of patterns.

New Teaching

Complete Activity Sheet

"Today's story is about a whale. Before we read the story, let's find out some facts about whales."

Whale Facts

Remove pages 147-148 from the *Leap into Reading* activity book.

Cut along the dotted lines on page 148. Stack the cards in numerical order with the cover page on top and staple the book together as indicated. Have your student refer to the book as you ask the following questions.

Point to the cover page. "What is the title of this book? Who is the author?"

> A few of the words on page 1 are not decodable yet (such as *types* and *glossary*), so you will read this page to your student.

"Turn to page 1. This is the table of contents. This page tells us what's inside the book: Whale Facts, Two Types of Whales, and Glossary. Let's say that we wanted to learn about different types of whales. In this table of contents, we learn that the information we want to find is on page 6."

Have your student turn to page 2 and encourage her to read pages 2 through 5.

"Now turn to page 6 and read the words next to the illustrations. These words are known as the *caption* of the photo. They describe the illustration."

"Turn to page 7. This is a *glossary*. A glossary is a list of words and definitions. It is like a dictionary, but a glossary only includes words that appear in a particular book. If you come across an unfamiliar word while reading, you can turn to the glossary for information. What does the word *pod* mean? Look in the glossary for the answer."

Point to the bold text on the glossary page. "See how these words are darker? This is *bold* text. Writers sometimes use bold text to bring attention to something important."

New Teaching
(continued)

Read the Warm-Up Sheet for "Whale Songs"

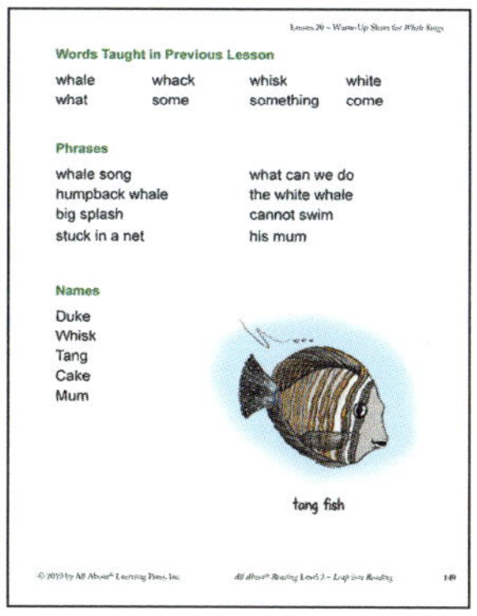

Words Taught in Previous Lesson

whale whack whisk white
what some something come

Phrases

whale song
humpback whale
big splash
stuck in a net
what can we do
the white whale
cannot swim
his mum

Names

Duke
Whisk
Tang
Cake
Mum

tang fish

Turn to page 149 in the activity book.

Have your student practice reading words and phrases that will be encountered in "Whale Songs."

Teach Vocabulary and Activate Prior Knowledge

Point out the last phrase on the Warm-Up Sheet: *his mum*. "*Mum* is another word for *mother*. Other words for *mother* are *mom, momma, ma,* and *mommy*. What do you call your mother?"

Point out the tang fish on the Warm-Up Sheet. "*Tang fish* are a colorful saltwater fish. They are between two inches and sixteen inches long. Some are striped and some have spots. Because tang fish are so pretty to look at, some people keep them in home aquariums."

"Have you ever wanted to do something big and important? Has anyone ever told you that you're too young or too small to do a big thing?"

"In our next story, a young humpback whale wants to do something big, but he is just a small whale. Let's find out what happens."

Read "Whale Songs"

"Turn to page 119 in your reader and read 'Whale Songs' aloud." Discuss your student's ideas for the questions below as you come to them.

After page 127: "Do you think Wade the crab will hear the song and come to help?"

After page 130: "Why do you think Duke swims off with a splash?"

New Teaching
(continued)

Discuss the Characters

"What could have happened to Whisk the white whale if his friends hadn't come to help him?"

"Who do you think is the main character in this story?" *Answer: Duke.*

"Can you explain why Duke is the main character?" *Answers may include: He is the most important character in the story. The story is about him. He is the hero.*

"There are four more characters in 'Whale Songs.' Can you name them all?" Encourage your student to look back at the story if she can't remember the characters' names.

> **Tip!**
>
> Consider recording your student as she reads the story again. It can be really helpful for kids to hear themselves reading—and having a recording session can be lots of fun! Just be sure to record a "hot" reading, not a cold reading.
>
> After recording, let your student assess her own work. How did it sound? Was it natural or choppy? Too fast, too slow, or just right? Did she pay attention to punctuation? Encourage her to notice one thing she did well and one thing that needs improvement. Then she can practice and re-record to see if she improved.

Read-Aloud Time

Read a Story or Poem

Read aloud to your student for twenty minutes.

Track Your Progress

Mark the Progress Chart

Have your student mark Lesson 20 on the Progress Chart.

Lesson 21 Blends with Silent E

Objective

This lesson teaches the concept of heteronyms and words that combine consonant blends with the Name Game pattern.

You Will Need

- ☐ *Leap into Reading* pages 151-163
- ☐ Word Cards 100-109

Before You Begin

Preview the Lesson

Your student knows how to read words with initial blends, and he knows how to read words with the Name Game syllable pattern. In this lesson, these two concepts will be combined and your student will read words like *smile* and *grape*.

The concept of *heteronyms* will also be introduced. Heteronyms are words that are spelled alike but pronounced differently, such as *lĭve* and *līve*. The pronunciation and meaning of heteronyms must be determined by context.

Review

Phonogram Cards

Review the Phonogram Cards that are behind the Review divider in your student's Reading Review Box. Show each card to your student and have him say the sound(s). If necessary, remind your student of the sound(s).

Word Cards

Shuffle and review the Word Cards that are behind the Review divider in your student's Reading Review Box. If your student has difficulty reading a word, build the word with letter tiles and have your student sound it out using the blending procedure shown in Appendix C.

Previous Concepts

Build the following word with letter tiles. Have your student divide the word using the One Consonant Tile rule, label with syllable tags, and read.

protect

Open Syllable	Closed Syllable
p r o	t e c t

New Teaching

Play "Change the Word"

Build the word *side*. s i d e

"What is this word?" *Side.*

"I'm going to add a tile to this word." Add an l to form the word *slide.*

s l i d e

"What does this new word say?" Encourage your student to sound out the new word, *slide.*

Build the word *sale.* s a l e

"Sound out this word." *Student sounds out the word* sale.

Add a t to form the word *stale.*

s t a l e

"What does this new word say?" Encourage your student to sound out the new word, *stale.*

Continue this activity using several of the words below.

dive → drive
sore → snore → store
bake → brake
save → slave
sake → snake
fame → frame → flame
dove → drove

New Teaching
(continued)

Complete Activity Sheet

"Let's flip some Silent E words."

Word Flippers for Blends with Name Game Syllables

Remove pages 151-157 from the *Leap into Reading* activity book.

There are four Word Flippers in this lesson. Each page will create one flipper.

Refer to Appendix I for assembly instructions.

Have your student turn the pages and read the words that are formed.

Teach Two Pronunciations of *Close*

Close and *close* are heteronyms. Other heteronyms that your student may already be familiar with include *lĭve* and *līve*, *wĭnd* and *wīnd*, *conflict* and *conflict*, *object* and *object*, and *use* (with /s/) and *use* (with /z/).

Take out Word Card 100.

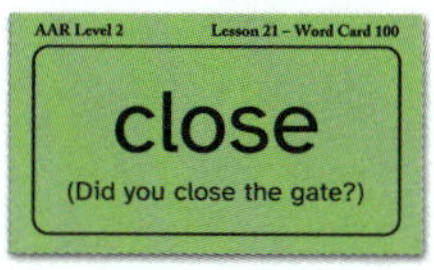

"This word can be pronounced two different ways. The first way is /clōs/, which means *near to,* as in *Sit close to the window.* The second way is /clōz/, which means *shut*, as in *Close the door.* We have to read the word in a sentence to know which meaning and pronunciation it has. Read the sentence on this card to figure out if this word should be pronounced /clōs/ or /clōz/." *Student reads the sentence using /clōz/.*

Practice Reading Words

Have your student practice reading the words on Word Cards 101-109.

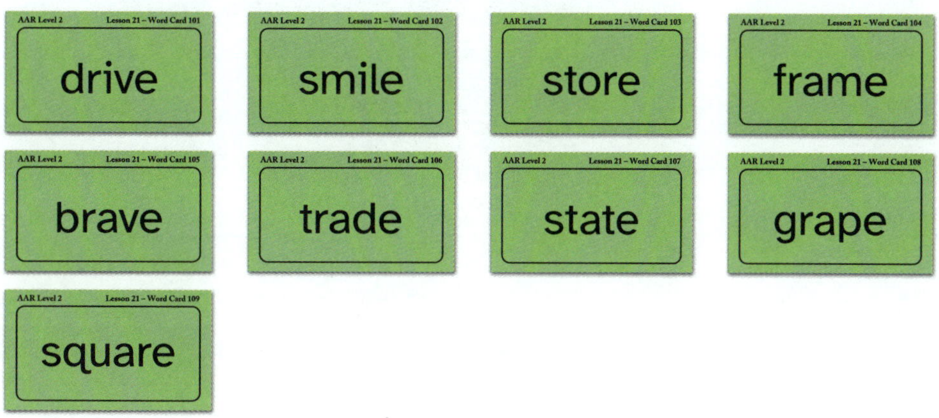

New Teaching
(continued)

File the Word Cards behind the Review divider of the Reading Review Box.

Practice Fluency

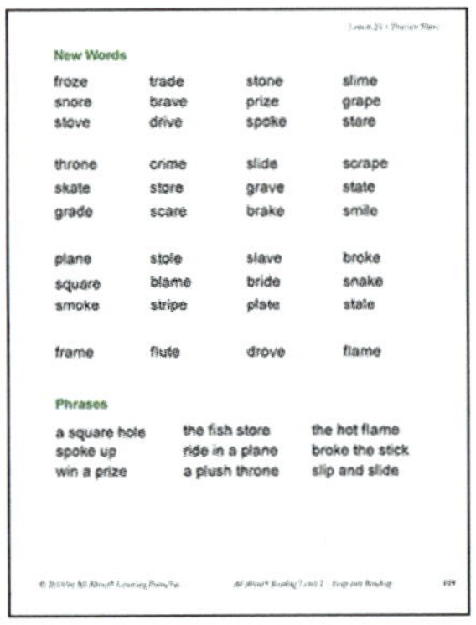
New Words

froze trade stone slime
snore brave prize grape
stove drive spoke stare

throne crime slide scrape
skate store grave state
grade scare brake smile

plane stole slave broke
square blame bride snake
smoke stripe plate stale

frame flute drove flame

Phrases

a square hole the fish store the hot flame
spoke up ride in a plane broke the stick
win a prize a plush throne slip and slide

Turn to pages 159-163 in the activity book.

Have your student read from the Practice Sheets.

To engage your student in the fluency exercises, try the activity "Word Hide and Seek." For instructions, look for this icon in Appendix K.

Read-Aloud Time

Read a Story or Poem

Read aloud to your student for twenty minutes.

Track Your Progress

Mark the Progress Chart

Have your student mark Lesson 21 on the Progress Chart.

Lesson 22 Read "Skunk Hotel"

Objective

In this lesson, students read a short story and practice sequencing.

You Will Need

- ☐ *Leap into Reading* pages 165-167
- ☐ *What Am I?* book

Before You Begin

Preview Story Sequencing

After reading the story, your student will complete a sequencing activity. Sequencing refers to the ability to identify, order, and retell events from a story, and it's a key strategy for reading comprehension.

Review

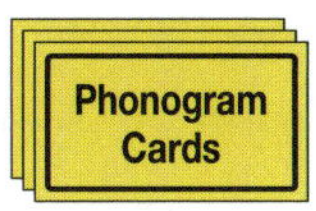

Review the Phonogram Cards that are behind the Review divider in your student's Reading Review Box. Show each card to your student and have him say the sound(s). If necessary, remind your student of the sound(s).

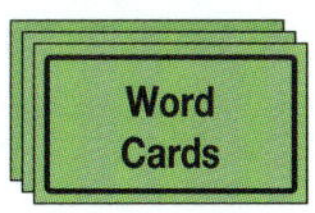

Shuffle and review the Word Cards that are behind the Review divider in your student's Reading Review Box. If your student has difficulty reading a word, build the word with letter tiles and have your student sound it out using the blending procedure shown in Appendix C.

New Teaching

Read the Warm-Up Sheet for "Skunk Hotel"

Words Taught in Previous Lesson

frame twine stripe stare
crate

Phrases

the man admits
an open shed
fix up a home

lone skunk
twine and rope
safe home

broken crate
bed frame
damp drafts

frozen for a moment
white stripe
skunk hotel

five skunk kits

Turn to page 165 in the *Leap into Reading* activity book.

Have your student practice reading words and phrases that will be encountered in "Skunk Hotel."

New Teaching
(continued)

Teach Vocabulary and Activate Prior Knowledge

Point out the skunk kits on the Warm-Up Sheet. "Baby skunks are called skunk *kits*. When they are newborns, they are deaf and blind, just like kittens. As they grow, they are playful and curious. They stick close to their mother while growing up. She protects them by lifting her tail and spraying enemies with a terrible-smelling liquid. Have you ever smelled a skunk?"

"What would happen if a wild skunk suddenly moved into your garage or shed? What would you do? What are some of the reasons that you might not want a skunk living in one of your buildings?"

"In our next story, a man is surprised to find a skunk in his shed. Let's find out what he does about it."

Read "Skunk Hotel"

"Turn to page 133 in your reader and read 'Skunk Hotel' aloud." Discuss your student's ideas for the questions below as you come to them.

After page 139: "What do you think the man will do about the skunk?"

After reading: "Do you think the man will let the whole skunk family stay in the shed? Would you?"

Complete Activity Sheet

"Let's see if we can remember what happens in the story you just read."

What Happens Next?
Remove pages 167-168 from the activity book.

Cut the page into three sections as indicated by the dotted lines. Place the sections on the table in random order, and then have your student rearrange the sections of the story so that they reflect the order in which they happened.

For your reference, the number on the back of each section indicates its placement in the sequence.

"Why do you think the story is titled 'Skunk Hotel'?"

Read-Aloud Time

Read a Story or Poem

Read aloud to your student for twenty minutes.

Read-Aloud Tip!

Explain New Vocabulary

If your student asks you what a word means during a read-aloud, by all means stop and define the word for her. But don't feel that you need to explain every unfamiliar word you come across. It would take a long time to get through a book if you did that!

Even if your student doesn't know the specific meaning of a word, more often than not she will pick up on context clues to form meaning. So as you read, choose just a few words to stop and define. You can always explain different new words the next time you read the book together.

Track Your Progress

Mark the Progress Chart

Have your student mark Lesson 22 on the Progress Chart.

Lesson 23 Plural Silent E Words

Objective

This lesson teaches how to read plural Silent E words.

You Will Need

- ☐ *Leap into Reading* pages 169-176
- ☐ Word Cards 110-119

Before You Begin

Preview Suffix S

Plural short-vowel words were taught in Level 1. We'll follow the same procedure to teach your student to read plural Silent E words:

1. Build the plural word with tiles. 

2. Cover the s with your finger. 

3. Ask your student to read the singular form of the word. Then uncover the s and ask for the plural form.

This strategy ensures that students don't misinterpret plural Silent E words as short-vowel words followed by suffix *es*: /gam/ + /ĕs/. They can easily see that the base word is a Name Game syllable type.

It is interesting to note that adding suffix *s* to a word generally does not add a syllable. For example, *ropes, vines*, and *kites* are all one-syllable words. But there are a handful of words where adding suffix *s* does add a syllable, as in *noses* and *prizes*. This extra syllable occurs when the base word ends in the sound of /z/. Following the procedure in this lesson allows students to read these words with confidence.

Review the Sound of S

In Level 1, students learned that at the end of a plural word, the s can say either /s/ or /z/. Most of the time, the student will naturally say the correct sound for the letter s. It is actually hard to say the wrong sound. But if your student has difficulty, remind him to say the singular form of the word first and then the plural form. He will naturally pronounce the word correctly.

Plural Silent E words ending in /s/:	**cakes**	**bites**	**votes**
Plural Silent E words ending in /z/:	**rules**	**holes**	**stores**

Review

Phonogram Cards

Review the Phonogram Cards that are behind the Review divider in your student's Reading Review Box. Show each card to your student and have him say the sound(s). If necessary, remind your student of the sound(s).

Word Cards

Shuffle and review the Word Cards that are behind the Review divider in your student's Reading Review Box. If your student has difficulty reading a word, build the word with letter tiles and have your student sound it out using the blending procedure shown in Appendix C.

> Test your student's Word Card memory with the game "Word Card Concentration." For instructions, look for this icon in Appendix M.

Previous Concepts

Build the following words with letter tiles. Have your student divide the words where necessary, label with syllable tags, and read. *Square* is a one-syllable word and is not divided. *Backbone* is divided using the Compound Words rule.

square

Name Game Syllable

s qu a r e

backbone

Closed Syllable | Name Game Syllable

b a ck | b o n e

"What does *plural* mean?" *More than one.*

"I'll say a word, and you say the plural form of that word."

"One *plate*, two ______." If necessary, prompt your student to say *plates*.

"One *prize*, two ______." *Prizes.*

"One *grape*, two ______." *Grapes.*

New Teaching

Teach Plural Silent E Words

Build the word *joke*. j o k e

"Read this word." *Joke.*

"Label the syllable type." *Student uses the Name Game syllable tag.*

Add an s to the word. j o k e s

"What does this word say now?" *Jokes.*

Build the word *cakes*. c a k e s

"Cover the s with your finger and read the word." *Cake.*

"Now uncover the s and read the word." *Cakes.*

> If your student ever struggles to read a plural word, remind her to cover up the s and decode the base word first. **Tip!**

Complete Activity Sheet

"Let's hunt for some bugs!"

Bug Hunt
Remove pages 169-172 from the *Leap into Reading* activity book.

Cut out the bug cards on page 171.

Mix the cards and place them in a pile with the words facing down. Have your student select a card, read the word aloud, and determine whether the word is plural or singular.

If the word is singular, he must first make the word plural by setting the card in the appropriate location next to the s. The student should then read the new version he created and add the word card to the bug net.

Continue until all the bugs have been caught.

New Teaching
(continued)

Practice Reading Words

Have your student practice reading the words on Word Cards 110-117.

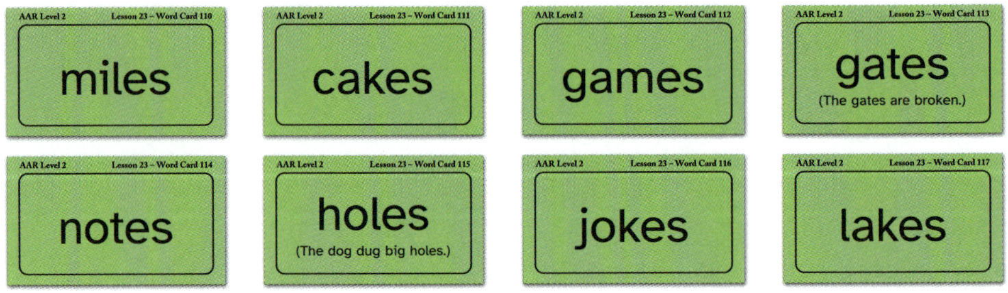

File the Word Cards behind the Review divider in the Reading Review Box.

Teach Two Leap Words: *pony* and *sandwich*

> The words *pony* and *sandwich* will be used in the story in the next lesson.

Show Word Card 118 to your student.

"This word is *pony*, as in *I love riding my pony*. The letter y often says /ē/ at the end of two-syllable words. We haven't studied that yet, so this is a Leap Word."

"What sound does the o make in this word?" */ō/.*

Show Word Card 119 to your student.

Cover up *wich* with your finger. "What does the first part of this word say?" *Sand.*

Uncover *wich*. "What does the second part of this word say?" *Wich.*

"Together they say *sandwich*, as in *I ate a sandwich*. This word follows a syllable division rule that you haven't learned yet, so that's why this is a Leap Word."

New Teaching
(continued)

Review these Leap Words several times today and then file them behind the Review divider in the Reading Review Box.

Practice Fluency

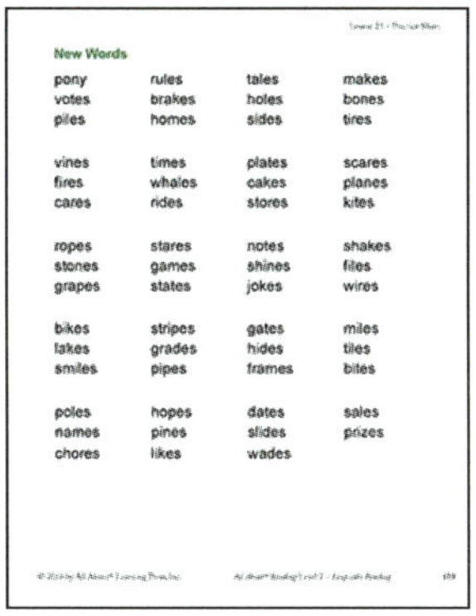

New Words

pony	rules	tales	makes
votes	brakes	holes	bones
piles	homes	sides	tires
vines	times	plates	scares
fires	whales	cakes	planes
cares	rides	stores	kites
ropes	stares	notes	shakes
stones	games	shines	files
grapes	states	jokes	wires
bikes	stripes	gates	miles
lakes	grades	hides	tiles
smiles	pipes	frames	bites
poles	hopes	dates	sales
names	pines	slides	prizes
chores	likes	wades	

Turn to pages 173-176 in the activity book.

Have your student read from the Practice Sheets.

To engage your student in the fluency exercises, try the activity "Eat Your Words." For instructions, look for this icon in Appendix K.

Read-Aloud Time

Read a Story or Poem

Read aloud to your student for twenty minutes.

Track Your Progress

Mark the Progress Chart

Have your student mark Lesson 23 on the Progress Chart.

Yum, yum, yum!
That bug hunt activity was
lip-smacking good.

How did you do with making
plural Silent E words?
Don't you just love the letter S? It's so ...
squishy
squirmy
slippery
slimy
swampy!

And now that we know how to use it
for plurals, we don't have to make just
one bug cake ... we can make
a hundred bug CAKES!
Ribbit!

Lesson 24 Read "Champ"

Objective

In this lesson, students learn about possessives and onomatopoeia and read a short story.

You Will Need

- ☐ *Leap into Reading* pages 177-181
- ☐ *What Am I?* book
- ☐ paper and pencil

Before You Begin

Preview Onomatopoeia

Onomatopoeia is a word that imitates the natural sound of a particular thing. For example, the words *plop, plip, splash, drizzle, drip, sprinkle,* and *gush* are all onomatopoeic words that can describe water.

Onomatopoeia is pronounced /ŏn–ō–mah–tō–pē–uh/.

Here are some other common examples of onomatopoeia.

buzz
blip
cackle
choo-choo
crash
ding-dong
groan
gurgle
honk
hoot
jingle
kerplunk
oink
pitter-patter
purr
quack
snarl
swish
thwack
whirr
zoom

Review

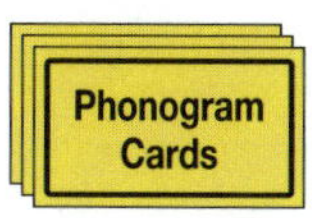

Review the Phonogram Cards that are behind the Review divider in your student's Reading Review Box. Show each card to your student and have him say the sound(s). If necessary, remind your student of the sound(s).

Engage your student in Phonogram Card review with the activity "Phonogram Card City." For instructions, look for this icon in Appendix L.

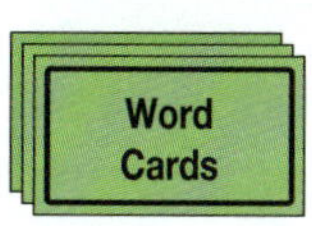

Shuffle and review the Word Cards that are behind the Review divider in your student's Reading Review Box. If your student has difficulty reading a word, build the word with letter tiles and have your student sound it out using the blending procedure shown in Appendix C.

New Teaching

Teach Onomatopoeia

"Some words imitate sound." Knock on a solid surface and say *knock knock.*

"You already know a lot of words that imitate sounds. What do cows say?" *Moo.*

"What do cats say?" *Meow* or *purr.*

"What do birds say?" *Tweet* or *chirp.*

"What does it sound like when a balloon breaks?" *Pop.*

"*Pop, moo, meow, tweet*—these are all examples of *onomatopoeia.* Onomatopoeia is when words imitate sound. Try saying this word: *onomatopoeia.*" *Student says the word.*

"Let's practice reading more words that imitate sounds."

Clip, Clop, Crack!

Remove pages 177-179 from the *Leap into Reading* activity book.

Cut out the word cards on page 179 and spread them out on the table with the words facing up. Have your student match each word with the drawing that makes that sound. For example, "clip-clop, clip-clop" should be matched with the drawing of the walking horse.

Continue until all word cards have been matched to their illustrations.

New Teaching
(continued)

Read the Warm-Up Sheet for "Champ"

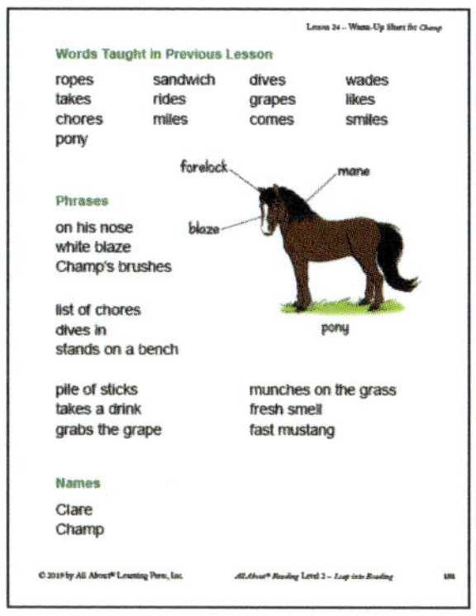

Words Taught in Previous Lesson

ropes	sandwich	dives	wades
takes	rides	grapes	likes
chores	miles	comes	smiles
pony			

Phrases

on his nose
white blaze
Champ's brushes

list of chores
dives in
stands on a bench

pile of sticks
takes a drink
grabs the grape

munches on the grass
fresh smell
fast mustang

Names

Clare
Champ

Turn to page 181 in the activity book.

Have your student practice reading words and phrases that are found in "Champ."

Point out the phrase *Champ's brushes.* "Champ is the name of a horse in the next story. The mark after his name is called an *apostrophe.* An apostrophe is a small mark that shows that something belongs to Champ. The brushes belong to Champ."

Write the words *Mom's shoes* on a piece of paper. "This apostrophe means that the shoes belong to Mom." Give several more written examples, such as *the girl's pillow*, *the dog's bone*, and *[student's name]'s book.*

Teach Vocabulary and Activate Prior Knowledge

Point out the illustration of the pony on the Warm-Up Sheet. "A *pony* is a small horse. A pony is shorter than a horse even when it is full grown."

"Have you ever ridden a pony? Have you ever had the opportunity to pet a pony's coat?"

"Several parts of a pony are mentioned in the next story. A *blaze* is a white stripe that runs down the face of a pony. The *mane* is hair that grows on top of the pony's neck. The mane helps keep the pony warm in the winter. The *forelock* is the front part of the mane that lays over the pony's forehead. The forelock helps protect the pony's eyes from flies and dust."

Read "Champ"

"Turn to page 145 in your reader and read 'Champ' aloud." Discuss your student's ideas for the questions below as you come to them.

After page 149: If your student didn't read the chore list on the blackboard, ask him to look at the illustration and read the list.

After page 155: "Why do you think it is silent?"

New Teaching
(continued)

Discuss Onomatopoeia

"'Champ' contains onomatopoeia. Turn to page 156. When it starts to rain, it thunders. What sound does the thunder make?" *Crash.*

"Have you ever been caught outside in a rain storm? What sounds do you hear when it rains?"

> There are other examples of onomatopoeia in "Champ," too:
>
> page 152: *Swish!*
> page 155: *the pony munches, insects buzz*
> page 156: *Drops begin to splash them.*

Read-Aloud Time

Read a Story or Poem

Read aloud to your student for twenty minutes.

> Read-Aloud Tip!
>
> **Try Buddy Reading for Expression**
> After listening to years of read-alouds, your student is probably familiar with how you interpret dialogue. Still, it can take a lot of practice for novice readers to get the hang of adding expression to their own voices.
>
> One fun way to encourage reading with expression is through buddy reading. You read a page first, using full expression for the dialogue and different characters, and then your student reads the same page. See if he can outdo you!

Track Your Progress

Mark the Progress Chart

Have your student mark Lesson 24 on the Progress Chart.

Wow, what a beautiful
story about Clare and Champ.
They make a great team, don't they?
It makes me want to say a few words.

Ahem.

I, Webfoot, King of the Swamp, am truly thankful to have YOU on my team. No frog could ask for a better study buddy. From daily review to reading stories, you've stuck with me through thick and thin. You are an inspiration!

Can I get a big RIBBIT
for teamwork?

Lesson 25 EE and Vowel Team Syllables

Objective

This lesson teaches phonogram ee, the Vowel Team syllable type, and words containing ee.

You Will Need

- ☐ *Leap into Reading* pages 183-188
- ☐ letter tile ee
- ☐ Phonogram Card 34
- ☐ Vowel Team syllable tag
- ☐ Vowel Team label
- ☐ Word Cards 120-129

Before You Begin

Preview Phonogram EE

Phonogram ee says /ē/ as in *need*. Read the following examples and listen for the /ē/ sound.

need	**green**	**queen**	**steep**	**seed**
teen	**tree**	**street**	**feed**	**deed**

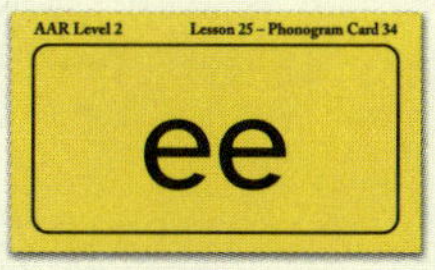

When we practice the Phonogram Card for ee, we say "/ē/, double e." This phrase distinguishes ee from the other ways of spelling /ē/, such as ea, which will be taught in Level 3. By learning the full wording for phonogram ee now, your student won't have to relearn the flashcard for spelling purposes later.

The ee tile is stored under the Vowel Teams category.

Refer to the Letter Tiles app or Phonogram Sounds app for a demonstration of the ee phonogram sound. When we use the ee letter tile, we only say the sound /ē/. To facilitate blending, we don't say the second part, "double e."

> Vowel team ee always says long e as in *sheep*, with one possible exception: the word *been*. In American English, *been* is pronounced with a short i or short e sound. In British English, though, *been* retains the long e sound. If your student pronounces this word with a long e sound, skip the part of the lesson in which we teach *been* as a Leap Word.

Before You Begin
(continued)

Preview Vowel Teams

In this lesson, your student will learn the first vowel team, phonogram ee. A vowel team is two or more letters working together to make one sound, such as ee, ea, oi, ay, and ou. Since the letters work together, the letters that make up a vowel team appear on a single letter tile. As you can guess by the name, vowel teams always contain a vowel. Examples of vowel teams are found in the words *sheep, heat, boil, stay,* and *house.*

Sometimes consonants are used in vowel teams, as in aw, ow, igh, and augh. Example words include *thaw, how, night,* and *daughter.*

Preview Vowel Team Syllables

Your student has already learned three syllable types: Closed, Open, and Name Game. Today he will learn the fourth syllable type, the Vowel Team syllable, which we label with the following syllable tag.

On the syllable tag, the team of horses represents a Vowel Team syllable. Just as a team of horses works together, the letters in a vowel team work together to make one sound.

Review

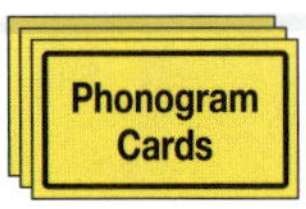

Review the Phonogram Cards that are behind the Review divider in your student's Reading Review Box. Show each card to your student and have him say the sound(s). If necessary, remind your student of the sound(s).

Shuffle and review the Word Cards that are behind the Review divider in your student's Reading Review Box. If your student has difficulty reading a word, build the word with letter tiles and have your student sound it out using the blending procedure shown in Appendix C.

Let your student get creative with the Word Card review with the activity "Color It." For instructions, look for this icon in Appendix M.

New Teaching

Teach New Phonogram EE

Hold up the ee Phonogram Card.

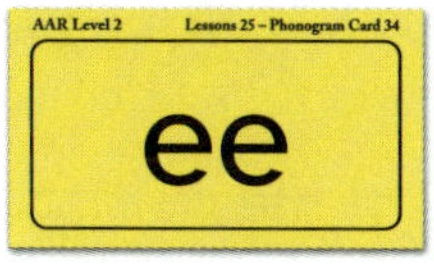

"E-e says /ē/. When we practice this card, we say */ē/, double /ē/.* Repeat after me: /ē/, double /ē/." *Student repeats the sound.*

Mix in several other Phonogram Cards for mixed review and practice until your student can say the sounds accurately. File the Phonogram Card behind the Review divider in the Reading Review Box.

Move the ee tile into the workspace. ee

Point to the ee tile. "When you see this tile, say its sound, /ē/. You don't have to say *double /ē/* when we are building with tiles, just when we are using the flashcards."

Mix in several other letter tiles for mixed review and practice with the new phonogram until your student can say the sound accurately.

For extra practice with the new phonogram, play the game "Phonogram Bingo." For instructions, look for this icon in Appendix L.

Blend Sounds with Letter Tiles

Build the word *feet.* f ee t

"I'll sound out this first word, and then you'll sound out the next word."

Touch under the f and say */f/.*

New Teaching
(continued)

Touch under the ee and say /ē/.

Touch under the t and say /t/.

Now go back to the beginning of the word. Slide your finger under the letters f-ee-t and say *feet* slowly.

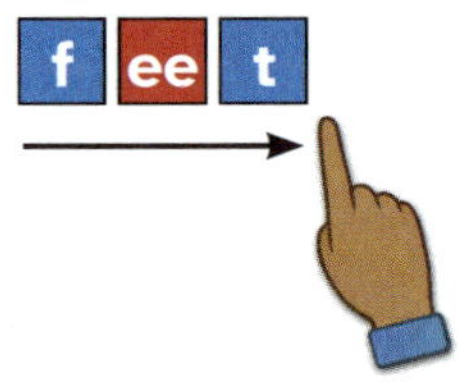

Finally, read the word *feet* at a normal pace as we do when we speak.

Using the same blending procedure, have your student sound out the word *weed*.

Leave the word *weed* in the workspace.

Play "Change the Word"

"I'm going to change the first part of this word."

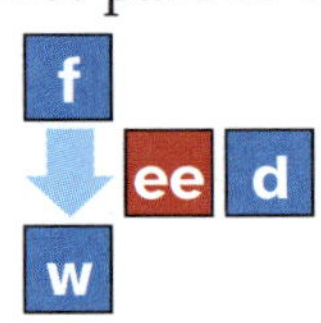

"What does this new word say?" Encourage your student to sound out the new word, *feed*.

Continue to change one or two tiles at a time to form the following words. Each time, have your student sound out the new word.

feed → need → seed → seem → seen → green

New Teaching
(continued)

Complete Activity Sheet

"Now it's time to wake up these sheep with some ee words."

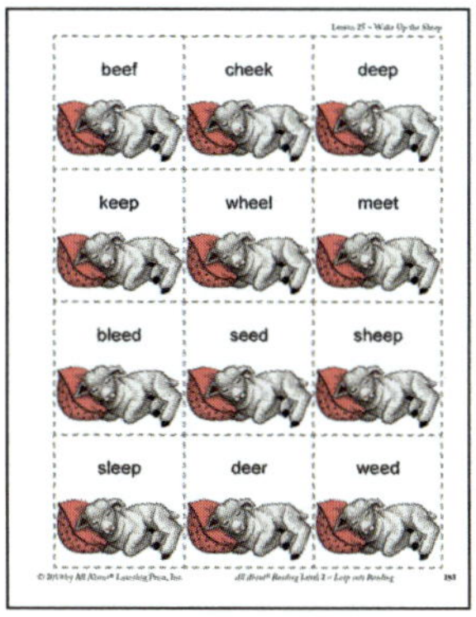

Wake Up the Sheep
Remove pages 183-184 from the *Leap into Reading* activity book.

Cut out the cards and place them in a pile with the words facing up. Have your student wake up the napping sheep by choosing a sleeping sheep card and reading the word. If he reads the word correctly, he can turn the card over to reveal a sheep that is awake.

Continue reading the cards until all the sleeping sheep have been awoken.

Teach the Fourth Syllable Type: Vowel Team

Place the Vowel Team syllable tag in the workspace. "We have a new syllable tag."

"This syllable tag shows a team of horses. A *team of horses* is two or more horses working together. We will use this to represent **vowel teams**, which are two or more letters working together to make one vowel sound.

Build the word *fifteen*. 

"When you divide a word into syllables, treat the vowel team the same as you would treat a vowel. When I look for the vowels in *fifteen*, I see the i tile and the ee tile."

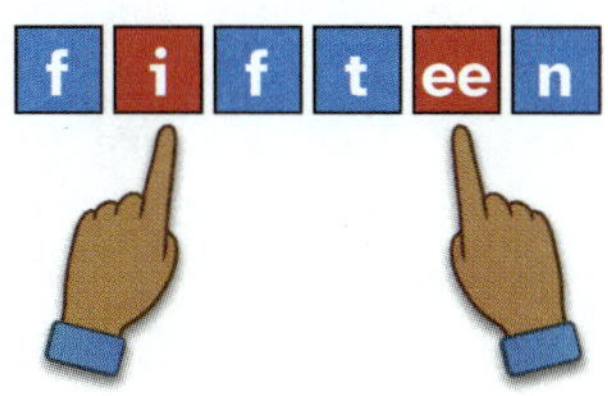

"There are two consonants between these tiles, so I divide between the consonants."

"Now I can put a tag above each syllable. What type is the first syllable?" *Closed.*

New Teaching
(continued)

"What type is the second syllable?" *Vowel Team.*

Closed Syllable	Vowel Team Syllable
f i f	t ee n

"Read the first syllable." *Fif.*

"Read the second syllable." *Teen.*

"Now read the word." *Fifteen.*

"Great! *Fifteen* is a real word, so you've divided the word correctly."

Build the word *weekend.* w ee k e n d

"Divide this word into syllables." *Student divides the word.*

"Put a tag above each syllable." *Student uses the Vowel Team and Closed tags.*

Vowel Team Syllable	Closed Syllable
w ee k	e n d

"Read each syllable and then read this word." *Week–end. Weekend.*

Complete Activity Sheet

"Those Party Monsters are back and now they want to form teams!"

Party Monsters Form Teams
Remove pages 185-186 from the activity book.

Cut out the four syllable type cards and lay them on the table. Cut out the monster cards and place them in a pile with the words facing down.

Have your student select a monster card and read the word on the back. He should then decide if the word is a Closed, Open, Name Game, or Vowel Team syllable and put the monster on the appropriate syllable type card.

Continue until all the monster cards have been read and sorted.

New Teaching
(continued)

<u>Answer Key</u>
Open: go, no, she
Closed: munch, plop, grunt
Name Game: rule, scare, slime
Vowel Team: seek, beep, teeth

Practice Reading Words

Have your student practice reading the words on Word Cards 120-128.

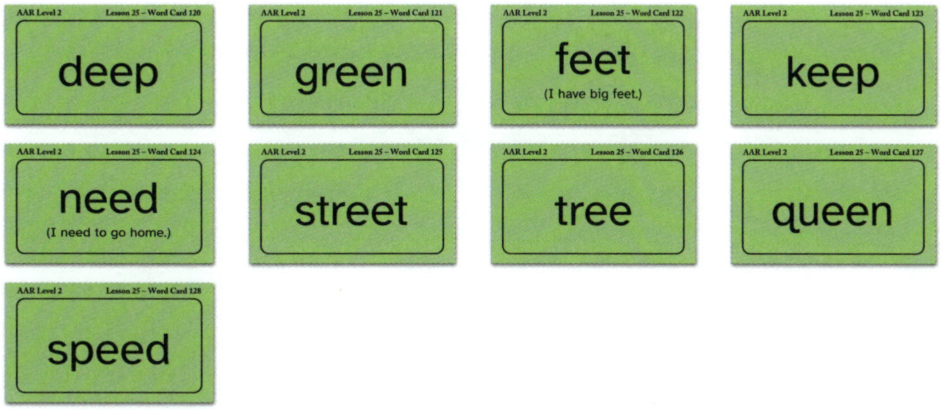

File the Word Cards behind the Review divider in the Reading Review Box.

Teach a Leap Word: *been*

> If *been* is pronounced with a long E in your region, you don't need to teach it as a Leap Word.

Show Word Card 129 to your student.

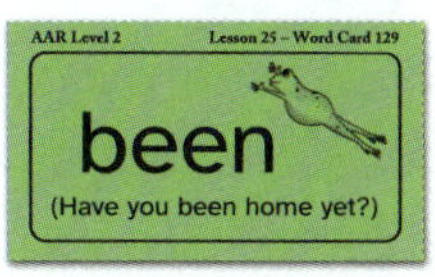

"This word is *been*, as in *Have you been home yet?* Vowel team <u>ee</u> always makes the long <u>e</u> sound, except in this word."

Review this Leap Word several times today and then file it behind the Review divider in the Reading Review Box.

New Teaching
(continued)

Practice Fluency

New Words

been	deer	jeep	sheet
greet	tree	beet	fifteen
sheep	meet	seed	beep
weed	bleed	sweet	free
steer	cheek	teeth	need
freeze	deep	speed	coffee
cheer	three	seem	seen
wheel	week	green	see
street	feed	bee	queen
sixteen	breeze	seventeen	sweep
sleep	weekend	keep	feel
feet	beef	tweed	

Turn to pages 187-188 in the activity book.

Have your student read from the Practice Sheets.

Some students will notice that the words *breeze* and *freeze* end in Silent E. <u>Z</u> is usually not alone at the end of a word. It's typically either doubled (as in *buzz*) or paired with Silent E (as in *freeze*).

To engage your student in the fluency exercises, try making his progress more concrete. For ideas on how to do that, look for this icon in Appendix K.

Read-Aloud Time

Read a Story or Poem

Read aloud to your student for twenty minutes.

Track Your Progress

Mark the Progress Chart

Have your student mark Lesson 25 on the Progress Chart.

Lesson 26 Read "Pine Tree Pet Shop"

Objective

In this lesson, students read a short story and discuss the main conflict.

You Will Need

- ☐ *Leap into Reading* pages 189-192
- ☐ *What Am I?* book
- ☐ sticky notes

Before You Begin

Avoid Making Corrections Too Soon

When your student misreads a word in a sentence, resist the temptation to correct him immediately. Let him reach the end of the sentence before you interrupt, giving him the chance to realize on his own that he made a mistake.

For example, if your student reads *The hot sat with a thud*, he will probably self-correct because the sentence obviously doesn't make sense. He will look back to see where his error is and reread the sentence correctly as *The hog sat with a thud.* If he does continue reading without correcting himself, ask him if the sentence he just read makes sense.

When you interrupt your student immediately after he makes an error, he is deprived of the opportunity to monitor what he is reading for meaning. In the example above, the phrase *The hot...* does make sense in itself, as it could be *The hot day* or *The hot lunch.* If you give your student time to reach the end of the sentence, though, it will most likely be clear to him that he has misread a word.

Review

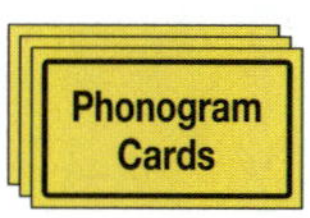

Review the Phonogram Cards that are behind the Review divider in your student's Reading Review Box. Show each card to your student and have him say the sound(s). If necessary, remind your student of the sound(s).

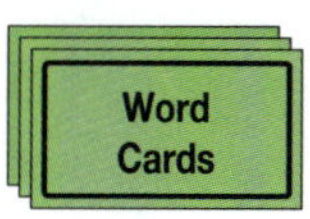

Shuffle and review the Word Cards that are behind the Review divider in your student's Reading Review Box. If your student has difficulty reading a word, build the word with letter tiles and have your student sound it out using the blending procedure shown in Appendix C.

Read the Warm-Up Sheet for "Pine Tree Pet Shop"

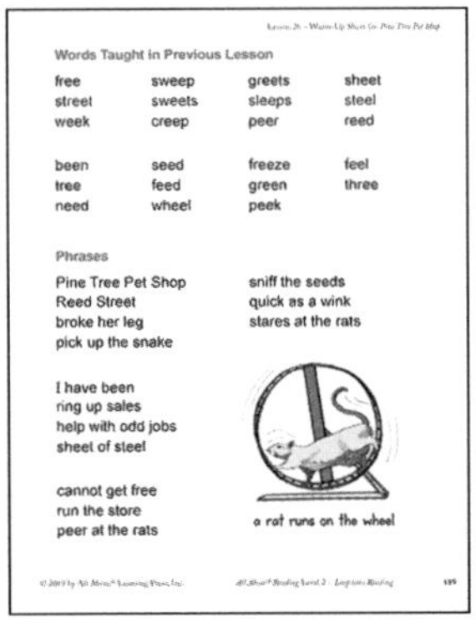
Words Taught in Previous Lesson

free, street, week, sweep, sweets, creep, greets, sleeps, peer, sheet, steel, reed

been, tree, need, seed, feed, wheel, freeze, green, peek, feel, three

Phrases

Pine Tree Pet Shop
Reed Street
broke her leg
pick up the snake

sniff the seeds
quick as a wink
stares at the rats

I have been
ring up sales
help with odd jobs
sheet of steel

cannot get free
run the store
peer at the rats

a rat runs on the wheel

Turn to page 189 in the *Leap into Reading* activity book.

Have your student practice reading words and phrases that are found in "Pine Tree Pet Shop."

Teach Vocabulary and Activate Prior Knowledge

Point out the illustration of the rat on the wheel on the Warm-Up Sheet. "Some people keep white rats as pets and give them a running wheel so they can exercise in their cages. You can buy pet rats and running wheels at a pet shop."

"Do you think it would be fun to work in a pet shop? You could feed the animals, sweep the floors, and give names to the pets. What would you name a puppy? How about a kitten? What would you name a pair of bunny rabbits?"

"In our next story, something unexpected happens at the Pine Tree Pet Shop. Let's find out what it is!"

Read "Pine Tree Pet Shop"

"Turn to page 161 in your reader and read 'Pine Tree Pet Shop' aloud. In this story, the main character faces a big problem. See if you can find out what this big problem is. Once you find it, put a sticky note next to it."

Discuss your student's ideas for the question below when you come to it.

After page 169: "Why do you think the main character says, 'I feel my skin creep'?"

New Teaching
(continued)

Discuss the Main Conflict

"In a story, the problem that a character faces is called the *conflict*. What do you think is the biggest conflict in this story?" Encourage your student to look for the sticky note(s) if necessary.

"What does the main character do to solve the problem?"

"What does the main character say that he or she would do to prevent that problem from happening again? Skim the text for the answer."

Complete Activity Sheet

"Now let's solve some other conflicts."

Solve Your Problem
Remove pages 191-192 from the activity book.

Cut out the cards. Place the Problem cards in a stack and arrange the Fix It! cards on the table with the solutions facing up. Have your student select a Problem card and read it aloud. Then have him select an appropriate Fix It! card to solve the problem. Some of the solutions are suitable for more than one problem. Discuss your student's choices.

Continue until all the problems have been solved.

Read-Aloud Time

Read a Story or Poem

Read aloud to your student for twenty minutes.

Track Your Progress

Mark the Progress Chart

Have your student mark Lesson 26 on the Progress Chart.

Lesson 27 Contractions

Objective

This lesson teaches common contractions.

You Will Need

- ☐ *Leap into Reading* pages 193-199
- ☐ apostrophe tile
- ☐ rubber band
- ☐ Word Cards 130-139

Before You Begin

Preview Contractions

In this lesson, your student will learn about contractions. A contraction is a shorter way of saying something. Contractions are formed by combining two words and using an apostrophe to replace the letters that have been removed.

Common contractions include:

aren't	**can't**	**didn't**	**hasn't**	**you'll**	**I'll**
she'll	**let's**	**wasn't**	**you've**	**it's**	**isn't**

The first word in a contraction doesn't change. Letters are always deleted from the second word and an apostrophe takes their place. There is one exception in which the first word of a contraction is changed: *won't*, which is a contraction for *will not*.

> *Won't* and *don't* will be taught in Lesson 29 when we teach the Find Gold rule: o is long when followed by two consonants.

This lesson also introduces the apostrophe tile. This tile is stored under the Other Tiles category.

Review

It's time to review the flashcards behind the **Mastered** dividers to ensure they stay fresh in your student's mind.

Shuffle the cards behind both dividers and choose a selection for review. See Appendix L and Appendix M for engaging ways to review Phonogram Cards and Word Cards.

Review
(continued)

Previous Concepts

Build the following words with letter tiles. Have your student divide the words where necessary, label with syllable tags, and read. *Grapevine* is divided using the Compound Words syllable division rule.

teeth	**grapevine**	
Vowel Team Syllable	Name Game Syllable	Name Game Syllable
t ee th	g r a p e	v i n e

New Teaching

Teach Contractions

In this exercise, you will use a rubber band to demonstrate the meaning of the words *contract* and *expand*. When you say the word *expand*, stretch out the rubber band.

"A rubber band can **expand** and **contract**. Watch: **Expand**. **Contract**."

Demonstrate the concept with the rubber band. "Is the rubber band smaller when it **expands** or when it **contracts**?" *When it contracts.*

"Today you are going to learn some contractions. A *contraction* is **two** words that have been made into **one** word. Say the word *contraction*." *Contraction.*

"We call it a contraction because the words **contract** and become smaller."

Build the words *we* and *will.* w e   w i l l

"Here is an example. Here are the words *we* and *will.*"

Remove the w-i and replace them with the apostrophe tile. "Now instead of two words, we have one word, *we'll.*"

w e ' l l

Point to the apostrophe tile. "I put an *apostrophe* in place of the letters that I took out. Say the word *apostrophe.*" *Apostrophe.*

"We often use contractions when we speak because they are a shorter way of saying something, and people like to take shortcuts when they speak."

New Teaching
(continued)

Build the following phrases. Have your student read each phrase and then form the contraction using the apostrophe tile.

he will → he'll
she will → she'll
she is → she's
she had → she'd

Complete Activity Sheet

"Now let's practice forming contractions."

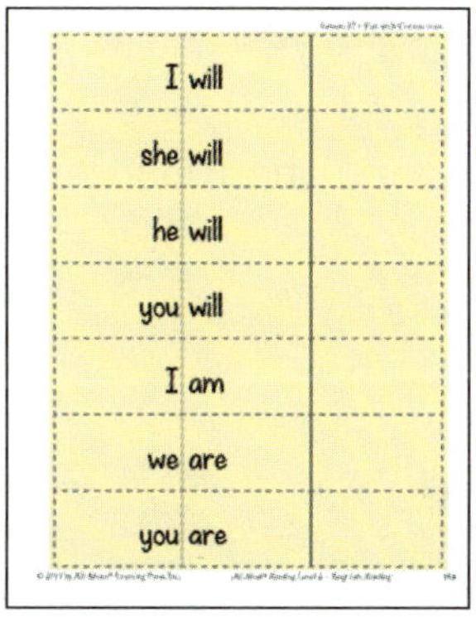

Fun with Contractions

Remove pages 193-196 from the *Leap into Reading* activity book.

Cut out the word strips along the dotted lines and place them in a pile. Do not cut on the solid lines.

Begin by having your student read the pair of words on the word strip (for example, *I will*.) Then have your student fold the word strip on the solid line to reveal the contraction (*'ll*) on the back of the word strip. Your student may then read the newly created contraction (*I'll*).

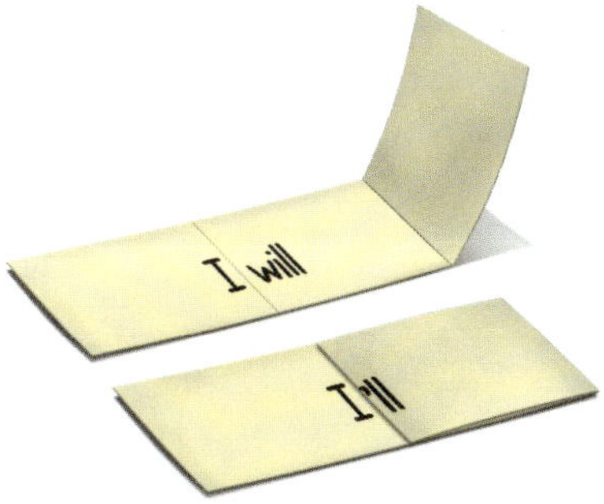

Continue until all the word strips and the new contractions have been read.

New Teaching
(continued)

Practice Reading Words

Have your student practice reading the words on Word Cards 130-139.

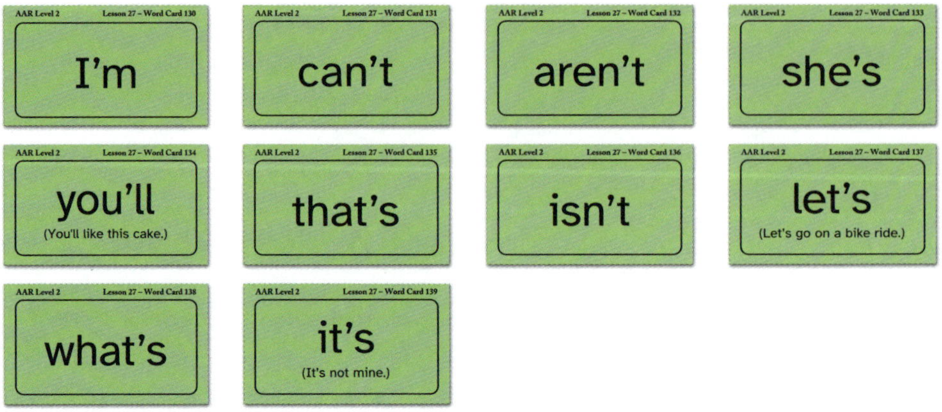

File the Word Cards behind the Review divider in the Reading Review Box.

Practice Fluency

New Words

haven't I'm we'll you're
she'll o'clock can't she's
it's we're aren't isn't

we've you'll he'll let's
here's he's hasn't what's
didn't wasn't that's I've
I'll you've

Phrases

haven't slept let's swim here's a hat
you're fun nine o'clock I'll try
he'll stomp isn't deep you'll begin

what's that can't see aren't frozen
you've been

Turn to pages 197-199 in the activity book.

Have your student read from the Practice Sheets.

To engage your student in the fluency exercises, try playing the game "Fluency Snowball Fight." For instructions, look for this icon in Appendix K.

Read-Aloud Time

Read a Story or Poem

Read aloud to your student for twenty minutes.

Read-Aloud Tip!

Choose a Wide Range of Books

If you've ever picked up a book outside of your expertise (such as a book on musical theory if you aren't a musician), then you've encountered unfamiliar vocabulary words that you don't understand. It would be difficult for you to read these books fluently because you wouldn't know what many of the words mean or how to pronounce them.

In the same way, it is difficult for your student to read fluently if he doesn't understand what the words mean. You can help your student develop a large listening vocabulary by reading aloud from a wide selection of books and discussing unfamiliar words.

Track Your Progress

Mark the Progress Chart

Have your student mark Lesson 27 on the Progress Chart.

Lesson 27!
Well, bounce me off the lily pad!
Can you believe how much stuff
we've learned?
Let's see ...

Open and Closed syllables
Silent E
wh and ee
syllable division rules
plurals
contractions
and a swampful of new words

Are you as proud of us
as I am?

Lesson 28 Read "Jake the Snake"

Objective

In this lesson, students read a poem and complete a Venn diagram.

You Will Need

- ☐ *Leap into Reading* pages 201-203
- ☐ *What Am I?* book

Before You Begin

Give Your Student an Audience

If your student enjoys a particular story in his *What Am I?* or *Queen Bee* reader, encourage him to read the story aloud to someone else, like a sibling, a visiting neighbor, Grandma, or a parent. Having an audience can be motivating and can give your student an opportunity to practice meaningful expression.

Review

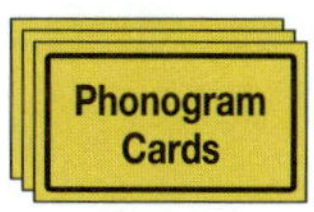

Review the Phonogram Cards that are behind the Review divider in your student's Reading Review Box. Show each card to your student and have him say the sound(s). If necessary, remind your student of the sound(s).

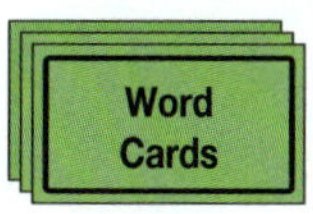

Shuffle and review the Word Cards that are behind the Review divider in your student's Reading Review Box. If your student has difficulty reading a word, build the word with letter tiles and have your student sound it out using the blending procedure shown in Appendix C.

Have fun with today's Word Card review with the activity "Word Card Racetrack." For instructions, look for this icon in Appendix M.

Read the Warm-Up Sheet for "Jake the Snake"

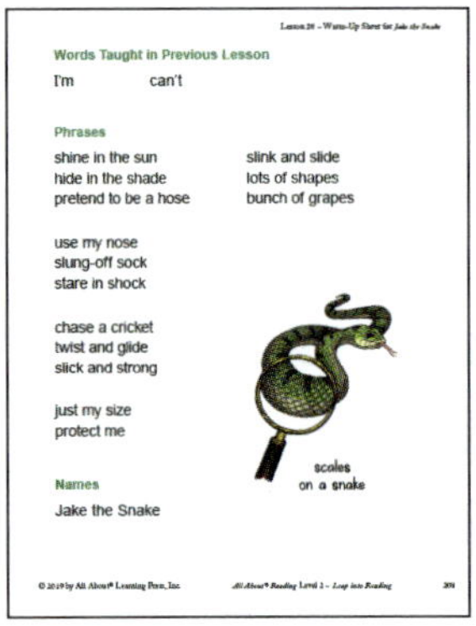

Words Taught in Previous Lesson

I'm can't

Phrases

shine in the sun
hide in the shade
pretend to be a hose

slink and slide
lots of shapes
bunch of grapes

use my nose
slung-off sock
stare in shock

chase a cricket
twist and glide
slick and strong

just my size
protect me

scales
on a snake

Names

Jake the Snake

Turn to page 201 in the *Leap into Reading* activity book.

Have your student practice reading words and phrases that are found in "Jake the Snake."

Teach Vocabulary and Activate Prior Knowledge

Point out the snake on the Warm-Up Sheet. "The skin of a snake is entirely covered in *scales*. Scales protect the snake's body and also help a snake move. Scales come in many different shapes, sizes, and colors depending on the species of snake."

"Have you ever watched the way a snake's tongue goes in and out of its mouth? It's probably smelling something, because a snake doesn't use its nose to smell—it uses its tongue."

"Have you ever watched a snake slither through the grass? Without making a sound, a snake can slink and slide along the ground, gliding and twisting as he goes."

"Snakes also possess another interesting characteristic: they shed their skin. Unlike the skin of animals and humans, the skin of a snake does not grow, so snakes shed the outer layer of their skin when they outgrow it."

"Our next story is actually a poem. It's about a snake who is very proud of his talents. He can do many unusual things."

New Teaching
(continued)

Read “Jake the Snake”

“Turn to page 177 in your reader and read ‘Jake the Snake’ aloud.” Discuss your student’s ideas for the questions below as you come to them.

After page 178: “How does Jake describe how he moves?” *Slip, slide, twist, glide.*

After reading: “What are some of the things that Jake is proud of? Skim the text for answers.”

Complete Activity Sheet

“Let’s see if you and Jake have anything in common.”

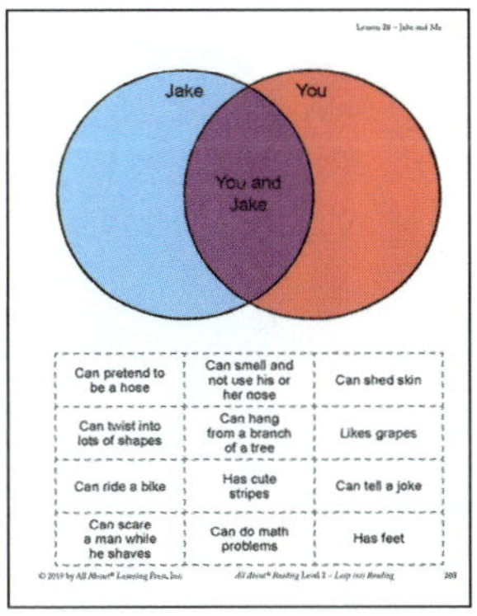

Jake and Me

Remove page 203 from the activity book.

Cut out the cards at the bottom of the page.

Guide your student in sorting the cards into the three areas of the Venn diagram. If the card lists something that only Jake can do, the card should be placed in Jake’s circle. If the card lists something that only your student can do, then the card should be placed in your student’s circle. If the card lists something that both can do, the card should be placed in the overlapping area between the two circles.

Continue until all the cards have been sorted.

Read-Aloud Time

Read a Story or Poem

Read aloud to your student for twenty minutes.

Track Your Progress

Mark the Progress Chart

Have your student mark Lesson 28 on the Progress Chart.

Lesson 29 The Find Gold Rule

Objective

This lesson teaches the Find Gold rule, which says that when the letters i or o are followed by two consonants, they may say their long sounds.

You Will Need

- ☐ *Leap into Reading* pages 205-212
- ☐ Word Cards 140-151

Before You Begin

Preview the Find Gold Rule

There are four ways to spell long vowel sounds. Your student has already learned three of these ways and today he will learn the fourth way. Here is an overview of the four ways:

1. A vowel can be long when it is placed at the end of an open syllable, as in *be*, *item (i-tem)*, and *open (o-pen)*.
2. Silent E can make a vowel long, as in *spine* and *home*.
3. A long vowel sound can be made using a vowel team, such as ee in the word *sheep*. More vowel teams representing long vowel sounds, such as oa in *road*, will be taught in Level 3.
4. Vowels i and o can be long before two consonants, as in *find* and *gold*.

Today's lesson will concentrate on number 4. Even though words like *colt* and *mind* are Closed syllables, the vowels are long, not short. Your student will learn that this is a special pattern: the letters i and o followed by two consonants may say their long vowel sound. We call this the Find Gold rule because *find* and *gold* are memorable examples.

Take a look at these other examples of the Find Gold rule.

-ild	**=**	**child**	**mild**	**wild**
-ind	**=**	**behind**	**blind**	**find**
-oll	**=**	**roll**	**droll**	**stroll**
-old	**=**	**bold**	**fold**	**hold**
-olt	**=**	**bolt**	**colt**	**jolt**
-ost	**=**	**most**	**post**	**host**

It is important to note that the Find Gold rule says that i and o *may* say their long vowel sound. They don't *always* say their long vowel sound. Examples of words in which i and o don't follow this rule are *build, gild, lost, frost,* and *cost*.

Wind is a homograph that can be pronounced with either a short i or a long i, depending on the context.

Review

Phonogram Cards

Review the Phonogram Cards that are behind the Review divider in your student's Reading Review Box. Show each card to your student and have him say the sound(s). If necessary, remind your student of the sound(s).

You may wish to have your student review phonograms by writing them in a salt tray. For instructions, look for this icon in Appendix L.

Word Cards

Shuffle and review the Word Cards that are behind the Review divider in your student's Reading Review Box. If your student has difficulty reading a word, build the word with letter tiles and have your student sound it out using the blending procedure shown in Appendix C.

Previous Concepts

Build the following words with letter tiles. Have your student label the words with syllable tags and read.

three	stick
Vowel Team Syllable	Closed Syllable
th r ee	s t i ck

New Teaching

Teach the Find Gold Rule

"Today you're going to learn a new pattern for one-syllable words."

Build the word *land*. l a n d

"What syllable type is this?" *Closed.*

"In a Closed syllable, is the vowel usually long or short?" *Short.*

"Right. In most cases, the vowel is short in a Closed syllable. What does this word say?" *Land.*

New Teaching
(continued)

Build the word *find*.

"This is also a Closed syllable, but in this case the i is long. What is this word?" *Find.*

"Good. In one-syllable words, if the letter i is followed by two consonants, the i is often long."

Leave the word *find* in the workspace. Next to it, build the word *gold*.

"The vowel in this word is also long. What does this word say?" *Gold.*

"Good. In one-syllable words, if the letter o is followed by two consonants, the o is often long."

"We call this the Find Gold rule for one-syllable words. The Find Gold rule says that when i and o are followed by two consonants, they often say their long sounds."

Leave the word *gold* in the workspace.

Play "Change the Word"

"I'm going to change the first part of this word."

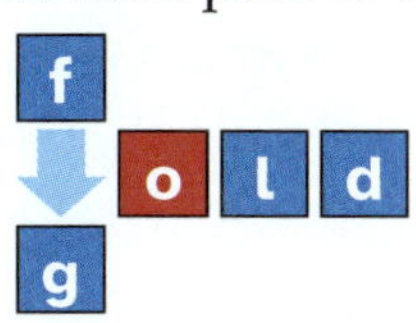

"What does this new word say?" Encourage your student to sound out the new word, *fold.*

Continue to change one or two tiles at a time to form the following words. Each time, have your student sound out the new word.

fold → cold → told

child* → wild → mild

*Use the ch tile for the word *child.*

New Teaching
(continued)

"Is the vowel in *mild* long or short?" *Long.*

"How many consonants are after the i?" *Two consonants.*

Complete Activity Sheet

"Let's pan for gold!"

Find Gold

Remove pages 205-208 from the *Leap into Reading* activity book.

Cut out the word cards and the pan for the gold.

Place the rectangular word cards along the river with the words facing down.

Have your student select a card from the river and read the word aloud. If he reads the word correctly, he may add the gold to his pan. If he reads the word incorrectly, return the card to the river for another try.

Continue until your student has all the gold in his pan.

Teach *Don't* and *Won't*

"You have already learned many contractions. Here are two that don't follow the same pattern as the others."

Build the words *do* and *not*. d o   n o t

"Here are the words *do* and *not*. The o in *do* says /o͞o/."

Remove the o in *not* and replace it with the apostrophe.

d o n ' t

"When I change this to the contraction *don't*, the o changes. What does the o say in the word *don't*?" */ō/.*

"Right. The o is no longer in an open syllable, but it is followed by two consonants, so it says its long sound."

New Teaching
(continued)

Change *don't* to *won't*. w o n ' t

"*Won't* is the contraction for *will not*." w i l l n o t

"Normally, we only change the second word in a contraction, but the contraction for *won't* is different. We change both words."

> *Won't* is an example of how our language changes over time. An older form of *will* was more similar to *would*; *woll*, *wolle*, and *wool* were some other forms of *will*. In some 19th-century writings, you can find the contraction *willn't*, but the shorter *won't* won out.

Practice Reading Words

Have your student practice reading the words on Word Cards 140-149.

told (Jan told me to sit.)	wild (That dog is wild!)	both	child
hold (Did you hold the cat?)	most	find (I can't find my bike.)	behind
don't	won't		

File the Word Cards behind the Review divider in the Reading Review Box.

Teach Two Leap Words: *who* and *move*

Show Word Card 150 to your student.

"This word is *who*, as in *Who is it?* This is a Leap Word because the wh doesn't say what we expect it to. It says /h/ instead of /hw/. The o says /o͞o/, which is the third sound of o."

New Teaching
(continued)

Show Word Card 151 to your student.

"This word is *move*, as in *Move the car.* This is a Leap Word because the o doesn't say what we expect it to. It says /ōō/ instead of /ō/. "

Review these Leap Words several times today and then file them behind the Review divider in the Reading Review Box.

Practice Fluency

New Words

who	move	roll	find
hold	kind	told	both
behind	cold	mild	blind
bold	child	old	mind
gold	wind	mold	don't
won't	sold		

Phrases

gold flute	both bikes
cold grapes	green mold
hold the child	old dog
find the snakes	the kind man
hold the hose	behind the tree
blind as a bat	wind the clock
she won't	

Turn to pages 209-212 in the activity book.

Have your student read from the Practice Sheets.

Give your student extra incentive for the fluency exercises by setting up a points system. For instructions, look for this icon in Appendix K.

Read-Aloud Time

Read a Story or Poem

Read aloud to your student for twenty minutes.

Track Your Progress

Mark the Progress Chart

Have your student mark Lesson 29 on the Progress Chart.

Hey there, buddy!
How's it going?
Are you leaping into reading?
Which stories have been your favorites so far?

And what about the lessons?
You know I only want the best for you,
so keep on reviewing ...
and having fun, too!

Lesson 30 Read "What Am I?"

Objective

In this lesson, students read a short story and create hints for a guessing game.

You Will Need

- ☐ *Leap into Reading* pages 213-215
- ☐ *What Am I?* book
- ☐ pencil

Before You Begin

Preview Parentheses

In today's story, your student will be introduced to parentheses, which are explanatory or additional words and phrases set off from the rest of the text by curved brackets. For example, the following sentence contains extra information that is not necessary for the sentence to make sense: *Maggie (who was always late) arrived at the birthday party at noon.*

Monitor Yourself for Excessive Feedback

We've already talked about how letting your student finish reading a sentence after he has misread a word encourages him to self-correct and read for meaning.

So as your student reads today's story, monitor yourself to see if you are offering immediate and constant feedback, interrupting the student for every misread word. Too often, such a stream of feedback causes the student to become dependent on the teacher to confirm that the word or phrase he just read is correct. The reader waits for the teacher to nod or say "good" or "uh-huh," which then becomes a cycle: the student reads a word or two, waits for affirmation, and then reads a few more words. This stop-and-go cycle works against the development of fluency.

If you feel yourself falling into this negative routine with your student, let him know that from now on, you will give feedback after the sentence has been completed instead of during his reading.

Review

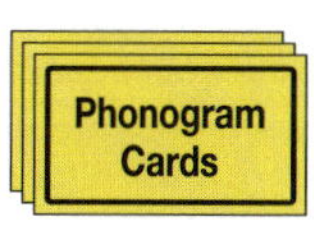

Review the Phonogram Cards that are behind the Review divider in your student's Reading Review Box. Show each card to your student and have him say the sound(s). If necessary, remind your student of the sound(s).

Review
(continued)

Shuffle and review the Word Cards that are behind the Review divider in your student's Reading Review Box. If your student has difficulty reading a word, build the word with letter tiles and have your student sound it out using the blending procedure shown in Appendix C.

New Teaching

Read the Warm-Up Sheet for "What Am I?"

Words Taught in Previous Lesson

gold mind find
move don't roll
won't hold

Phrases

drift on the wind
tales of brave deeds
with your chores

crash on the rocks
splash on the shore
dig holes in the sand

swim with the whales
make up a quiz
here is a prize

here is a prize
wake you up
tap a tune

won't be late
long string
make you smile

don't be shy
what am I

Turn to page 213 in the *Leap into Reading* activity book.

Have your student practice reading words and phrases that are found in "What Am I?"

Teach Vocabulary and Activate Prior Knowledge

Point out the illustration of the quill on the Warm-Up Sheet. "A *quill* is a feather from the wing or tail of a large bird such as a goose, turkey, or swan. Many years ago, before pens were invented, people used quills for writing. They would sharpen the shaft to a point and dip it in a bottle of ink."

"I have some riddles for you. What has six wheels and flies?" *Answer: a garbage truck.*

"Here's another one: I have to be broken before I can be used. What am I?" *Answer: an egg.*

"A riddle is a question or problem that can be solved. It is a type of game. Today you'll read some riddles and try to guess the answers."

New Teaching
(continued)

Read "What Am I?"

"Turn to page 187 in your reader and read 'What Am I?' aloud." Discuss your student's ideas for the questions below as you come to them.

After page 188: Point out the pair of parentheses. "These are parentheses. Inside the parentheses is extra information for the reader. In this case, what is the extra information?" *That the hints are free.*

After each riddle: Stop after each of the five riddles and try to guess the object with your student.

Complete Activity Sheet

"Let's write our own riddles!"

What Am I?

Object you have in mind:

Hints:

1

2

3

Can your pals tell what it is?

What Am I?
Remove page 215 from the activity book.

Guide your student in creating a "What Am I?" activity. The student should first think of an object and then write the word or draw a picture of the object in the space provided. Encourage your student to think of at least three hints that describe the object.

Have several friends or family members try to guess what the object is.

Read-Aloud Time

Read a Story or Poem

Read aloud to your student for twenty minutes.

Read-Aloud Tip!

Explore the Whole Book
Before diving into a new book for the first time, explore the front and back covers, the spine, and the jacket flaps. Read and discuss the title, the author, and the illustrator, and look for interesting info about them on the flaps. If you're reading a picture book, spend some time admiring the endpapers, too!

Track Your Progress

Mark the Progress Chart

Have your student mark Lesson 30 on the Progress Chart.

Lesson 31 ER and Bossy R Syllables

Objective

This lesson teaches phonogram er, the Bossy R syllable type, and words containing er.

You Will Need

- ☐ *Leap into Reading* pages 217-227
- ☐ letter tiles ur, ir, purple or, ear, and our from your Levels 3-4 baggie
- ☐ letter tile er
- ☐ Phonogram Card 35
- ☐ Bossy R syllable tag
- ☐ Sound of /er/ label
- ☐ Word Cards 152-161

Before You Begin

Preview Phonogram ER

Phonogram er says /er/ as in *her.* Read the following examples and listen for the /er/ sound.

winter	**paper**	**tender**	**summer**	**under**
never	**over**	**perfect**	**after**	**stern**

Phonogram er is found in relatively few one-syllable words, but it is found in thousands of multisyllable words. In Level 3, your student will learn that er is also used as a suffix in words like *bigger* and *shorter.*

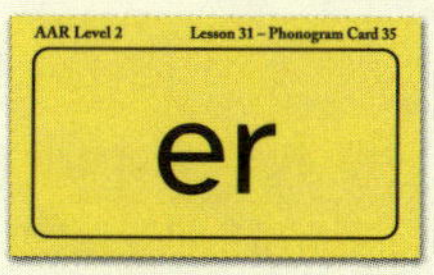

When we practice the Phonogram Card for er, we say "/er/ as in *her*" to distinguish er from the other ways of spelling /er/. This extra bit of information is important to know for spelling. By learning the full wording for phonogram er now, your student won't have to relearn the flashcard for spelling purposes later.

The er tile is stored under the Sound of /er/ category.

Refer to the Letter Tiles app or Phonogram Sounds app for a demonstration of the er phonogram sound. When we use the er letter tile, we only say the sound /er/. To facilitate blending, we don't say the second part, "as in *her.*"

Before You Begin
(continued)

Preview Multiple Ways to Say /er/

Phonogram er is by far the most common way to spell the sound of /er/. The sound of /er/ can also be represented in the following ways:

- er as in *her* (taught in this lesson)
- ir as in *first* (taught in Level 3, Lesson 19)
- ur as in *nurse* (taught in Level 3, Lesson 21)
- or as in *work* (taught in Level 3, Lesson 23) and in *doctor* (taught in Level 4, Lesson 26)
- ear as in *early* (taught in Level 4, Lesson 8)
- our as in *journey* (taught in Level 4, Lesson 50)
- In an unaccented syllable, phonogram ar is muffled and can sound like /er/, as in *dollar.*

Preview Bossy R Syllables

Today your student will learn the fifth syllable type, the Bossy R syllable.

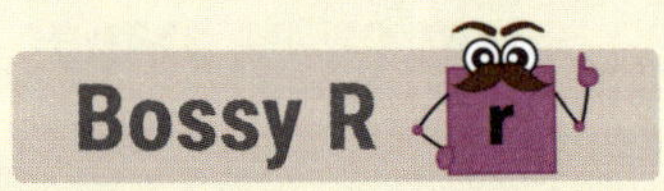

A Bossy R syllable contains a vowel followed by the letter r. The r controls the vowel and changes the way it is pronounced, as in the words *her*, *car*, and *firm*. On the syllable tag, the Bossy R syllable is represented by a bossy-looking r letter tile.

Adding this new syllable type helps students see that words like *herd* and *fur* aren't Closed syllables and therefore they shouldn't expect the vowels to be short like they would be in a Closed syllable. Instead, this is a different syllable type in which the r controls the sound of the vowel that comes before it.

Review

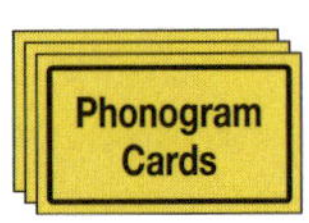

Review the Phonogram Cards that are behind the Review divider in your student's Reading Review Box. Show each card to your student and have him say the sound(s). If necessary, remind your student of the sound(s).

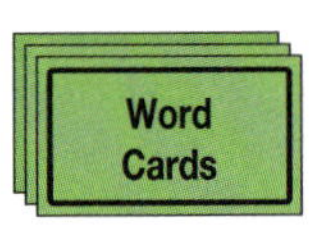

Shuffle and review the Word Cards that are behind the Review divider in your student's Reading Review Box. If your student has difficulty reading a word, build the word with letter tiles and have your student sound it out using the blending procedure shown in Appendix C.

Review
(continued)

Previous Concepts

Build the following words with letter tiles. Have your student divide the words where necessary, label with syllable tags, and read. *Campfire* is divided using the Compound Words syllable division rule.

campfire

Closed Syllable: c a m p | Name Game Syllable: f i r e

need

Vowel Team Syllable: n ee d

New Teaching

Teach New Phonogram ER

Hold up the er Phonogram Card.

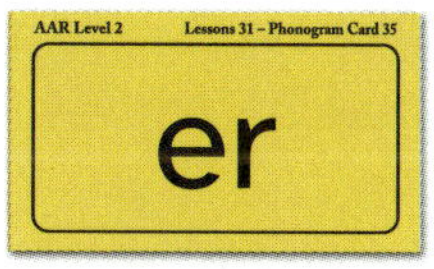

"E-r says /er/ as in *her*. Repeat after me: /er/ as in *her*." *Student repeats the sound.*

Mix in several other Phonogram Cards for mixed review and practice until your student can say the sounds accurately. File the Phonogram Card behind the Review divider in the Reading Review Box.

Move these letter tiles into the workspace. er ir ur or ear our

"All of these letter tiles say /er/."

Point to the er. "We need a way to tell the difference between them, so we call this one */er/, the /er/ of her*."

Build the word *her*. h er

"Er is used in the word *her*."

Point to the er tile again. "When you see this tile, say its sound, /er/. You don't have to say *as in her* when we are building with tiles, just when we are using the flashcards."

New Teaching
(continued)

If your student is interested in the names of the other phonograms, you can share this information with him:

er as in *her*	or as in *work*
ir as in *first*	ear as in *early*
ur as in *nurse*	our as in *journey*

In the following sentence, these spellings are represented in order of frequency in English words: *Her first nurse works early on the journey.*

Remove the letter tiles ir, ur, or, ear, and our from the workspace, leaving just the er tile.

Mix in several other letter tiles for mixed review and practice with the new phonogram until your student can say the sound accurately.

For extra practice with the new phonogram, play some file folder games. For instructions, look for this icon in Appendix L.

Blend Sounds with Letter Tiles

Build the word *herd.* h er d

"I'll sound out this first word, and then you'll sound out the next word."

Touch under the h and say */h/.*

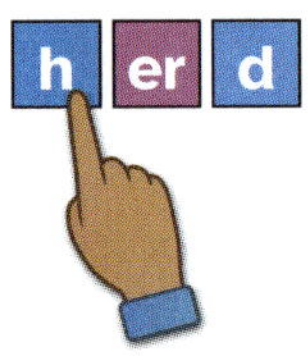

Touch under the er and say */er/.*

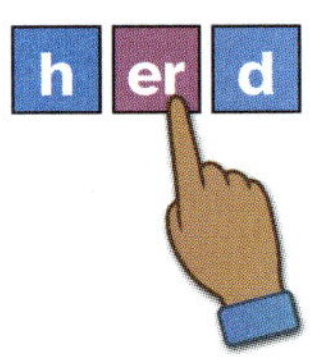

Touch under the d and say */d/.*

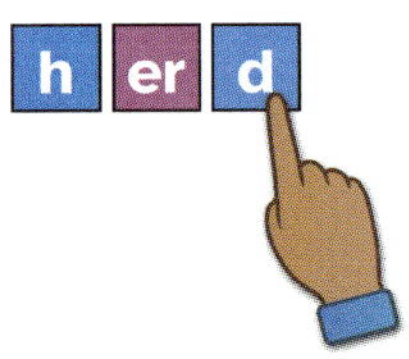

New Teaching
(continued)

Now go back to the beginning of the word. Slide your finger under the letters h-er-d and say *herd* slowly.

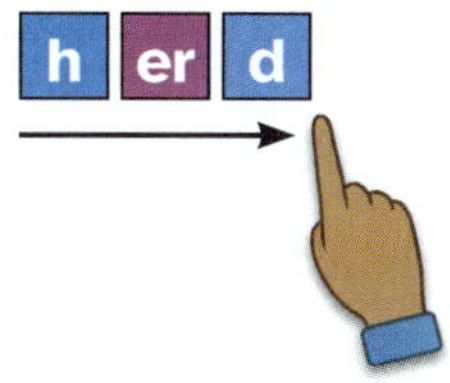

Finally, read the word *herd* at a normal pace as we do when we speak. "*Herd*, as in *a herd of buffalo*."

Using the same blending procedure, have your student sound out the word *fern*.

Leave the word *fern* in the workspace.

Teach the Fifth Syllable Type: Bossy R

Point to the word *fern*. "This is a new syllable type. When a vowel and an r are on the same letter tile, the r makes the vowel say a different sound. We pretend that r bosses the vowels around, telling them what to do."

Move the Bossy R syllable tag into the workspace.

"On this syllable tag, we see that the r tile looks rather bossy."

Point to the er tile. "When we see a vowel and an r on the same letter tile, we know that the syllable will be a Bossy R syllable and we need to use the Bossy R syllable tag."

"Label this syllable." *Student uses the Bossy R tag.*

New Teaching
(continued)

Decode Words with Bossy R Syllables

Build the word *paper.* p | a | p | er

"I'd like to read this word together, but first let's divide the word into syllables. Point to the vowels."

p | a | p | er

"How many consonants are between the two vowels?" *One.*

> You may need to help your student see that e is still considered a vowel even though it is part of phonogram er. **Tip!**

"When there is just one consonant, we usually divide before the consonant. Divide the word."

p | a   p | er

"Label the syllable types."

Open Syllable	Bossy R Syllable
p a	p er

"Read the first syllable." *Pā.*

"Read the second syllable." *Per.*

"Now read the word." *Paper.*

"Great! *Paper* is a real word, so you've divided the word correctly."

Using the same procedure for blending, have your student sound out the following words by applying the appropriate syllable division rules and labeling the syllable types.

better = Two Consonant Tiles rule
river = One Consonant Tile rule, Part 2
ruler = One Consonant Tile rule, Part 1
winter = Two Consonant Tiles rule

New Teaching
(continued)

Complete Activity Sheet

"The Party Monsters are back and they've invited Bossy R over for dinner. Bossy R is a very picky eater, but you can help!"

<u>**Party Monsters Make Dinner**</u>

Remove pages 217-221 from the *Leap into Reading* activity book.

Place the refrigerator and menu pages in front of your student. Cut out the Bossy R strip and place it next to the refrigerator. Cut out the word cards and place them in a pile in the refrigerator with the words facing down.

Have your student select two word cards from the refrigerator and place them on one of the pairs of empty spaces on the menu. He can then read aloud the recipe title that he has created. Possible menu items include a radish and cracker sandwich or a hot dog and jam cake. Next, ask Bossy R if he would like to eat this menu item. But be forewarned—he will only eat it if it has a Bossy R syllable type in the menu item! If it's an item that Bossy R will eat, your student may move the word cards to the Bossy R strip.

Continue playing until the refrigerator has been emptied.

Practice Reading Words

Have your student practice reading the words on Word Cards 152-158.

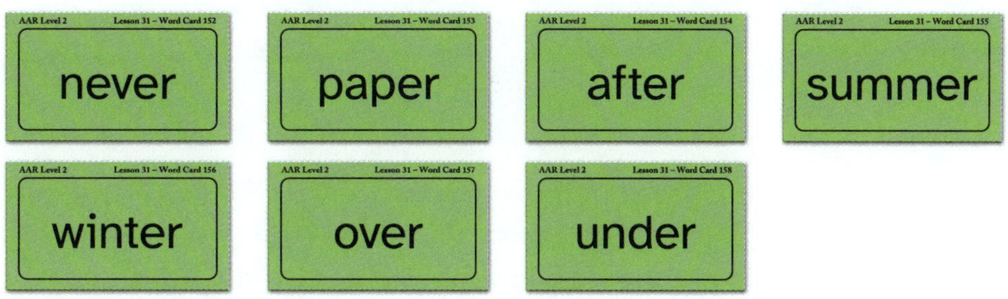

File the Word Cards behind the Review divider in the Reading Review Box.

New Teaching
(continued)

Teach Three Leap Words: *done, none,* and *one*

Show Word Card 159 to your student.

"This word is *done*, as in *I am done with lunch.* What sound does the o make in the word *done*?" */ŭ/.*

"This is the fourth sound of o. You haven't studied words with the fourth sound of o yet, so this is a Leap Word."

"Silent E has a different job in this word, too, which you haven't learned yet."

Cover the e to show the word *don*.

"Silent E has been added so we don't confuse this word with the name *Don*."

Show Word Card 160 to your student.

"This word is *none*, as in *None of us can fly*. *None* rhymes with *done*, and the o also has the fourth sound. Silent E has been added so we don't confuse this word with the word *non*."

Show Word Card 161 to your student.

"This word is *one*, as in *We will plant one tree*. *One* also rhymes with *done* and *none*. The o says /wŭ/, which is unusual. Silent E has been added so we don't confuse this word with the word *on*. The frog will remind you to stop and remember this special Leap Word."

Review these Leap Words several times today and then file them behind the Review divider in the Reading Review Box.

New Teaching
(continued)

Practice Fluency

New Words

done	after	ruler	tiger
ever	member	one	finger
river	shelter	gather	none
summer	over	desert	glitter
number	paper	dinner	super
cracker	herd	winter	never
perhaps	enter	blister	pepper
zipper	under	ladder	hammer
supper	thunder	rubber	dresser
fever	silver	spider	sister
fern	shiver	robber	better
butter	later	hunger	
different	fantastic	cucumber	remember

Turn to pages 223-227 in the activity book.

Have your student read from the Practice Sheets.

Let your student get emotional with the fluency exercise with a fun emoticon activity. For instructions, look for this icon in Appendix K.

Read-Aloud Time

Read a Story or Poem

Read aloud to your student for twenty minutes.

Read-Aloud Tip!

A Picture Is Worth...

Before, during, or after reading, be sure to take the time to talk about the book's illustrations. Not only do the illustrations in picture books tell half the story, there are often secondary "silent" stories going on as well.

Have your child point out favorite characters, objects, colors, and recurring elements, or ask him why the artist drew something a certain way.

Track Your Progress

Mark the Progress Chart

Have your student mark Lesson 31 on the Progress Chart.

Whoa!
This ER sound came in handy as I was hopping around the pond visiting my friends today. We had fun giving each other new nicknames. Can you guess who my friends are from their names?

Leggy Skater
Busy Builder
Mister Hisser
Buzzy Biter
Hide-n-Seeker
Graceful Glider
Hover 'Copter
Whisker Swisher

Answers:
pond skater, beaver, snake,
mosquito, turtle, swan,
dragonfly, catfish

Lesson 32 Read "Ruben and the Secret Gift"

Objective

In this lesson, students read a short story and compare settings.

You Will Need

- ☐ *Leap into Reading* pages 229-231
- ☐ *Queen Bee* book
- ☐ pencil

Before You Begin

Today your student will read the first story in the *Queen Bee* reader.

As with *What Am I?*, the story-related lessons help your student apply the new concepts she's learned and practice comprehension skills.

Remember to check out the tips in Appendix N if your student runs into difficulties while reading the stories.

The story-related lessons contain important activities, so don't skip them!

Review

Phonogram Cards Review the Phonogram Cards that are behind the Review divider in your student's Reading Review Box. Show each card to your student and have him say the sound(s). If necessary, remind your student of the sound(s).

Word Cards Shuffle and review the Word Cards that are behind the Review divider in your student's Reading Review Box. If your student has difficulty reading a word, build the word with letter tiles and have your student sound it out using the blending procedure shown in Appendix C.

> **?** For extra practice with the Word Cards, play the game "Guess the Word." For instructions, look for this icon in Appendix M.

Teach the Words *Secret* and *Husband*

Build the word *secret*. s e c r e t

"I'll divide this word into syllables and you see if you can read it."

s e   c r e t

"What is this word?" *Secret.*

> You may wish to explain to your student that *secret* doesn't follow the normal syllable division rule. Instead of dividing this word *between* the middle consonants as we usually do, we divide it *before* the middle consonants.

Build the word *husband*. h u s b a n d

"Divide this word into syllables." *Student divides between the s and the b.*

h u s   b a n d

Point to the s. "The s says /z/ in this word. Read this syllable." *Hus.*

Push the syllables together and point to the a. "When we say this word in everyday conversation, the sound of the a gets muffled because we say it so fast. The word sounds like *husb'nd* in normal speech."

"What is this word?" *Husband.*

Read the Warm-Up Sheet for "Ruben and the Secret Gift"

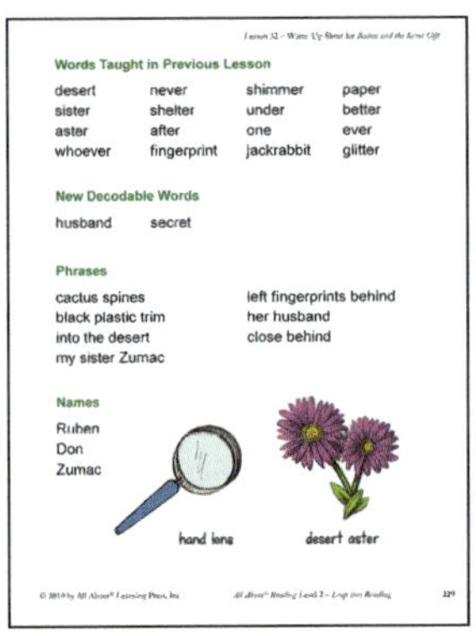

Words Taught in Previous Lesson

desert	never	shimmer	paper
sister	shelter	under	better
aster	after	one	ever
whoever	fingerprint	jackrabbit	glitter

New Decodable Words

husband   secret

Phrases

cactus spines
black plastic trim
into the desert
my sister Zumac
left fingerprints behind
her husband
close behind

Names

Ruben
Don
Zumac

Turn to page 229 in the *Leap into Reading* activity book.

Have your student practice reading words and phrases that are found in "Ruben and the Secret Gift."

Point out the first word, *desert*. "In *desert*, the s says /z/ because it is between two vowels."

Point out the words *whoever, fingerprint,* and *jackrabbit* on the fourth line. "These words are compound words. Can you find the smaller words that make up these compound words?"

New Teaching
(continued)

Teach Vocabulary and Activate Prior Knowledge

Point out the illustration of the hand lens on the Warm-Up Sheet. “Another name for a hand lens is a *magnifying glass*. A magnifying glass is a tool you can use to make things look bigger so you can see them in more detail.”

Point out the illustration of the aster. “An *aster* is a type of flower. There are many types of asters and they come in many different colors. They have yellow centers that attract bees and butterflies. In our next story, you’ll see a specific type of aster called a *desert aster*.”

“In this story, a boy named Ruben receives a gift but he doesn’t know who it is from. Let’s see if you can figure out who gave him the gift.”

Read “Ruben and the Secret Gift”

“Turn to page 9 in your reader and read ‘Ruben and the Secret Gift’ aloud.” Discuss your student’s ideas for the question below when you come to it.

After page 27: “Before we turn the page, see if you can figure out who gave Ruben the hand lens. Look closely at the fingerprints on the card in Ruben’s hand and compare them to the fingerprint in Ruben’s notebook. Who gave Ruben the gift?”

Complete Activity Sheet

“Let’s compare Ruben’s home to yours.”

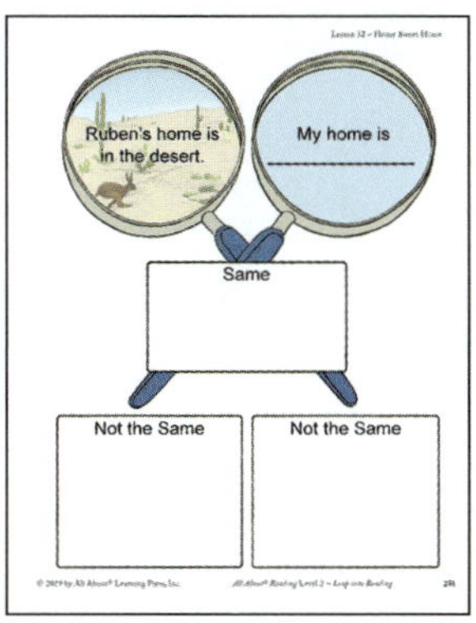

Home Sweet Home
Remove page 231 from the activity book.

Encourage your student to think of a phrase to fill in the blank at the top of the page: *My home is* ____. Choose a descriptive phrase such as *near the ocean*, *by a lake*, *in a big city*, *in a small town*, *in a subdivision*, or *on a farm*.

Guide your student in recording the similarities and differences between his own location and the setting of Ruben’s story.

Read-Aloud Time

Read a Story or Poem

Read aloud to your student for twenty minutes.

Track Your Progress

Mark the Progress Chart

Have your student mark Lesson 32 on the Progress Chart.

Lesson 33 AR

Objective

This lesson teaches phonogram ar, words containing ar, and how to decode three-syllable words.

You Will Need

- ☐ *Leap into Reading* pages 233-240
- ☐ letter tile ar
- ☐ Phonogram Card 36
- ☐ Word Cards 162-171

Before You Begin

Preview Phonogram AR

Phonogram ar says /ar/ as in *car.* Read the following examples and listen for the /ar/ sound.

star **jar** **start** **barn** **march**

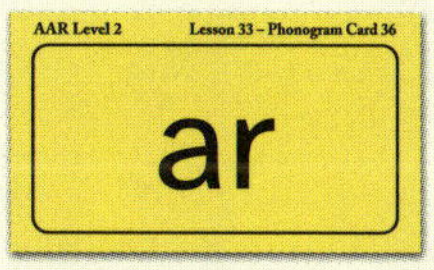

When we practice the Phonogram Card for ar, we say "/ar/".

The ar tile is stored under the Other Tiles category.

Refer to the Letter Tiles app or Phonogram Sounds app for a demonstration of the ar phonogram sound.

Review

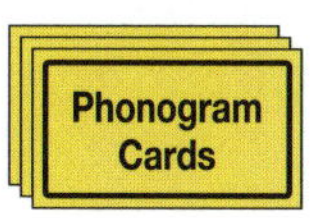

Review the Phonogram Cards that are behind the Review divider in your student's Reading Review Box. Show each card to your student and have him say the sound(s). If necessary, remind your student of the sound(s).

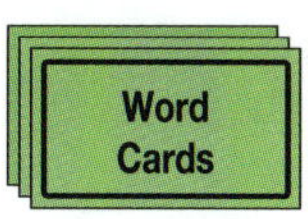

Shuffle and review the Word Cards that are behind the Review divider in your student's Reading Review Box. If your student has difficulty reading a word, build the word with letter tiles and have your student sound it out using the blending procedure shown in Appendix C.

Review
(continued)

Previous Concepts

Build the following words with letter tiles. Have your student divide the words, label with syllable tags, and read. *Thunder* uses the Two Consonant Tiles rule; *tiger* uses the One Consonant Tile rule.

thunder		**tiger**	
Closed Syllable	Bossy R Syllable	Open Syllable	Bossy R Syllable
th u n	d er	t i	g er

New Teaching

Teach New Phonogram AR

Hold up the ar Phonogram Card.

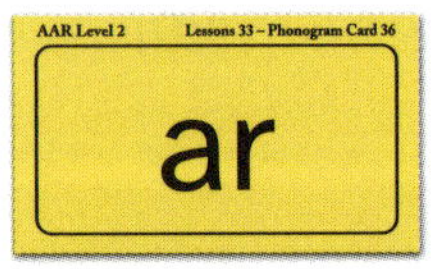

"A-r says /ar/. Repeat after me: /ar/." *Student repeats the sound.*

Mix in several other Phonogram Cards for mixed review and practice until your student can say the sound accurately. File the Phonogram Card behind the Review divider in the Reading Review Box.

Move the ar tile into the workspace. ar

Mix in several other letter tiles for mixed review and practice with the new phonogram until your student can say the sound accurately.

For extra practice with the new phonogram, try the activity "Jump On It." For instructions, look for this icon in Appendix L.

New Teaching
(continued)

Blend Sounds with Letter Tiles

Build the word *barn*. 

"I'll sound out this first word, and then you'll sound out the next word."

Touch under the b and say */b/.*

Touch under the ar and say */ar/.*

Touch under the n and say */n/.*

Now go back to the beginning of the word. Slide your finger under the letters b-ar-n and say *barn* slowly.

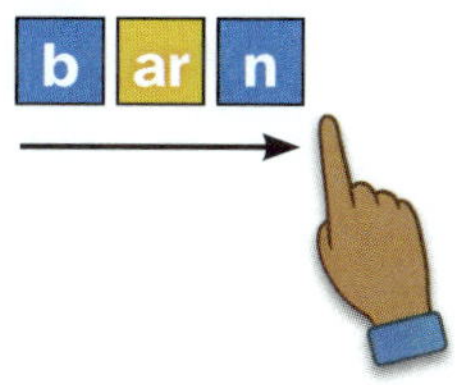

Finally, read the word *barn* at a normal pace as we do when we speak.

Using the same procedure for blending, have your student sound out the word *bark*.

Leave the word *bark* in the workspace.

Play "Change the Word"

"I'm going to change the first part of this word."

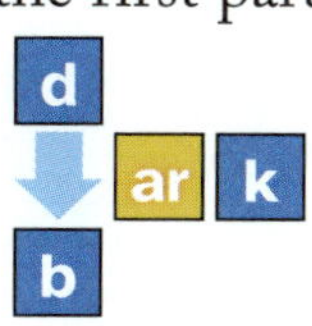

"What does this new word say?" Encourage your student to sound out the new word, *dark*.

New Teaching
(continued)

Continue to change one tile at a time to form the following words. Each time, have your student sound out the new word.

dark → mark → park → spark → shark*

*Use the <u>sh</u> tile for the word *shark*.

Leave the word *shark* in the workspace.

Label Syllable Types

"Let's label this syllable."

Point to the <u>ar</u> tile. "In this syllable, we have a tile with a vowel and an <u>r</u>. This is a Bossy R syllable. Label it with the Bossy R syllable tag."

Build the following words with letter tiles. Have your student divide the words into syllables where necesssary, label with syllable tags, and read. *Garden* is divided using the Two Consonant Tiles rule.

start **garden**

Decode Longer Words

Build the word *fantastic*.

"This is a long word that you've probably never read before. But if you divide it into syllables, you'll be able to read it."

"Just follow the normal steps for dividing a word into syllables. Point to the first two vowels." *Student points to the vowels.*

"There are two consonant tiles between the vowels, so divide between them."

New Teaching
(continued)

"Point to the next two vowels."

f a n   t a s t i c

"There are two consonant tiles between these vowels as well, so divide between them."

f a n   t a s   t i c

"Now you can read the word one syllable at a time." Guide your student in decoding each syllable and then have him read the word at normal speed. *Fantastic.*

> If necessary, help your student see that all three syllables are Closed syllables, so the vowels are short. **Tip!**

"You followed all the normal syllable division rules, but instead of dividing the word once, you did it twice. How many syllables does this word have?" *Three.*

Build the word *different.* d i f f er e n t

"Divide this word into three syllables." *Student divides the word in two steps:*

d i f   f er e n t

d i f   f er   e n t

> If your student asks why r doesn't go with the second e when dividing *different*, explain that we rarely split up phonograms. This rule will be covered later in the series.

"Place a syllable tag over each syllable."

Closed Syllable	Bossy R Syllable	Closed Syllable
d i f	f er	e n t

"Now sound out the word." *Dif-fer-ent.*

"Say the word." *Different.*

New Teaching
(continued)

Repeat the process with *cucumber*.

Open Syllable	Closed Syllable	Bossy R Syllable
c u	c u m	b er

> If your student ever tries to use a short vowel sound in a Bossy R syllable, remind him that Bossy R always makes the vowel say a different sound.
>
> **Tip!**

Complete Activity Sheet

"Now let's get some work done on the farm."

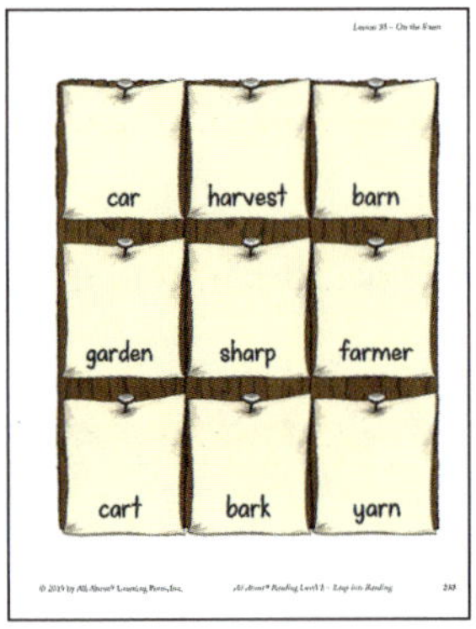

On the Farm

Remove pages 233-235 from the *Leap into Reading* activity book.

Cut out the cards on page 235. Mix them up and place them on the table.

Ask your student to read the first word on the game sheet (*car*) and to locate the card with an illustration of a car. Once he has found the correct match, he should place the illustration above its corresponding word on the game board.

Continue until all nine words have been read and matched with their corresponding illustrations.

Practice Reading Words

Have your student practice reading the words on Word Cards 162-167.

barn	sharp	hard	start
March (It is cold in March.)	dark		

File the Word Cards behind the Review divider in the Reading Review Box.

New Teaching
(continued)

Teach Four Leap Words: *warm, Mr., Mrs.,* and *too*

Show Word Card 168 to your student.

"This word is *warm*, as in *It's warm in the sun*. The ar says /or/ instead of /ar/, so this is a Leap Word."

> In some regions, *warm* is pronounced with /ar/. If that is the case in your region, it doesn't need to be treated as a Leap Word. Instead, teach *warm* as a normal Word Card.

Show Word Card 169 to your student.

"An abbreviation is a shortened form of a word. *Mr.* is a shortened way of writing the word *mister*. Notice that in this abbreviation, we capitalize the m and add a period at the end. The abbreviation is *Mr.*, as in *Mr. Smith.*"

Show Word Card 170 to your student.

"*Mrs.* is a shortened way of writing the word *missus*. To make this abbreviation, we give it a capital m and put a period at the end. This gives us the abbreviation *Mrs.*, as in *Mrs. Lane.*"

Show Word Card 171 to your student.

"This word is *too*, as in *This dress is too big*. It is a common word, but it doesn't follow the rules that you have learned so far. The two o's work together to say the sound /o͞o/. What is this word?" *Too.*

Review these Leap Words several times today and then file them behind the Review divider in the Reading Review Box.

New Teaching
(continued)

Practice Fluency

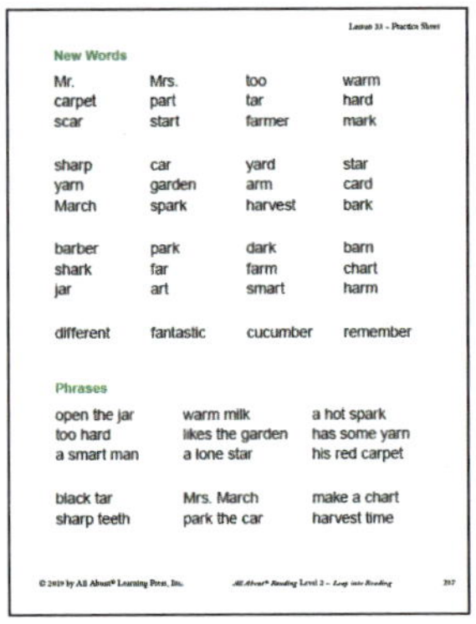

New Words

Mr.	Mrs.	too	warm
carpet	part	tar	hard
scar	start	farmer	mark
sharp	car	yard	star
yarn	garden	arm	card
March	spark	harvest	bark
barber	park	dark	barn
shark	far	farm	chart
jar	art	smart	harm
different	fantastic	cucumber	remember

Phrases

open the jar	warm milk	a hot spark
too hard	likes the garden	has some yarn
a smart man	a lone star	his red carpet
black tar	Mrs. March	make a chart
sharp teeth	park the car	harvest time

Turn to pages 237-240 in the activity book.

Have your student read from the Practice Sheets.

Have some fun with the fluency exercises with a silly sentence activity. For instructions, look for this icon in Appendix K.

Read-Aloud Time

Read a Story or Poem

Read aloud to your student for twenty minutes.

Track Your Progress

Mark the Progress Chart

Have your student mark Lesson 33 on the Progress Chart.

Lesson 34 Read "Mrs. Marvel's Garden"

Objective

In this lesson, students read a short story and learn about the five senses in literature.

You Will Need

- ☐ *Leap into Reading* pages 241-243
- ☐ *Queen Bee* book

Before You Begin

Preview the Purpose of the Activity Sheet

Authors often use the five senses of taste, sight, sound, touch, and smell in their imagery and description. In today's activity, your student will practice distinguishing and discussing the five senses.

Review

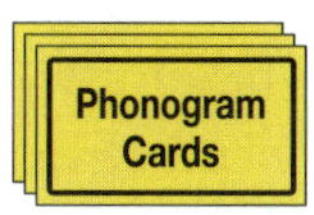

Review the Phonogram Cards that are behind the Review divider in your student's Reading Review Box. Show each card to your student and have him say the sound(s). If necessary, remind your student of the sound(s).

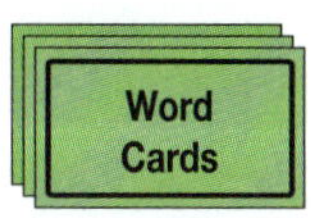

Shuffle and review the Word Cards that are behind the Review divider in your student's Reading Review Box. If your student has difficulty reading a word, build the word with letter tiles and have your student sound it out using the blending procedure shown in Appendix C.

Your student may enjoy reviewing today's Word Cards with the activity "Word Cloud." For instructions, look for this icon in Appendix M.

Read the Warm-Up Sheet for "Mrs. Marvel's Garden"

Words Taught in Previous Lesson

warm, garden, art, part, too, star, park, jars, Mrs.

Phrases

last summer
art sale
in the park

garden gate
old bed frame
bare feet

green moss
cucumber vine
twist on my finger

old milk crate
under a frond
part of a plant

peek under here
made a star
twigs and twine

pots and silverware
Mrs. Marvel's Garden
this butterfly

Names

Mrs. Marvel

Turn to page 241 in the *Leap into Reading* activity book.

Have your student practice reading words and phrases that are found in "Mrs. Marvel's Garden."

Teach Vocabulary and Activate Prior Knowledge

Point out the illustration of the fern frond on the Warm-Up Sheet. "The leaves of ferns are called *fronds*. We can see six fronds on this fern."

Point out the illustration of the wind chime. "Have you ever heard a *wind chime*? When the wind blows, a wind chime makes sounds. Some wind chimes sound like music, while others make a twinkling sound. Wind chimes can be made of bells, wood, metal, or anything else that makes a sound when it is moved."

"Have you ever been to a garden? Was it a vegetable garden or a flower garden?"

"What things might you hear when you go to a garden?"

"What things might you smell when you go to a garden?"

"When you go to a garden, you can experience it with all five of your senses: sight, hearing, touch, smell, and taste."

"The girl in the next story can't see very well, so she uses her other senses to help her experience the world around her."

New Teaching
(continued)

Read "Mrs. Marvel's Garden"

"Turn to page 31 in your reader and read 'Mrs. Marvel's Garden' aloud." Discuss your student's ideas for the questions below as you come to them.

After page 41: "Do you recognize the names of any of the plants Mrs. Marvel mentions?"

After reading: "What is Mrs. Marvel going to do with the star that they just made?"

Complete Activity Sheet

"Authors often use words that appeal to the five senses. They may describe sounds, sights, or smells to create a better picture in the reader's mind."

That Makes Sense!
Remove page 243 from the activity book.

Cut apart the cards at the bottom of the page and place them in a pile.

"Let's pretend that the girl in the story has come to your house and you have just taken her to your kitchen."

Encourage your student to select one of the cards from the pile and decide if the girl in the story would use her sense of sight, hearing, taste, smell, or touch to experience that particular item. Your student should then place the card in the appropriate box. There are no absolutely right answers—one student might think that a cucumber represents sound (*crunch*), while another might think that it represents sight, smell, taste, or touch.

Continue until all the cards have been distributed on the game board.

Read-Aloud Time

Read a Story or Poem

Read aloud to your student for twenty minutes.

Read-Aloud Tip!

Motivate a Reluctant Reader

If you have a reluctant reader on your hands, use read-aloud time to help motivate him. Here are some tips:

- Avoid making reading feel like a chore by scheduling a leisurely read-aloud time that isn't squished between other activities.
- Try books of different genres until you hit upon some that interest your student. Possibilities include horse books, how-to books related to hobbies or current interests, nature topics, mysteries, fairy tales, and many more.
- Let your student peruse the aisles at the library or bookstore and choose the next read-alouds. Check out the magazines, comic books, and joke books as well as chapter book series.

Track Your Progress

Mark the Progress Chart

Have your student mark Lesson 34 on the Progress Chart.

Lesson 35 OR

Objective

This lesson teaches phonogram or and words containing or.

You Will Need

- ☐ *Leap into Reading* pages 245-252
- ☐ Phonogram Card 37
- ☐ yellow or letter tile
- ☐ Word Cards 172-181

Before You Begin

Preview Phonogram OR

Phonogram or can say two sounds:

- /or/ as in *corn* (emphasized in this lesson)
- /er/ as in *work* (emphasized in Level 3, Lesson 23)

In this lesson, your student will learn words in which or says /or/. Read the following examples and listen for the /or/ sound.

corn	**fork**	**morning**	**forest**	**short**
storm	**for**	**north**	**order**	**forget**

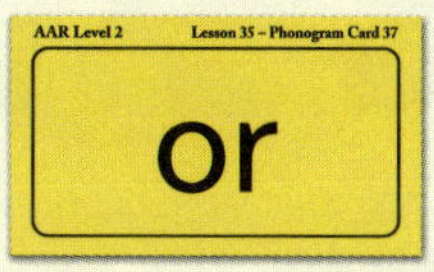

When we practice the Phonogram Card for or, we say "/or/–/er/ as in *work*."

or

The yellow or tile is stored under the Other Tiles category. This tile represents the first sound of or, /or/. In Level 3, we'll use the purple or tile to represent the sound of /er/ as in *work*. If your student doesn't know which sound or says in a word, he should try each sound in sequence until he finds the right one.

Refer to the Letter Tiles app or Phonogram Sounds app for a demonstration of the or phonogram sound.

> When working with letter tiles, some words can be built with or + e or with o r + e. Both of these examples are correct: sh or e   sh o r e
>
> Other words that contain or end in -ore include *more, core, bore, chore,* and *forecast.*

Review

Phonogram Cards

Review the Phonogram Cards that are behind the Review divider in your student's Reading Review Box. Show each card to your student and have him say the sound(s). If necessary, remind your student of the sound(s).

Word Cards

Shuffle and review the Word Cards that are behind the Review divider in your student's Reading Review Box. If your student has difficulty reading a word, build the word with letter tiles and have your student sound it out using the blending procedure shown in Appendix C.

Previous Concepts

Build the following words with letter tiles. Have your student divide the words using the Two Consonant Tiles rule, label with syllable tags, and read.

number

Closed Syllable	Bossy R Syllable
n u m	b er

harvest

Bossy R Syllable	Closed Syllable
h ar	v e s t

New Teaching

Teach New Phonogram OR

Hold up the or Phonogram Card.

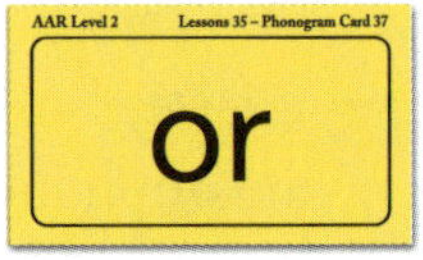

"O-r says /or/–/er/ as in *work*. Repeat after me: /or/–/er/ as in *work*." *Student repeats the sounds.*

Mix in several other Phonogram Cards for mixed review and practice until your student can say the sounds accurately. File the Phonogram Card behind the Review divider in the Reading Review Box.

Move the yellow or tile into the workspace. or

New Teaching
(continued)

"We use the yellow or tile for the /or/ sound. Later we'll have a purple or tile for the sound of /er/ as in *work*."

Mix in several other letter tiles for mixed review and practice with the new phonogram until your student can say the sound accurately.

For extra practice with the new phonogram, try the "Phonogram Cup Hunt." For instructions, look for this icon in Appendix L.

Blend Sounds with Letter Tiles

"Today you will learn words with the sound of /or/. Repeat these words after me and listen for the /or/ sound: *fort, torn, storm, corn*." *Student repeats the words.*

Build the word *fork*.

"I'll sound out this first word, and then you'll sound out the next word."

Touch under the f and say */f/*.

Touch under the or and say */or/*.

Touch under the k and say */k/*.

Now go back to the beginning of the word. Slide your finger under the letters f-or-k and say *fork* slowly.

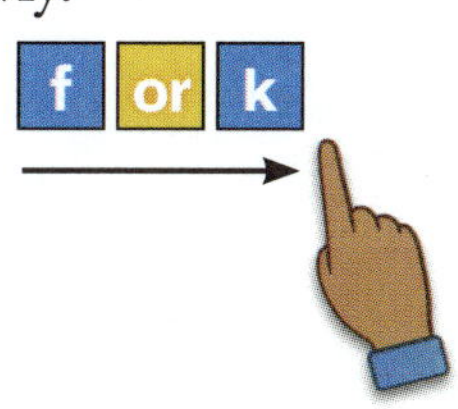

New Teaching
(continued)

Finally, read the word *fork* at a normal pace as we do when we speak.

Using the same procedure for blending, have your student sound out the word *fort*.

f | or | t

Leave the word *fort* in the workspace.

Play "Change the Word"

"I'm going to change the first part of this word."

sh ↓ f | or | t

"What does this new word say?" Encourage your student to sound out the new word, *short*.

Continue to change one tile at a time to form the following words. Each time, have your student sound out the new word.

short → port → sport

Label Syllable Types

Build the word *forest*. f | or | e | s | t

"Divide this word into syllables." *Student divides the word between the r and the e using the One Consonant Tile rule.*

Point to the or tile. "In the first syllable, we have a tile with a vowel and an r. This is a Bossy R syllable. Label it with the Bossy R syllable tag."

Bossy R Syllable: f | or   Closed Syllable: e | s | t

Build the following words with letter tiles. Have your student divide the words into syllables, label with syllable tags, and read. *Report* is divided using the One Consonant Tile rule; *order* is divided using the Two Consonant Tiles rule.

report

Open Syllable: r | e   Bossy R Syllable: p | or | t

order

Bossy R Syllable: or   Bossy R Syllable: d | er

New Teaching
(continued)

Complete Activity Sheet

"Now it's time to bring in the corn!"

<u>**It's Harvest Time!**</u>

Remove pages 245-248 from the *Leap into Reading* activity book.

Cut out the corn cards on page 247. Mix the cards and position them along the corn stalks.

Have your student harvest the corn by selecting a card, flipping it over, and reading the word aloud. If he reads the word correctly, he can keep the harvested corn card. If he reads the word incorrectly, the card should be returned to the game board for another try.

The activity continues until all the corn has been harvested.

Practice Reading Words

Have your student practice reading the words on Word Cards 172-181.

File the Word Cards behind the Review divider in the Reading Review Box.

New Teaching
(continued)

Practice Fluency

New Words

porch	forest	torn	corner
snort	forget	north	sort
acorn	stork	form	horn
forgot	cork	pork	sport
short	or	corn	storm
morning	thorn	popcorn	born
fork	fort	forever	order

Phrases

forgot to tell	harvest the corn	torn cloth
a short man	go north	was born
on the corner	late morning	a big storm
ate popcorn	a deep forest	this or that
take my order	the sharp thorn	use a fork

Turn to pages 249-252 in the activity book.

Have your student read from the Practice Sheets.

Have some fun with the fluency exercises with the "Feed the Monster" activity. For instructions, look for this icon in Appendix K.

Read-Aloud Time

Read a Story or Poem

Read aloud to your student for twenty minutes.

Track Your Progress

Mark the Progress Chart

Have your student mark Lesson 35 on the Progress Chart.

Lesson 36 Read "Storm in the North"

Objective

In this lesson, students complete a concept map and read a short story.

You Will Need

- ☐ *Leap into Reading* pages 253-255
- ☐ pencil
- ☐ *Queen Bee* book

Before You Begin

Preview the Purpose of the Activity Sheet

Before reading the story, your student will use a graphic organizer to collect and categorize her knowledge about animals in winter. This type of exercise, also called concept mapping, is an excellent tool for deepening your student's understanding of words and concepts.

Review

Phonogram Cards

Review the Phonogram Cards that are behind the Review divider in your student's Reading Review Box. Show each card to your student and have him say the sound(s). If necessary, remind your student of the sound(s).

Word Cards

Shuffle and review the Word Cards that are behind the Review divider in your student's Reading Review Box. If your student has difficulty reading a word, build the word with letter tiles and have your student sound it out using the blending procedure shown in Appendix C.

Give your student extra incentive for today's Word Card review with the activity "Snack Stack." For instructions, look for this icon in Appendix M.

New Teaching

Complete Activity Sheet

"Let's see how much we know about animals in winter."

Critters in Winter

Remove page 253 from the *Leap into Reading* activity book.

Cut along the dotted line to remove the Brainstorming section of the activity sheet.

1. Brainstorm. With your student, brainstorm a list of words that come to mind when you think of animals in winter. If necessary, use some of the following questions as prompts.

"A *critter* is an animal. What kinds of animals would you expect to see in the woods in the winter?" *Possible answers: deer, otter, bobcat, fox, beaver, birds.*

"What sounds might they make?" *Possible answers: plop, swish, chirp, squeak, splash.*

"What do they do all day?" *Possible answers: eat, hunt, sleep, leave tracks in the snow, play, hibernate.*

"Where do they live?" *Possible answers: trees, holes, dens, riverbank, the woods.*

"What do they look like?" *Possible answers: thick fur, fluffy tail, sharp claws, long nose, small ears.*

Write the brainstorm words in the space provided.

2. Categorize. Now have your student categorize the brainstorm words on the concept map. Three categories have been provided, but you can add another. Possible categories are *animals that hibernate* (chipmunks, skunks, badgers, bears, frogs), *animals that do not hibernate* (deer, otters, foxes, bobcats), *animals with wings* (birds, ducks), and *animals with fur* (bear, fox, deer).

New Teaching
(continued)

Read the Warm-Up Sheet for "Storm in the North"

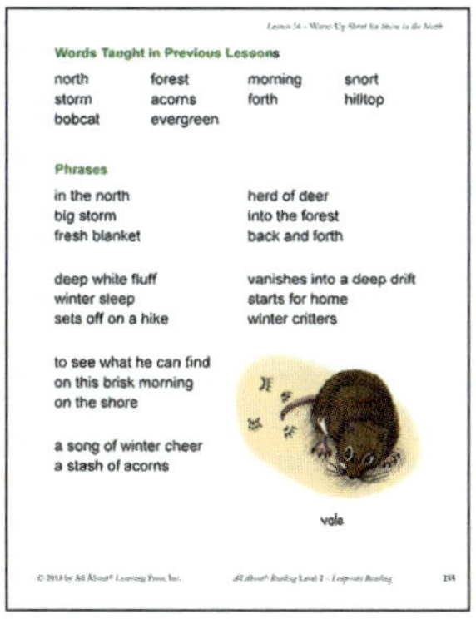
Words Taught in Previous Lessons

north forest morning snort
storm acorns forth hilltop
bobcat evergreen

Phrases

in the north
big storm
fresh blanket

herd of deer
into the forest
back and forth

deep white fluff
winter sleep
sets off on a hike

vanishes into a deep drift
starts for home
winter critters

to see what he can find
on this brisk morning
on the shore

a song of winter cheer
a stash of acorns

vole

Turn to page 255 in the activity book.

Have your student practice reading words and phrases that are found in "Storm in the North."

Teach Vocabulary

Point out the illustration of the vole on the Warm-Up Sheet. "A *vole* is similar to a mouse, but it has a rounder body and shorter tail. Voles live underground in burrows and like to eat flower bulbs and the roots of plants and trees. If a plant suddenly dies without warning, it could be because a little vole has been munching away underground. In our next story, you'll see a vole in the winter time."

Read "Storm in the North"

"Turn to page 53 in your reader and read 'Storm in the North' aloud." Discuss your student's ideas for the questions below as you come to them.

After page 61: "The pup is careful not to wake the sleeping chipmunk because she is *hibernating*." Explain that some animals hibernate during the winter.

After reading: "Which animals would you want to see while taking a walk in the snow?"

"Which animals would you *not* want to meet up with? Why not?"

Read-Aloud Time

Read a Story or Poem

Read aloud to your student for twenty minutes.

> **Read-Aloud Tip!**
>
> **Build Comprehension with Wordless Picture Books**
> Yes, that's right—sometimes less is a lot more! You can practice comprehension and other reading skills by sharing wordless picture books and simply asking questions. For example, practice comprehension by asking, "What is happening here?" Questions like "What makes you think that?" strengthen inferring skills, while prediction and oral language skills can be honed with questions like "What do you think will happen next?" and "Why?"

Track Your Progress

Mark the Progress Chart

Have your student mark Lesson 36 on the Progress Chart.

Lesson 37 The Third Sound of U

Objective

This lesson teaches words with the third sound of u.

You Will Need

- ☐ *Leap into Reading* pages 257-263
- ☐ Word Cards 182-191

Before You Begin

Review Phonogram U

In Level 1, your student learned the three sounds of u:

- /ŭ/ as in *udder* (emphasized in Level 1, Lesson 12)
- /ū/ as in *unit* (emphasized in Level 2, Lesson 17)
- /o͝o/ as in *put* (emphasized in this lesson)

The majority of the time, the letter u says its long or short sound. But there are a small number of common words in which u says its third sound, /o͝o/ as in *put*. In this lesson, your student will become very familiar with these words. Read the following examples and listen for the /o͝o/ sound.

push **pull** **full** **put**

u When we practice the Phonogram Card for u, we say all three sounds: /ŭ/–/ū/–/o͝o/. When we use the u letter tile, we only say the sound that the phonogram says in the word. To facilitate blending, we don't say all the sounds. If your student doesn't know which sound u says in a word, he should try each sound in sequence until he finds the right one.

Review

Phonogram Cards

Review the Phonogram Cards that are behind the Review divider in your student's Reading Review Box. Show each card to your student and have him say the sound(s). If necessary, remind your student of the sound(s).

Word Cards

Shuffle and review the Word Cards that are behind the Review divider in your student's Reading Review Box. If your student has difficulty reading a word, build the word with letter tiles and have your student sound it out using the blending procedure shown in Appendix C.

Review
(continued)

Previous Concepts

Build the following words with letter tiles. Have your student divide the words where necessary, label with syllable tags, and read. *Popcorn* uses the Compound Words rule.

popcorn **sleep**

New Teaching

Teach the Third Sound of U

Move the u letter tile into the workspace.

"Tell me the sounds of u." */ŭ/–/ū/–/o͝o/.*

Build the word *push.*

Point to the u. "What sound is the u making in the word *push*?" */o͝o/.*

Leave the word *push* in the workspace.

Play "Change the Word"

"I'm going to change the first part of this word."

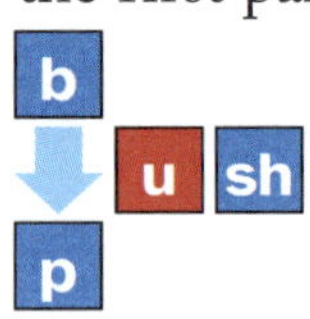

"What does this new word say?" Encourage your student to sound out the new word, *bush.*

Continue to change one or two tiles at a time to form the following words. Each time, have your student sound out the new word.

bush → bull → pull → put → full

New Teaching
(continued)

Play "Guess What I'm Saying"

> In this activity, pronounce the second syllable like the word *on*, as a beginning reader might do when first sounding out a word.

"I will say two syllables and you will guess what word I am saying: *lem...ŏn.*" *Student says* lemon *at normal conversational speed.*

Repeat this activity using the following words. Be sure to pause between the syllables as you say them.

drag...on **wag...on** **ba...con**

Build the word *bacon*. b a c o n

"Divide this word into syllables." *Student divides the word between the* a *and the* c.

b a   c o n

"Read each syllable." *Bā–con.*

Point to the o. "When we say this word in everyday conversation, the sound of the o gets muffled because we say it so fast. The word sounds like *bac'n* in normal speech."

"When you sound out a two-syllable word like this, you can get very close to the correct pronunciation. Sound out each syllable and then say the syllables together like a normal word."

Complete Activity Sheet

"Let's practice some muffled o words with this little dragon."

A Dragon and a Wagon

Remove pages 257-259 from the *Leap into Reading* activity book.

Cut out the objects on page 257. Cut out the game cards and place them on the table with the words facing up.

Have your student choose a game card and read the sentence aloud. Encourage your student to

New Teaching
(continued)

follow the instructions on the game card. For example, if the card says "Put the dragon in the wagon," then your student should place the dragon card on the wagon card.

Continue until your student has read and followed the instructions on each game card.

Practice Reading Words

Have your student practice reading the words on Word Cards 182-189.

File the Word Cards behind the Review divider in the Reading Review Box.

Teach Two Leap Words: *where* and *there*

Show Word Card 190 to your student.

"This word is *where*, as in *Where are my socks?* The e-r-e doesn't say what we expect it to, so this is a Leap Word."

Show Word Card 191 to your student.

"This word is *there*, as in *The duck is over there*. This is another word in which the e-r-e doesn't say what we expect it to. Do *where* and *there* rhyme?" *Yes.*

Review these Leap Words several times today and then file them behind the Review divider in the Reading Review Box.

New Teaching
(continued)

Practice Fluency

New Words

lemon	full	there	dragon
where	push	bull	bacon
pull	wagon	bush	put
person	button		

Compound Words

bullfrog	dragonfly	somewhere	bulldog

Phrases

lemon twist	full of moths
where we are	push the wagon
eggs and bacon	a big dragon
pull the tab	didn't go there
put it here	a mad bull
a green bush	one person

Turn to pages 261-263 in the activity book.

Have your student read from the Practice Sheets.

Engage your student in the fluency exercises with a letter search activity. For instructions, look for this icon in Appendix K.

Read-Aloud Time

Read a Story or Poem

Read aloud to your student for twenty minutes.

Track Your Progress

Mark the Progress Chart

Have your student mark Lesson 37 on the Progress Chart.

Bravo!
You did such a great job
with that lesson! You deserve some
belly laughs, so here are my
best jokes just for you.

Why are frogs so happy?
They eat whatever bugs them!

Why don't frogs park on the side of the road?
They are afraid of getting toad!

What do frogs like to drink?
Hot croako!

Hahahahaha.
I croak myself up.

Lesson 38 Read "Dragon in the Wagon"

Objective

In this lesson, students learn about alliteration and read a short story.

You Will Need

- ☐ *Leap into Reading* pages 265-269
- ☐ *Queen Bee* book

Before You Begin

Preview Alliteration

Writers often use figurative language to stir the reader's emotions or convey a certain feeling. One type of figurative language is called *alliteration*. Alliteration is when the same starting sound is repeated in words, such as the /p/ sound in *Peter Piper picked a peck of pickled peppers.*

Other examples of alliteration are *hairy hippo*, *sunset on the sea*, and *jar of jiggly jello*. In today's activity, your student will create her own examples of alliteration and then read a story containing alliteration.

Review

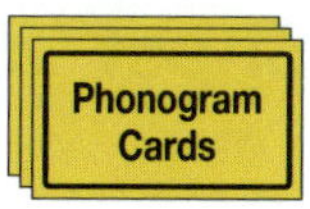

Review the Phonogram Cards that are behind the Review divider in your student's Reading Review Box. Show each card to your student and have him say the sound(s). If necessary, remind your student of the sound(s).

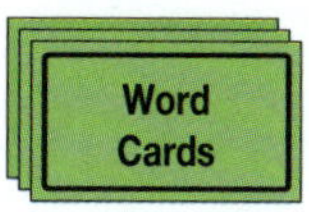

Shuffle and review the Word Cards that are behind the Review divider in your student's Reading Review Box. If your student has difficulty reading a word, build the word with letter tiles and have your student sound it out using the blending procedure shown in Appendix C.

For today's Word Card review, let your student express her artistic side with an illustration activity. For instructions, look for this icon in Appendix M.

New Teaching

Complete Activity Sheet

"Have you ever heard the tongue twister *Peter Piper picked a peck of pickled peppers*? Most of the words start with the same sound of /p/. That's called *alliteration*. This activity is called 'Smiling Suns,' which is also an example of alliteration because both words start with the /s/ sound. Let's see if you can make your own examples of alliteration."

Smiling Suns

Remove pages 265-268 from the *Leap into Reading* activity book.

Cut out the cards on pages 265 and 267. Mix the cards and place them on the table with the words facing up. Encourage your student to group the cards by their beginning sounds: all the words that begin with s, all the words that begin with c, and so on.

After your student has successfully sorted the cards into groups, have her create some alliterative phrases such as *big black bull* and *skip, skid, slide.*

Read the Warm-Up Sheet for "Dragon in the Wagon"

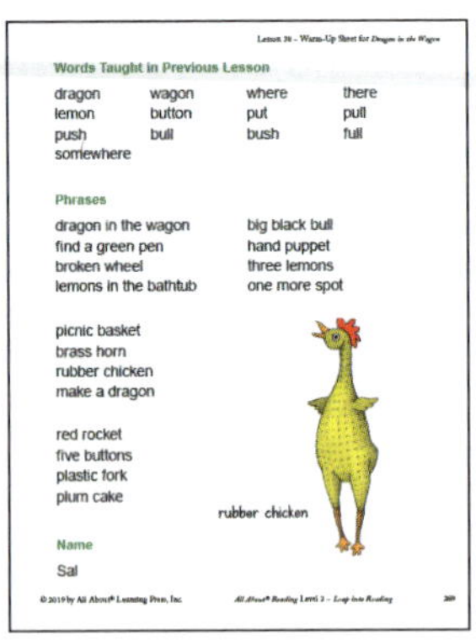

Words Taught in Previous Lesson

dragon wagon where there
lemon button put pull
push bull bush full
somewhere

Phrases

dragon in the wagon
find a green pen
broken wheel
lemons in the bathtub
big black bull
hand puppet
three lemons
one more spot

picnic basket
brass horn
rubber chicken
make a dragon

red rocket
five buttons
plastic fork
plum cake

rubber chicken

Name

Sal

Turn to page 269 in the activity book.

Have your student practice reading words and phrases that are found in "Dragon in the Wagon."

New Teaching
(continued)

Teach Vocabulary and Activate Prior Knowledge

Point to the illustration of the rubber chicken on the Warm-Up Sheet. "A *rubber chicken* is a funny object used in comedy shows. It looks like a plucked chicken and is made of rubber."

"Do you like art? What's your favorite tool for making art? Pencils? Paint? Clay?"

"What kinds of things do you like to make?"

"Have you ever looked and looked for something but couldn't find it? What was it? What did you do?"

"In the story you are about to read, the main character can't find an item he needs to create his work of art. Let's see what he does instead."

Read "Dragon in the Wagon"

"Turn to page 71 in your reader and read 'Dragon in the Wagon' aloud." Discuss your student's ideas for the questions below as you come to them.

After page 73: "Where should Sal look for a green pen?"

After page 81: "Where do you think Sal will look?"

After page 89: "Can you see the dragon in the wagon?"

Find Examples of Alliteration

Guide your student in finding and reading one or two of the following examples of alliteration.

Page 76: Third paragraph: *slip, skid, slide; slips on the slick tiles*
Page 77: Third paragraph: *Sal snorts*
Page 79: First sentence: *crash, clank, clunk*
Page 80: List of items: *red rocket*
Page 86: List of items: *big black bull; plate of plum cake*

Read-Aloud Time

Read a Story or Poem

Read aloud to your student for twenty minutes.

> Read-Aloud Tip!
>
> **Read Fairy Tales**
>
> If your student isn't familiar with classic fairy tales, now is a good time to read them aloud! Here are some you might consider:
>
> - Goldilocks and the Three Bears
> - The Ugly Duckling
> - Rumpelstiltskin
> - Beauty and the Beast
> - The Gingerbread Man
> - The Steadfast Tin Soldier
> - Tom Thumb
> - Aladdin

Track Your Progress

Mark the Progress Chart

Have your student mark Lesson 38 on the Progress Chart.

Lesson 39 Soft C and the Second Job of Silent E

Objective

This lesson teaches the second job of Silent E and words containing soft c.

You Will Need

- ☐ *Leap into Reading* pages 271-277
- ☐ Word Cards 192-201
- ☐ Jobs of Silent E chart

Before You Begin

Review Phonogram C

c Phonogram c can say two sounds:

- /k/ as in *cat,* also known as hard c (emphasized in Level 1, Lesson 3)
- /s/ as in *city,* also known as soft c (emphasized in this lesson)

In almost every instance, c is soft when followed by e, i, or y. Read the following examples and listen for the /s/ sound.

city	**dance**	**ice**	**pencil**	**center**
place	**nice**	**face**	**twice**	**space**

This is a highly reliable pattern with very few exceptions. The exceptions occur in higher level words of foreign origin, such as *cello* and *concerto* (in which c followed by e says /ch/) and *Celtic* (in which c followed by e says /k/).

In *All About Spelling* Level 1, your student learns that the letter k is used when the /k/ sound is needed before the vowels e, i, and y, as in the words *kept, kind,* and *sky.*

Preview the Second Job of Silent E

The second job of Silent E is to make c and g soft, as in the words *prince* and *hinge.*

Today's lesson will focus on soft c and Lesson 42 will focus on soft g.

Review

Phonogram Cards

Review the Phonogram Cards that are behind the Review divider in your student's Reading Review Box. Show each card to your student and have him say the sound(s). If necessary, remind your student of the sound(s).

Word Cards

Shuffle and review the Word Cards that are behind the Review divider in your student's Reading Review Box. If your student has difficulty reading a word, build the word with letter tiles and have your student sound it out using the blending procedure shown in Appendix C.

Previous Concepts

Build the following words with letter tiles. Have your student divide the words where necessary, label with syllable tags, and read. *Lemon* uses the One Consonant Tile rule.

New Teaching

Determine the Sound of C

Move the c tile into the workspace. c

"You know that the letter c can say /k/ or /s/. We have a way to tell which of these two sounds the c is going to make."

Move the e, i, and y tiles into the workspace and arrange them next to the c tile.

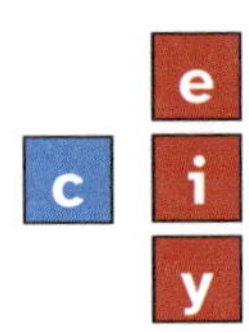

"If c is followed by an e, i, or y, it says /s/."

Show the c tile visiting the letters e, i, and y one at a time. "In front of the e it says /s/. In front of the i it says /s/. In front of the y it says /s/."

New Teaching
(continued)

Move the a, o, u, l, and r tiles into the workspace and arrange them like this:

"If the c is before any other letter, it says /k/."

Show the c tile visiting the letters one at a time. "In front of the a it says /k/." Repeat for o, u, l, and r.

Once your student understands this concept, mix up the e, i, and y with the a, o, u, l, and r and place the c in front of each one. Ask your student to tell you whether the c says /k/ or /s/.

Continue this activity until it has been mastered by your student.

Teach the Terms *Hard C* and *Soft C*

Leave the c tile in the workspace. 

"When c says /s/, we say that the c is **soft**."

"When c says /k/, we say that the c is **hard**."

"Tell me the **hard** sound of c." */k/.*

"Tell me the **soft** sound of c." */s/.*

New Teaching
(continued)

Blend Words with Soft C

Build the word *cent*.

"We just learned that when c is followed by e, i, or y, it says /s/. I will sound out this word."

Touch under the c and say */s/.*

Touch under the e and say */ĕ/.*

Touch under the n and say */n/.*

Touch under the t and say */t/.*

Now go back to the beginning of the word. Slide your finger under the letters c-e-n-t and say *cent* slowly.

Finally, read the word *cent* at a normal pace as we do when we speak.

Using the same procedure for blending, have your student sound out the word *cell*.

New Teaching
(continued)

Teach the Second Job of Silent E

Build the word *fence*.

"Today you will learn the second job of Silent E. Silent E makes the c say /s/. I will sound out this word."

Touch under the f and say */f/*.

Touch under the e and say */ĕ/*.

Touch under the n and say */n/*.

Touch under the c and say */s/*.

Touch under the e. "This is Silent E."

Now go back to the beginning of the word. Slide your finger under the letters f-e-n-c-e and say *fence* slowly.

Finally, read the word *fence* at a normal pace as we do when we speak.

"Silent E usually doesn't jump over two consonants to make the vowel say its name."

New Teaching
(continued)

Point to the first e. "This e is short. The only job of Silent E here is to make the c say /s/."

Using the same procedure for blending, have your student sound out the word *prince*.

For words like *fence* and *prince* in which Silent E does its second job, we won't label with syllable tags. These words don't fall into a clear-cut category like most other words do. They could be considered Closed syllables with Silent E added, but that information isn't needed in order to read the words.

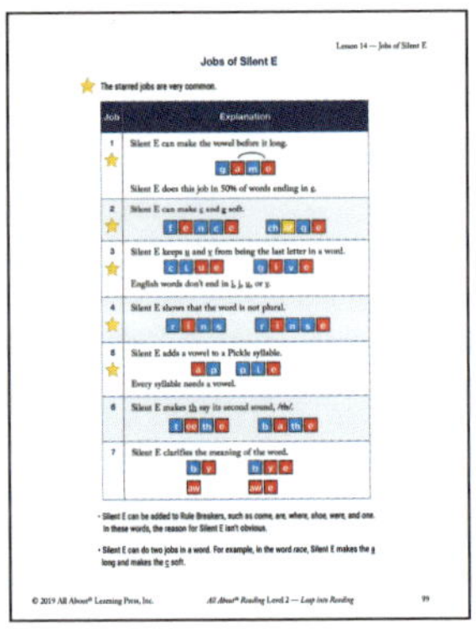
Jobs of Silent E

Take out the Jobs of Silent E chart and read Job #2 with your student. "This is the second job of Silent E. In a later lesson, you'll learn words in which g is soft. Today we are learning just about soft c."

Complete Activity Sheet

"Let's discover whether these c's are hard or soft."

Hammers and Feathers

Remove pages 271-274 from the *Leap into Reading* activity book.

Cut out the hammer, the feather, and the word cards. Mix up the cards and place them in a pile with the words facing down.

Have your student choose a card, locate the letter c in the word, and then decide whether c says its hard or soft sound. If the c is hard, he can hit the word with the hammer. If the c is soft, he can tickle the word with the feather. Place the word cards in separate piles depending on their sound.

After all the words have been sorted, have your student read each word aloud.

New Teaching
(continued)

Answer Key

Hammer pile: carpet, cold, cake, creek, plastic, cry, craft, cart
Feather pile: dance, force, fence, prince, since, chance, glance, cent

Practice Reading Words

Have your student practice reading the words on Word Cards 192-201.

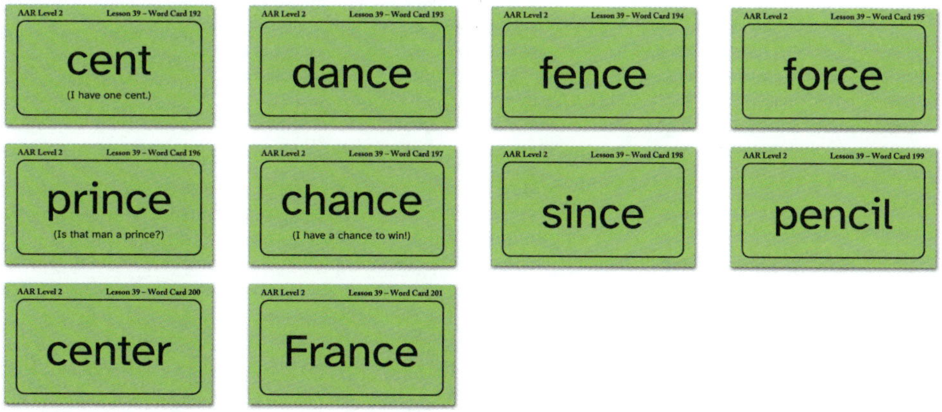

File the Word Cards behind the Review divider of the Reading Review Box.

Practice Fluency

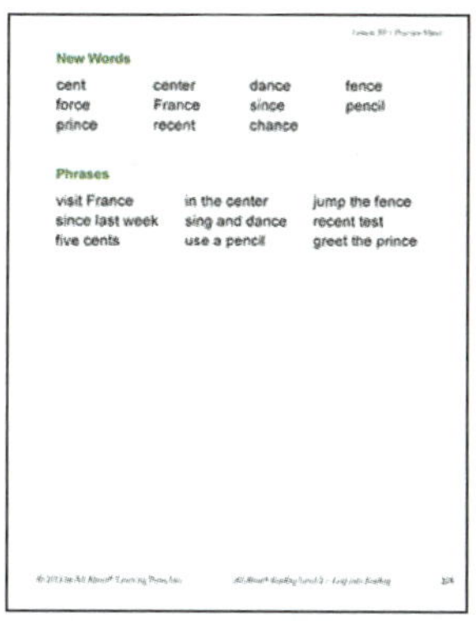

Turn to pages 275-277 in the activity book.

Have your student read from the Practice Sheets.

Read-Aloud Time

Read a Story or Poem

Read aloud to your student for twenty minutes.

Track Your Progress

Mark the Progress Chart

Have your student mark Lesson 39 on the Progress Chart.

Lesson 40 Silent E Can Have Two Jobs

Objective

This lesson teaches that Silent E can have two jobs in the same word. It also teaches more words containing Silent E.

You Will Need

- ☐ *Leap into Reading* pages 279-286
- ☐ Word Cards 202-211
- ☐ Jobs of Silent E chart

Before You Begin

Preview Two Jobs for Silent E

Sometimes Silent E has two jobs in the same word, as in the words *space* and *page*. Silent E makes the vowel long and softens the c̲ or g.

Review

Phonogram Cards

Review the Phonogram Cards that are behind the Review divider in your student's Reading Review Box. Show each card to your student and have him say the sound(s). If necessary, remind your student of the sound(s).

Word Cards

Shuffle and review the Word Cards that are behind the Review divider in your student's Reading Review Box. If your student has difficulty reading a word, build the word with letter tiles and have your student sound it out using the blending procedure shown in Appendix C.

Previous Concepts

Build the following words with letter tiles. Have your student divide the words, label with syllable tags, and read. *Starfish* uses the Compound Words rule; *princess* uses the Two Consonant Tiles rule.

starfish

Bossy R Syllable	Closed Syllable
s t ar	f i sh

princess

Closed Syllable	Closed Syllable
p r i n	c e s s

New Teaching

Teach that Silent E Can Have Two Jobs

"Sometimes Silent E can have two jobs, like in this word."

Build the word *mice*.

Point to the Silent E. "Silent E will make the i say its name and make the c say /s/. I will sound out this word."

Touch under the m and say */m/*.

Touch under the i and say */ī/*.

Touch under the c and say */s/*.

Touch under the e. "This is Silent E."

Now go back to the beginning of the word. Slide your finger under the letters m-i-c-e and say *mice* slowly.

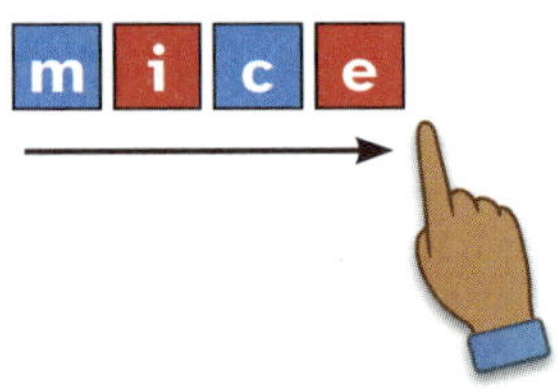

Finally, read the word *mice* at a normal pace as we do when we speak.

Using the same procedure for blending, have your student sound out the word *place*.

New Teaching
(continued)

Leave *place* in the workspace.

"Silent E has two jobs in this word. Can you figure out what they are?" *Silent E makes the vowel long (or say its name), and Silent E makes the c say /s/.*

Build the word *since* next to *place*. 

"Silent E only has one job in this word. It makes the c say /s/."

"Sound out this word." *Since.*

Point to Silent E. "What is the job of Silent E in this word?" *To make the c soft.*

Point to *place* and *since*. "As you can see, sometimes Silent E has one job in a word, as in *since*, and sometimes it has two jobs in a word, as in *place*.

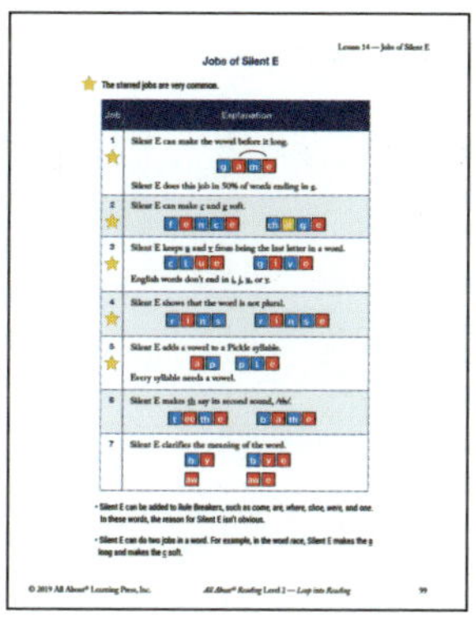
Jobs of Silent E

Take out the Jobs of Silent E chart and review Jobs #1 and #2 with your student.

Complete Activity Sheet

"It's time to put on your detective hat and help Detective Dog break the code of Silent E."

Detective Dog Breaks the Code
Remove pages 279-282 from the *Leap into Reading* activity book.

Cut out the word cards. Mix them up and place them in a pile with the question marks facing up.

Have your student select a card from the pile. Explain that the word on the code card isn't a real word and that something will have to be done to the word before it can be read.

New Teaching
(continued)

Have your student place the card in the empty box next to the Silent E on the Detective Dog sheet. Your student will then read the new word that Detective Dog has decoded with Silent E and determine how many jobs the Silent E is performing: one or two. (The number of question marks in the thought bubble on the back of the card is a hint as to the number of jobs.)

Continue until your student has helped Detective Dog decode all the cards.

Practice Reading Words

Have your student practice reading the words on Word Cards 202-211.

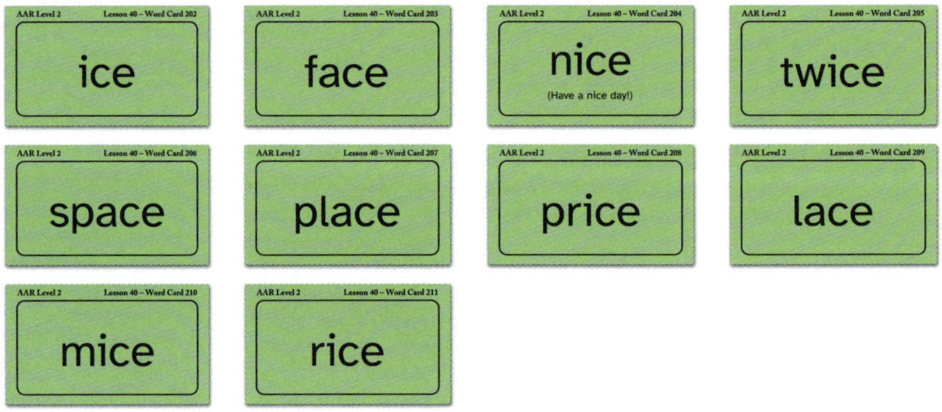

File the Word Cards behind the Review divider of the Reading Review Box.

Practice Fluency

Turn to pages 283-286 in the activity book.

Have your student read from the Practice Sheets.

Consider breaking up the Practice Sheets into more manageable chunks. For instructions, look for this icon in Appendix K.

Read-Aloud Time

Read a Story or Poem

Read aloud to your student for twenty minutes.

Track Your Progress

Mark the Progress Chart

Have your student mark Lesson 40 on the Progress Chart.

Lesson 40!
We are SO smart!.
We need to celebrate!
Let's give ourselves
a pat on the back and a giant tub of
horsefly pudding.
We deserve it!

Lesson 41 Read "Under the Carpet"

Objective

In this lesson, students read a short story and imagine an alternate ending.

You Will Need

- ☐ *Leap into Reading* pages 287-289
- ☐ *Queen Bee* book
- ☐ flashlight

Before You Begin

Help Your Student Read Critically

After reading today's story, your student will be asked to imagine alternate endings. Talking about other ways a story could end is a great way for you to assess your student's understanding of plot, character, and narrative, and for your student to be creative.

Review

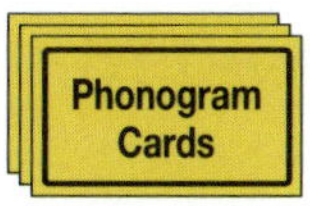

Review the Phonogram Cards that are behind the Review divider in your student's Reading Review Box. Show each card to your student and have him say the sound(s). If necessary, remind your student of the sound(s).

Shuffle and review the Word Cards that are behind the Review divider in your student's Reading Review Box. If your student has difficulty reading a word, build the word with letter tiles and have your student sound it out using the blending procedure shown in Appendix C.

Get silly with today's Word Card review with the activity "Yucky Snacks." For instructions, look for this icon in Appendix M.

Complete Activity Sheet

"Let's look at some shapes and try to guess what they are."

Guess the Shadow

Remove pages 287-288 from the *Leap into Reading* activity book.

Cut out the flashlight and the cards. If you have a real flashlight handy, you may want to use that instead. Place the cards in a pile with the shadows facing up.

Have your student select a card and ask him to imagine what the shadow on the card could be. Discuss your student's ideas. Then have him shine the real or pretend flashlight on the shadow, turn the card over, and read the word aloud.

Continue until all the shadows have been guessed and the items revealed.

Read the Warm-Up Sheet for "Under the Carpet"

Words Taught in Previous Lesson

place	race	face	ice
center	twice	mice	space

Phrases

What do you do
a place in the center
that place

pile of red beets
frozen in ice
a safe place

forgot to finish
roll over
bolt from bed

seven mice
shelter from the storm
none of those things

up to my face
peek at it twice

Turn to page 289 in the activity book.

Have your student practice reading words and phrases that are found in "Under the Carpet."

Teach Vocabulary and Activate Prior Knowledge

Point out the illustration of the stork on the Warm-Up Sheet. "*Storks* are large birds with long, thin legs, long necks, and long, thick bills. They can't sing like most birds do; instead, they clack with their beaks to talk to each other. They build very large nests. In fact, their nests are bigger than your bed."

New Teaching
(continued)

"Have you ever seen a shadow in your bedroom at night and been afraid of what it might be?"

"What would happen if you suddenly noticed a large lump under the carpet or rug in your bedroom? Would you spend some time imagining what the lump might be? Sometimes it's fun to imagine silly things and pretend."

"In our next story, a strange lump appears under the bedroom carpet. Let's find out what it could be!"

Read "Under the Carpet"

"Turn to page 93 in your reader and read 'Under the Carpet' aloud." Discuss your student's ideas for the question below when you come to it.

After page 101: "What do you think is causing the strange lump under the carpet?"

Imagine an Alternate Ending

"At the end of the story, were you surprised to discover that the lump under the carpet is just a ham sandwich?"

"What if the lump had been a duck that needed a safe place to hide? Or a basket full of soft kittens? How would that have changed the outcome of this story? Would you have been more surprised?" Discuss different possible outcomes for this story and encourage your student to imagine an alternate ending for "Under the Carpet."

Read-Aloud Time

Read a Story or Poem

Read aloud to your student for twenty minutes.

Track Your Progress

Mark the Progress Chart

Have your student mark Lesson 41 on the Progress Chart.

Lesson 42 Soft G

Objective

This lesson teaches words containing soft g.

You Will Need

- ☐ *Leap into Reading* pages 291-300
- ☐ Word Cards 212-221
- ☐ Jobs of Silent E chart

Before You Begin

Review Phonogram G

g Phonogram g can say two sounds:

- /g/ as in *goat,* also known as hard g (emphasized in Level 1, Lesson 3)
- /j/ as in *gem,* also known as soft g (emphasized in this lesson)

G is soft when followed by an e, i, or y **most of the time**. Read the following examples and listen for the /j/ sound.

gem **large** **cage** **orange** **danger**

It would be nice if the pattern for soft g was as reliable as the pattern for soft c, but with our given alphabet, this is not possible. For the sound of /k/, the letters c and k are available, so if we need a hard c sound before e, i, or y, the letter k can fill in. But for the sound of /g/, the only letter available is the g. G must do double duty, and the reader must be prepared to try both the /g/ and /j/ sounds before the letters e, i, and y.

Notice the hard g sound in these words, despite the e, i, or y.

get **girl** **gift** **begin** **saggy**

It is helpful to know that most of the time, g says /j/ before e, i, or y. In fact, g is soft in over seven hundred words. It is hard in only forty or so words.

Review

It's time to review the flashcards behind the **Mastered** dividers to ensure they stay fresh in your student's mind.

Shuffle the cards behind both dividers and choose a selection for review. See Appendix L and Appendix M for engaging ways to review Phonogram Cards and Word Cards.

Review
(continued)

Previous Concepts Build the following words with letter tiles. Have your student divide the words using the Two Consonant Tiles rule, label with syllable tags, and read.

pencil		**farmer**	
Closed Syllable	Closed Syllable	Bossy R Syllable	Bossy R Syllable
p e n	c i l	f ar	m er

New Teaching

Determine the Sound of G

Move the g tile into the workspace. g

"Tell me the two sounds of this letter." */g/–/j/.*

Move the e, i, and y tiles into the workspace and arrange them next to the g tile.

g e / i / y

"If g is followed by an e, i, or y, it **usually** says /j/."

Show the g tile visiting the letters e, i, and y one at a time. "Followed by an e, it **usually** says /j/. Followed by an i, it **usually** says /j/. Followed by a y, it **usually** says /j/."

Build the word *gem*. g e m

"What sound does the g say in the word *gem*?" */j/.*

"Why?" *Because of the e.*

Change *gem* to *gel*. g e l

"Read this word." *Gel.*

"Good. Gel is a thick, jelly-like substance that is used in a lot of products, like hair gel."

"Now remember that e, i, and y can make g say /j/, but they don't *always* make g say /j/. In this next word, the g says /g/."

New Teaching
(continued)

Replace the l with a t. g e t

"What is this word?" *Get.*

"So you see that g **usually** says /j/ before an e, i, or y, but not always. Sometimes it says /g/."

> If your student says *jet* instead of *get*, tell her to try the other sound of g. She already knows this word from Level 1, but may try to apply the new concept of soft g.
>
> **Tip!**
>
> Remind her that g can be soft before e, i, or y, but it isn't always. You can show her these three common words that retain the hard g: *gift, begin, give.*

Move the a, o, u, l, and r tiles into the workspace and arrange them like this:

"If g is before any letter that isn't e, i, or y, it says /g/." Show the g tile visiting the letters one at a time.

"In front of the a, it says /g/." Repeat for letters o, u, l, and r.

Once your student understands this concept, mix up the e, i, and y with the a o, u, l, and r.

"In front of which letters can g say /j/?" *E, i, or y.*

Continue this activity until it has been mastered by your student.

Teach the Terms *Hard G* and *Soft G*

Leave the g tile in the workspace. g

"When g says /j/, we say that the g is **soft**."

"When g says /g/, we say that the g is **hard**."

New Teaching
(continued)

"Tell me the **hard** sound of g." */g/*.

"Tell me the **soft** sound of g." */j/*.

Emphasize the Second Job of Silent E

Build the word *large*. 

"You know that the second job of Silent E is to make c say /s/ and g say /j/. I will sound out this word."

Touch under the l and say */l/*. 

Touch under the ar and say */ar/*. 

Touch under the g and say */j/*. 

Touch under the e. "This is Silent E." 

Now go back to the beginning of the word. Slide your finger under the letters l-ar-g-e and say *large* slowly.

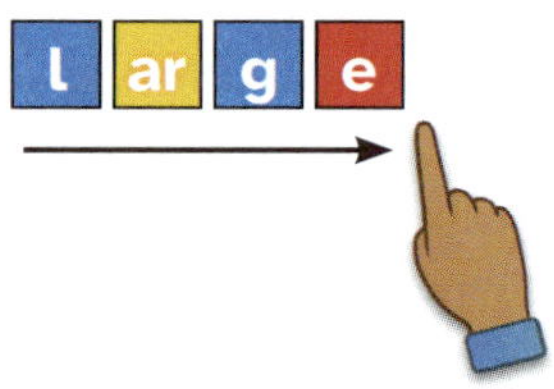

Finally, read the word *large* at a normal pace as we do when we speak.

Point to Silent E. "The only job of Silent E here is to make the g say /j/."

New Teaching
(continued)

Blend Words with Silent E

Build the word *huge*. 

"This word ends in Silent E, so I know that the u will probably be long. And we just learned that when g is followed by e, i, or y, it usually says /j/. I will sound out this word."

Touch under the h and say */h/*.

Touch under the u and say */ū/*.

Touch under the g and say */j/*.

Touch under the e. "This is Silent E."

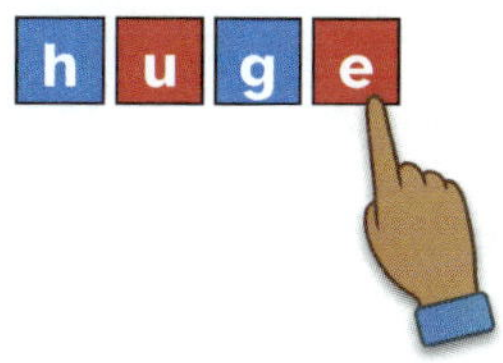

Now go back to the beginning of the word. Slide your finger under the letters h-u-g-e and say *huge* slowly.

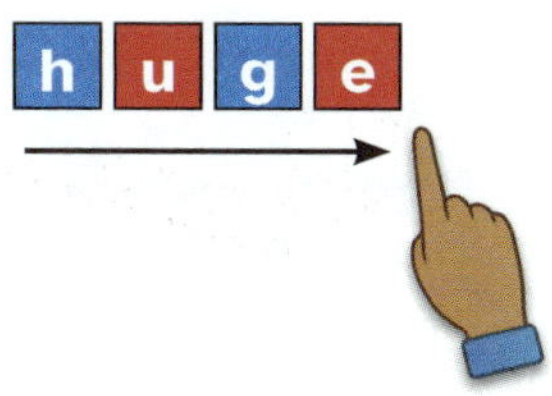

Finally, read the word *huge* at a normal pace as we do when we speak.

"Silent E has two jobs in this word. What are the two jobs?" *It makes the u long and the g soft.*

Using the same procedure for blending, have your student sound out the word *stage*.

Leave the word *stage* in the workspace.

New Teaching
(continued)

Emphasize that Silent E Can Have Two Jobs

"In some words, Silent E has one job, and in other words it has two. In the word *stage*, Silent E has two jobs: it makes the a long and it makes the g soft."

Build the word *hinge*. 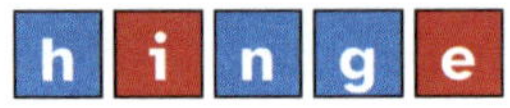

"In the word *hinge*, Silent E has just one job. What is it?" Help your student see that the job of Silent E is to make the g say /j/.

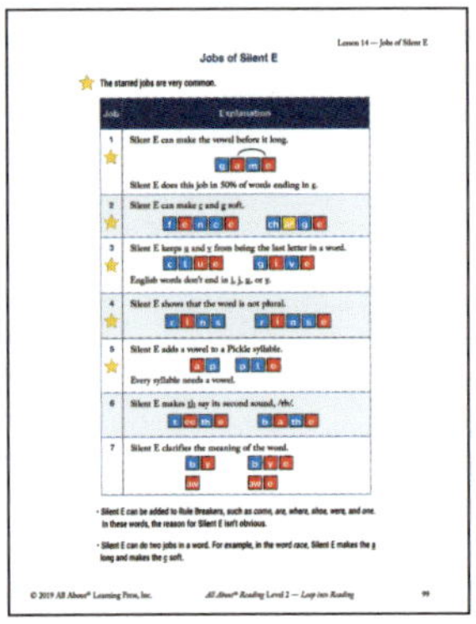

Take out the Jobs of Silent E chart and review Job #2 with your student.

Complete Activity Sheet

"Let's use some soft g words to build a gerbil cage."

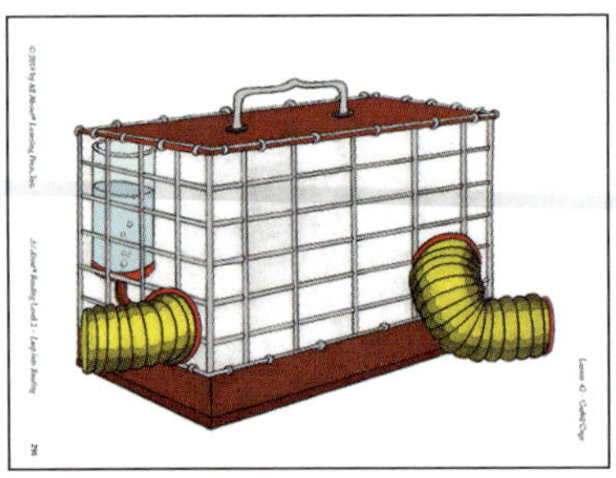

Gerbil Cage

Remove pages 291-296 from the *Leap into Reading* activity book.

Cut out the word cards. Locate the gerbil card, have your student read the word on the back, and encourage him to give the gerbil a name.

Place the tunnel sections in a pile. Now it's time to build the cage. Have your student choose a section of the tunnel, read the word on the back, and add the tunnel to the cage.

Continue until all the cards have been read and the gerbil cage is complete. Your student can then pretend to run his gerbil through the maze.

A different cage can be constructed each time your student plays.

New Teaching
(continued)

Practice Reading Words

Regarding the Word Cards for *change, danger,* and *orange*:

As discussed in Level 1, when phonogram ng comes after a as in *danger* and *change*, a doesn't say its pure short vowel sound. Instead, the sound of a falls between its short and long vowel sounds, as in the words *sang* and *bang*.

This concept is generally easy for students to grasp since it is difficult to say the pure short vowel sound of a in these words. It is easier to say these words correctly.

In the word *orange*, the a is in an unaccented syllable and the vowel sound is muffled.

Have your student practice reading the words on Word Cards 212-220.

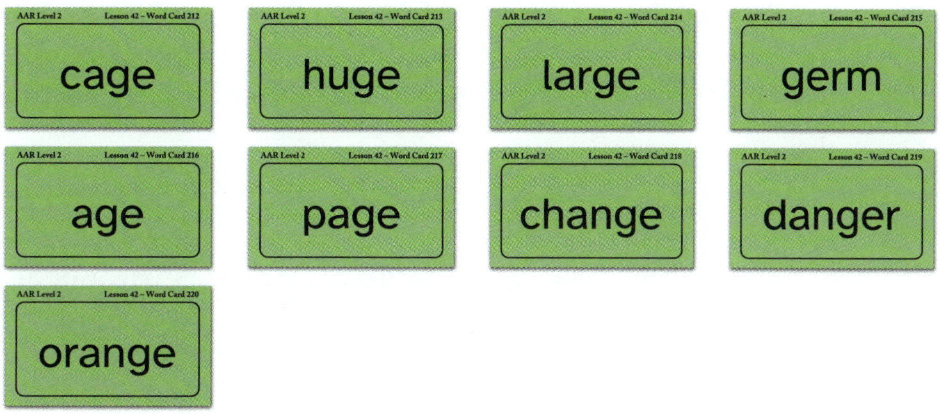

File the Word Cards behind the Review divider of the Reading Review Box.

Teach a Leap Word: *pumpkin*

Show Word Card 221 to your student.

Cover up *kin* with your finger. "What does the first part of this word say?" *Pump.*

Uncover *kin*. "What does the second part of this word say?" *Kin.*

New Teaching
(continued)

"Together they say *pumpkin*, as in *Let's make a pumpkin pie.* This word follows a syllable division rule that you haven't learned yet, so that's why it is a Leap Word."

> The word *pumpkin* will be used in the story in the next lesson.

Review this Leap Word several times today and then file it behind the Review divider in the Reading Review Box.

Practice Fluency

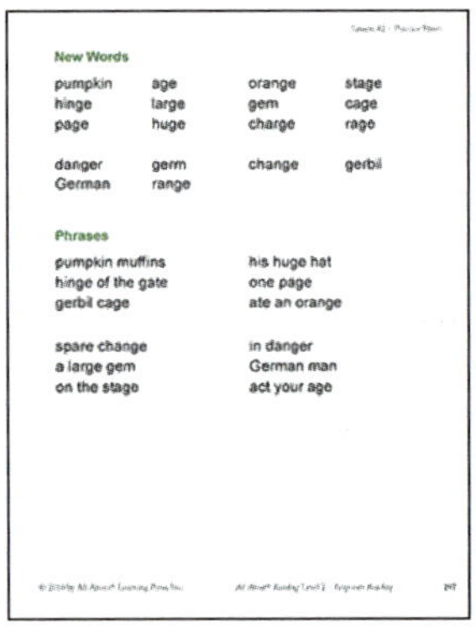

New Words

pumpkin	age	orange	stage
hinge	large	gem	cage
page	huge	charge	rage
danger	germ	change	gerbil
German	range		

Phrases

pumpkin muffins	his huge hat
hinge of the gate	one page
gerbil cage	ate an orange
spare change	in danger
a large gem	German man
on the stage	act your age

Turn to pages 297-300 in the activity book.

Have your student read from the Practice Sheets.

> To engage your student in the fluency exercises, try the activity "Eat Your Words." For instructions, look for this icon in Appendix K.

Read-Aloud Time

Read a Story or Poem

Read aloud to your student for twenty minutes.

Track Your Progress

Mark the Progress Chart

Have your student mark Lesson 42 on the Progress Chart.

Hey, there!
I was just thinking about what a busy guy
Silent E is. I had no idea he had so much to do.
I admit I was getting a mushed-bug-brain
feeling with the soft c and soft g, but now I've got
it all figured out.

One thing I noticed is that there aren't enough froggy words with
soft c and soft g, so I invented my own.
What do you think?

ribbitdigits: frog toes
summer frogstice: the froggiest day of the year
croakage: the number of croaks croaked per day
frogface: a huge compliment!

Lesson 43 Read "In My Backpack"

Objective

In this lesson, students read a poem, learn about rhyme and stanzas, and relate the poem to life.

You Will Need

- ☐ *Leap into Reading* pages 301-303
- ☐ *Queen Bee* book
- ☐ pencil

Before You Begin

Preview the Purpose of the Activity Sheet

After reading the poem, your student will complete an activity that points out rhyme, stanzas, and other elements and styles that are common to poetry. See the reading tip in the Read-Aloud Time section of the lesson for more information about sharing poetry with your student.

Review

Phonogram Cards

Review the Phonogram Cards that are behind the Review divider in your student's Reading Review Box. Show each card to your student and have him say the sound(s). If necessary, remind your student of the sound(s).

Liven up today's Phonogram Card review with the "Snowball Fight" activity. For instructions, look for this icon in Appendix L.

Word Cards

Shuffle and review the Word Cards that are behind the Review divider in your student's Reading Review Box. If your student has difficulty reading a word, build the word with letter tiles and have your student sound it out using the blending procedure shown in Appendix C.

New Teaching

Read the Warm-Up Sheet for "In My Backpack"

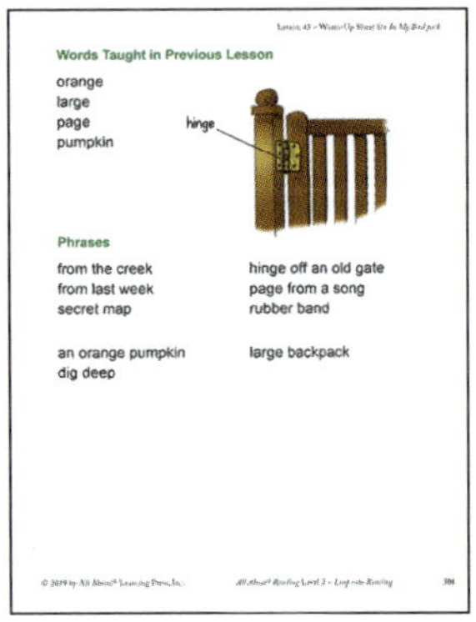
Words Taught in Previous Lesson

orange
large
page
pumpkin

hinge

Phrases

from the creek
from last week
secret map

an orange pumpkin
dig deep

hinge off an old gate
page from a song
rubber band

large backpack

Turn to page 301 in the *Leap into Reading* activity book.

Have your student practice reading words and phrases that are found in the poem "In My Backpack."

Teach Vocabulary and Activate Prior Knowledge

Point out the illustration of the hinge on the Warm-Up Sheet. "This is a *hinge* from a gate. Hinges are used to help things open and close, such as gates, doors, furniture, and suitcases."

"Do you like to go camping? When you go on a camping trip, you have to bring important things like food, a flashlight, and clothes. To carry all these things, you need a large backpack. What do you like to carry in your backpack?"

"Today you'll read a poem about a backpack with lots of interesting things in it—including some surprises!"

Read "In My Backpack"

"Turn to page 106 in your reader and read 'In My Backpack' aloud." Discuss your student's ideas for the question below when you come to it.

After reading: "The last line of 'In My Backpack' is 'I'm glad I have a large backpack!' But what would happen if you had a *small* backpack and could only carry a few things in it? What do you think would be the most important items to include if you were going on an overnight trip?"

New Teaching
(continued)

Complete Activity Sheet

"You already know that some words rhyme, like *cat* and *bat*, but rhyming is also an important feature of many poems. Let's look at 'In My Backpack' again."

In My Backpack

A frog.
A flag.
A hot dog.
A bag.
A rock from the creek.
A sandwich from last week.
A secret map to find gold.
An orange pumpkin you can hold.
The wing of a bee.
Seeds I got for free.

If I dig deep,
there are *more* things I'd like to keep!
A zipper from a tent.
A card my sister sent.
A hinge off an old gate.
The bag from some chips I ate.
A page from a song.
A rubber band that's strong.

I'm glad I have a large backpack!

Poem Practice
Remove page 303 from the activity book.

Encourage your student to study the poem. "Is this a rhyming poem? Let's underline some rhyming pairs." Offer suggestions if your student needs guidance. *Rhyme pairs: frog/hot dog, flag/bag, creek/week, gold/hold, bee/free, deep/keep, tent/sent, gate/ate, song/strong.*

For the next questions, you may need to explain *complete sentence* and *sentence fragment.*

A **complete sentence** has both a subject (noun) and a verb, as in *The cat caught the mouse.* A complete sentence can stand by itself.

A **sentence fragment** is a group of words that cannot stand by itself. Examples include: *caught the mouse, a leaf and a pen, both the boys and the girls.*

"Some poems break the rules and don't have complete sentences. Can you spot any sentence fragments in this poem? Put a checkmark next to those. Then put an asterisk next to the complete sentences."

"Is this poem made of mostly sentence fragments or complete sentences?" *The poem is made of mostly fragments. There are only two complete sentences in the poem: "If I dig deep..." and the last line.*

"Some poems have *stanzas.* A stanza is a group of lines in a poem. Stanzas are separated by an empty space. Let's count the stanzas in this poem." *There are three stanzas.*

After your student has finished discovering the features of this poem, encourage him to read it again.

Read-Aloud Time

Read a Story or Poem

Read aloud to your student for twenty minutes.

Read-Aloud Tip!

Read Poetry

Besides being a delightful and engaging form of writing, poetry benefits students in many ways.

- Rhyming poems help develop your student's memory, memorization skills, and rhythmic awareness.
- Poetry helps develop an awareness of language and phonic patterns.
- The distilled nature of poetry helps students focus on sentence-level skills such as adjectives, adverbs, powerful verbs, and specific nouns.
- Poetry helps students express their own experiences through writing.

Check out our poetry picture book library list on our blog at blog.allaboutlearningpress.com/poetry-books-for-kids for some ideas to get you started.

Track Your Progress

Mark the Progress Chart

Have your student mark Lesson 43 on the Progress Chart.

Lesson 44 The Third Job of Silent E

Objective This lesson teaches the third job of Silent E.

You Will Need

- ☐ *Leap into Reading* pages 305-312
- ☐ Word Cards 222-231
- ☐ Jobs of Silent E chart

Before You Begin

Preview the Third Job of Silent E

The third job of Silent E is to keep u and v from being the last letter in a word. Notice the Silent E in the following words.

clue **give** **carve** **twelve** **blue**

The letter v is never used as the last letter of an English word. Silent E is always added to the end words that end in the sound of /v/.

As a general rule, English words don't end in u, but there are a few notable exceptions.

- *You* is the most common exception your student will encounter. It was first introduced as a Leap Word in Lesson 2.
- *Thou* is no longer in common usage.
- *Ecru, emu, guru, haiku, impromptu, lieu, gnu,* and *menu* are all borrowed from foreign languages.
- *Flu* and *thru* are abbreviations for *influenza* and *through.*

Review

Review the Phonogram Cards that are behind the Review divider in your student's Reading Review Box. Show each card to your student and have him say the sound(s). If necessary, remind your student of the sound(s).

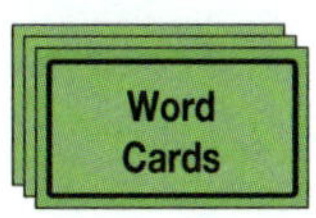

Shuffle and review the Word Cards that are behind the Review divider in your student's Reading Review Box. If your student has difficulty reading a word, build the word with letter tiles and have your student sound it out using the blending procedure shown in Appendix C.

Review
(continued)

Previous Concepts

Build the following words with letter tiles. Have your student label the words with syllable tags and read.

huge	**beep**
Name Game Syllable	Vowel Team Syllable
h u g e	b ee p

New Teaching

Teach the Third Job of Silent E

Build the words *clue* and *give.* c l u e   g i v e

"Silent E has a special job that we haven't talked about before. English words don't end in u or v, so Silent E is added to keep u and v from being the last letters in a word."

"In the word *give*, the only job of Silent E is to keep v from being the last letter. It doesn't make the i long."

Change *give* to *gave*. g a v e

"In this word, Silent E has two jobs. It makes the a long and it keeps v from being the last letter. Read this word." *Gave.*

Build the following words one at a time. Have your student read the word and state the job of Silent E.

g l u e	Keeps u from being the last letter in the word.
s o l v e	Keeps v from being the last letter in the word.
b l u e	Keeps u from being the last letter in the word.
h a v e	Keeps v from being the last letter in the word.

"This is the third job of Silent E."

New Teaching
(continued)

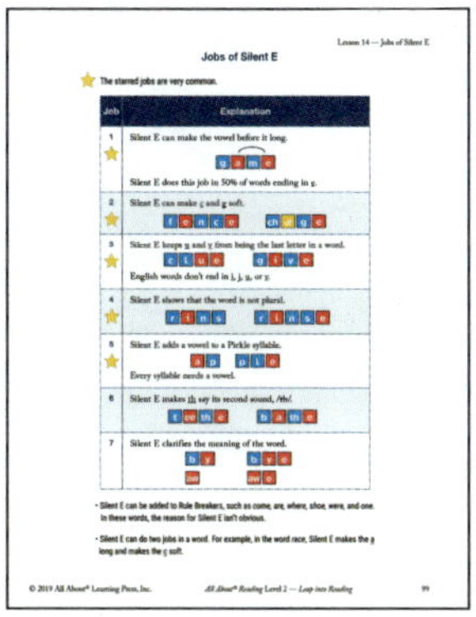

Take out the Jobs of Silent E chart and read Job #3 with your student.

Complete Activity Sheet

"Looks like Detective Dog needs our help again!"

Detective Dog Gets a Clue

Remove pages 305-308 from the *Leap into Reading* activity book.

Cut out the word cards and place them in a pile with the words *Clue Card* facing up. Cut out the detective hat and magnifying glass markers and fold them in half.

Have your student select the marker of his choice to use during the activity.

Your student can help Detective Dog reach the missing bone. Have your student select a Clue Card from the pile and read the word aloud. If he reads the word correctly, he can move his marker forward by the number of spaces indicated by the number on the corner of the card.

The game continues until your student reaches the end of the game board and Detective Dog finds his lost bone.

If desired, this activity can also be played as a two-person game.

New Teaching
(continued)

Practice Reading Words

Have your student practice reading the words on Word Cards 222-231.

File the Word Cards behind the Review divider of the Reading Review Box.

Practice Fluency

Turn to pages 309-312 in the activity book.

Have your student read from the Practice Sheets.

Engage your student in the fluency exercises by making a word road. For instructions, look for this icon in Appendix K.

Read-Aloud Time

Read a Story or Poem

Read aloud to your student for twenty minutes.

Track Your Progress

Mark the Progress Chart

Have your student mark Lesson 44 on the Progress Chart.

Lesson 45 Read "Pumpkin and the Kitten"

Objective

In this lesson, students read a short story and make inferences from text and illustrations.

You Will Need

- ☐ *Leap into Reading* pages 313-316
- ☐ pencil
- ☐ *Queen Bee* book

Before You Begin

Preview the Purpose of the Activity Sheet

In most picture books and stories for young children, illustrations and text work together to create meaning. Illustrations also help make the text more interesting and accessible. And since children are naturally observant and therefore drawn to images, we can help develop their ability to "read" images for meaning and express their ideas about the text they are reading.

The activity for today's short story asks your student to make inferences about the main character based on both illustrations and text.

Review

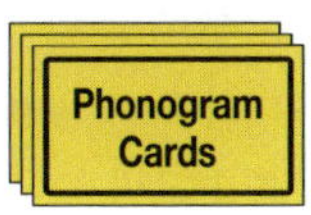

Review the Phonogram Cards that are behind the Review divider in your student's Reading Review Box. Show each card to your student and have him say the sound(s). If necessary, remind your student of the sound(s).

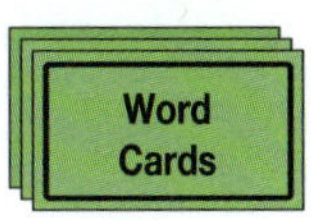

Shuffle and review the Word Cards that are behind the Review divider in your student's Reading Review Box. If your student has difficulty reading a word, build the word with letter tiles and have your student sound it out using the blending procedure shown in Appendix C.

Liven up today's Word Card review with the game "Go Fish." For instructions, look for this icon in Appendix M.

Read the Warm-Up Sheet for "Pumpkin and the Kitten"

Words Taught in Previous Lesson

true live give forgive
forgave

Phrases

orange stripes
sharp teeth
hunt for his supper

did not understand
woke up with a jolt
for a short time

twinge of hunger
square boxes
fake mice

hide and seek
swing on the drapes
push paperclips

have to share
with a blanket
large teeth

Names

Pumpkin Kate Nick

Turn to page 313 in the *Leap into Reading* activity book.

Have your student practice reading words and phrases that are found in the short story "Pumpkin and the Kitten."

Teach Vocabulary and Activate Prior Knowledge

Point out the illustration of the bed fringe on the Warm-Up Sheet. "Some bedspreads have *fringe* along the bottom. This is one type of fringe. Fringe can be made from knotted strings, fuzzy balls, crocheted lace, or fancy tassels. Sometimes drapes have fringe on the bottom edge."

"What's your favorite food?"

"What if we only had one [insert student's favorite food, such as *piece of cake, cookie, hot dog, bowl of ice cream*] left and someone else ate it in front of you? You wouldn't get to have your favorite food! How would that make you feel?"

"Do you know what it means to be *jealous*? If a person is jealous, it means that he is sad or mad because he wants something that someone else has. Sometimes we want something that we can't have or we want the attention that someone else is getting. This can make us feel jealous."

"In our next story, a cat named Pumpkin gets jealous of someone else. Let's find out what happens."

New Teaching
(continued)

Read "Pumpkin and the Kitten"

"Turn to page 109 in your reader and read 'Pumpkin and the Kitten' aloud." Discuss your student's ideas for the questions below as you come to them.

After page 117: "Do you think Pumpkin is going to be happy about having a new kitten in the house?"

After page 118: "Why do you think Pumpkin wants to scare and chase the kitten and make her cry?"

After reading: "Turn to page 118 and look for the text that is slanted. Slanted text is called *italics*, and writers sometimes use italics to show what a character is thinking. Whose thoughts are in italics on this page?" *Pumpkin's.*

"Skim the story to find other places where italics are used." *Pages 122 and 123.*

Complete Activity Sheet

"We learned a few things about Pumpkin as we read his story. Let's discuss some of the things we discovered."

How Is Pumpkin Feeling?
Remove pages 315-316 from the activity book.

Guide your student as he fills in the answers to the questions on each side of the activity sheet. Discuss your student's responses.

Read-Aloud Time

Read a Story or Poem

Read aloud to your student for twenty minutes.

Track Your Progress

Mark the Progress Chart

Have your student mark Lesson 45 on the Progress Chart.

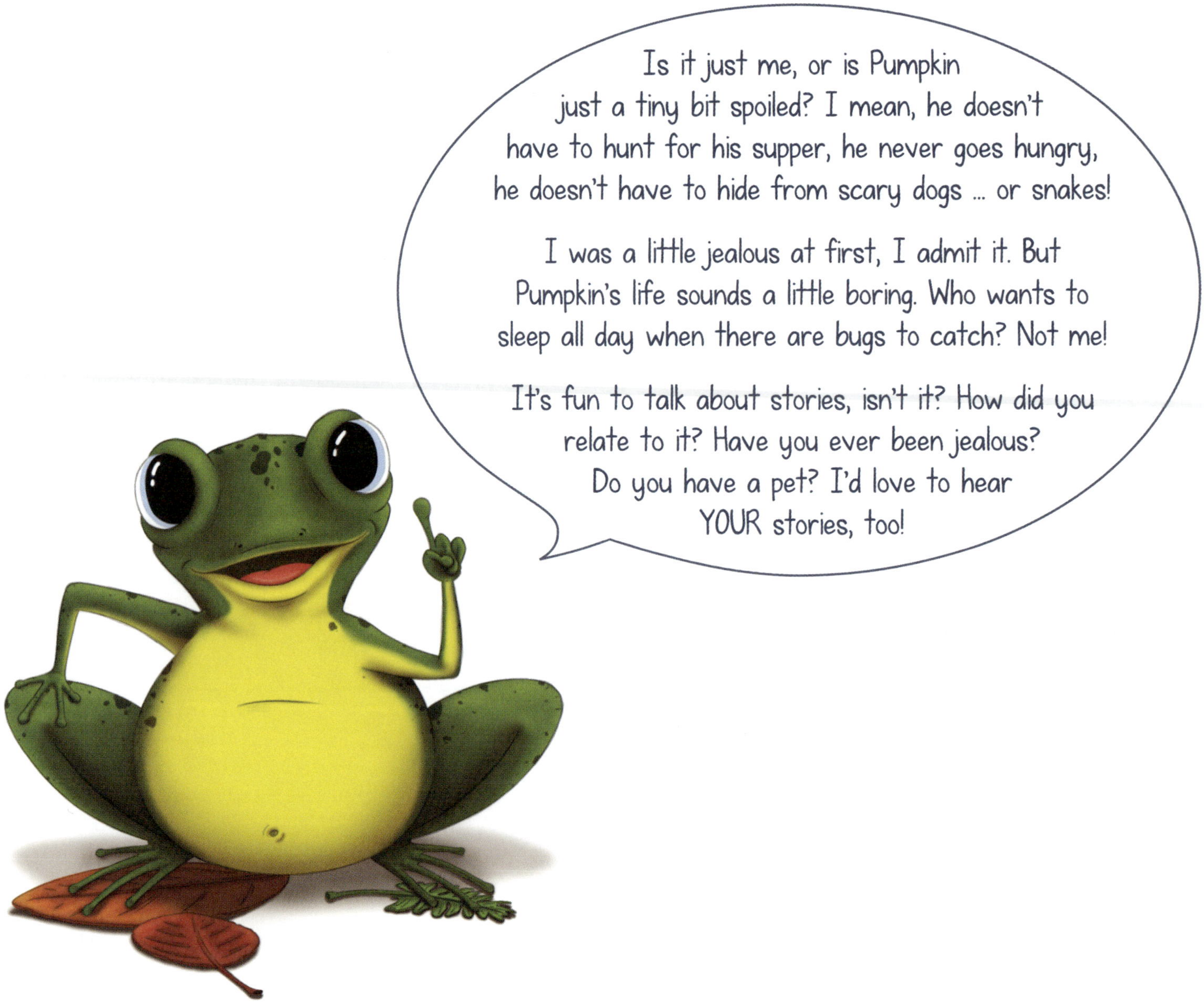

Lesson 46 The Fourth Sound of O and the Fourth Job of Silent E

Objective

This lesson teaches the fourth job of Silent E and words containing the fourth sound of o.

You Will Need

- ☐ *Leap into Reading* pages 317-321
- ☐ Word Cards 232-242
- ☐ Jobs of Silent E chart

Before You Begin

Review Phonogram O

Your student already knows the four sounds of o, as follows:

- /ŏ/ as in *otter* (emphasized in Level 1, Lesson 10)
- /ō/ as in *open* (emphasized in Level 1, Lesson 46)
- /o͞o/ as in *to* (used in Leap Words in Levels 1 and 2)
- /ŭ/ as in *oven* (emphasized in this lesson)

Today's lesson will teach words containing the fourth sound of o, pronounced /ŭ/ as in *love* and *mother*. Read the following examples and listen for the /ŭ/ sound.

love	**mother**	**nothing**	**month**	**Monday**

Approximately thirty more words with the fourth sound of o are covered in Lesson 47 of Level 3, including *dozen* and *wonderful*.

> The fourth sound of o is a clear vowel sound that occurs in accented syllables. It is not a schwa, which is a sound that occurs in *unaccented* syllables.

o When we use the o letter tile to represent the sound of /ŭ/, we only say the sound /ŭ/. To facilitate blending, we don't say all four sounds. If your student doesn't know which sound o says in a word, she should try each sound in sequence until she finds the right one.

Preview the Fourth Job of Silent E

The fourth job of Silent E is to show that a word is not plural. Take a look at the following examples.

cheese	**goose**	**sparse**	**horse**	**noise**
mouse	**glimpse**	**false**	**rinse**	**pause**

Without the Silent E, these words look like plurals.

Review

Phonogram Cards

Review the Phonogram Cards that are behind the Review divider in your student's Reading Review Box. Show each card to your student and have him say the sound(s). If necessary, remind your student of the sound(s).

Word Cards

Shuffle and review the Word Cards that are behind the Review divider in your student's Reading Review Box. If your student has difficulty reading a word, build the word with letter tiles and have your student sound it out using the blending procedure shown in Appendix C.

Previous Concepts

Build the following words with letter tiles. Have your student divide the words where necessary, label with syllable tags, and read. *Windstorm* uses the Compound Words rule.

brace	**windstorm**	
Name Game Syllable	Closed Syllable	Bossy R Syllable
b r a c e	w i n d	s t or m

New Teaching

Teach Words with the Fourth Sound of O

Build the word *love*. l o v e

"What sound does the o make in the word *love*?" /ŭ/.

"/ŭ/ is the fourth sound of o."

"Today you will learn words with the fourth sound of o."

Build the word *front*. f r o n t

"I'll sound out this first word, and then you'll sound out the next word."

Touch under the f and say /f/. f r o n t

New Teaching
(continued)

Touch under the r and say */r/.*

Touch under the o and say */ŭ/.*

Touch under the n and say */n/.*

Touch under the t and say */t/.*

Now go back to the beginning of the word. Slide your finger under the letters f-r-o-n-t and say *front* slowly.

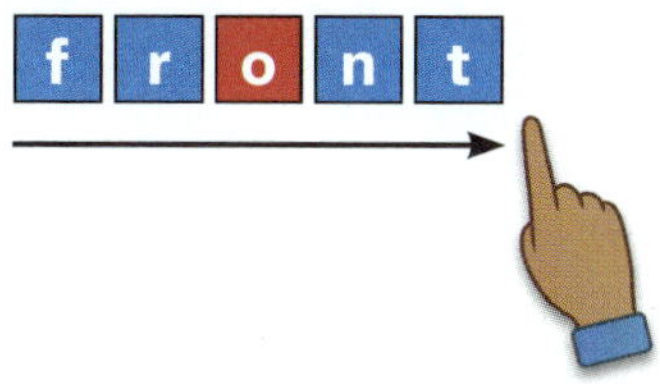

Finally, read the word *front* at a normal pace as we do when we speak.

Using the same procedure for blending, have your student sound out the word *won*.

Teach the Fourth Job of Silent E

Build the word *rinse.*

"In this word, Silent E is added to keep *rinse* from looking like a plural word."

Remove Silent E.

New Teaching
(continued)

"Without Silent E, the reader would have to figure out whether *rins* is a plural word."

Replace Silent E. "What is this word?" *Rinse.*

Build the word *cheese.* ch ee s e

"Here is another word that would look like a plural without Silent E. What is this word?" *Cheese.*

"This is the fourth job of Silent E."

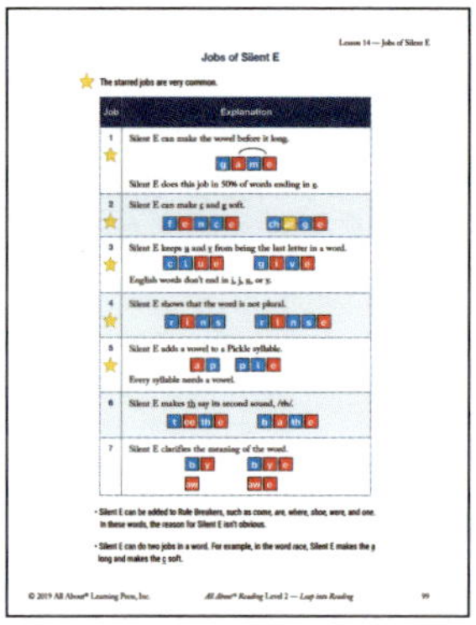

Take out the Jobs of Silent E chart and read Job #4 with your student.

Complete Activity Sheet

"Are you ready to round up some geese?"

Gather the Geese

Remove pages 317-318 from the *Leap into Reading* activity book.

Cut out the goose cards and lay them out on the table with the illustrations facing up.

Have your student select one card at a time, turn it over, and read the word aloud. If the word is read correctly, the student may keep the card. If it is read incorrectly, he should return it to the table to try again later.

Continue until your student has read all the words correctly and gathered all the geese.

New Teaching
(continued)

Practice Reading Words

Have your student practice reading the words on Word Cards 232-241.

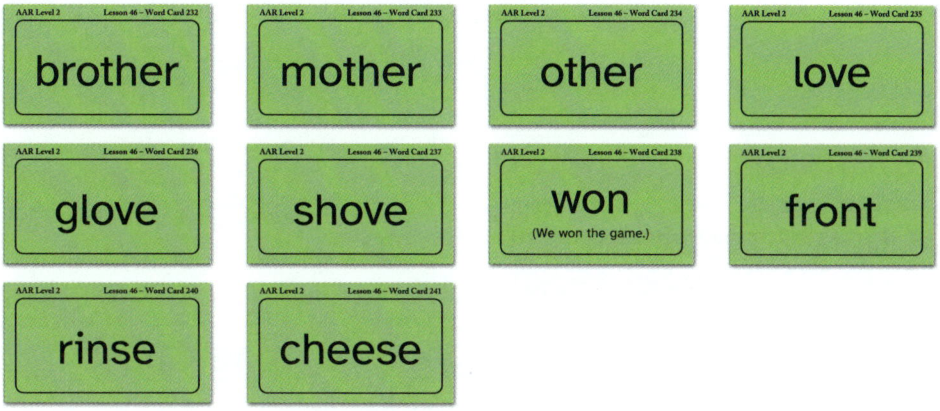

File the Word Cards behind the Review divider in the Reading Review Box.

Teach a Leap Word: *oh*

Show Word Card 242 to your student.

"This word is *oh*, as in *Oh, there you are!* This is a Leap Word because the h is silent."

"What is this word?" *Oh.*

Review this Leap Word several times today and then file it behind the Review divider in the Reading Review Box.

Practice Fluency

New Words

oh brother front glove
love mother nothing other
shovel won cover shove

ton son cheese rinse
geese grandmother

Phrases

my brother cover the tracks rinse the dish
the front step won the game the lost glove
a big shovel lots of love a ton of bricks

nothing to do
slice of cheese
oh, brother

Turn to pages 319-321 in the activity book.

Have your student read from the Practice Sheets.

Read-Aloud Time

Read a Story or Poem

Read aloud to your student for twenty minutes.

Track Your Progress

Mark the Progress Chart

Have your student mark Lesson 46 on the Progress Chart.

Lesson 47 Read "Oh, Brother!"

Objective

In this lesson, students discuss words with multiple meanings, read a short story, and make predictions.

You Will Need

- ☐ *Leap into Reading* pages 323-325
- ☐ *Queen Bee* book

Before You Begin

Preview Multiple Meanings

This lesson will give your student experience with words with multiple meanings such as the homographs *bark* and *bark*. The concept is introduced in today's activity and then expanded on in Lesson 57.

In the story "Oh, Brother!" the main characters pretend to misunderstand the use of words with multiple meanings, leading to some silly results.

Review

Review the Phonogram Cards that are behind the Review divider in your student's Reading Review Box. Show each card to your student and have him say the sound(s). If necessary, remind your student of the sound(s).

> Let your student make her mark during Phonogram Card review with a stamping activity. For instructions, look for this icon in Appendix L.

Shuffle and review the Word Cards that are behind the Review divider in your student's Reading Review Box. If your student has difficulty reading a word, build the word with letter tiles and have your student sound it out using the blending procedure shown in Appendix C.

Complete Activity Sheet

"Some words can have two meanings. For example, *bow* can mean to bend at the waist, or it can mean the front part of a ship. Let's see if you can figure out the two meanings of some words."

What Do You Mean?

Remove pages 323-324 from the *Leap into Reading* activity book.

Cut apart the puzzle pieces on the dotted lines. Mix up the pieces and place them on the table with the illustrations facing up.

Have your student match the five pairs of puzzle pieces that represent a word with multiple meanings. For example, the pieces that feature the sandhill crane and the construction crane illustrate two meanings of the word *crane*. If your student needs a hint, the appropriate word is included on the back of each puzzle piece.

Continue until your student has matched all the puzzle pieces.

Read the Warm-Up Sheet for "Oh, Brother!"

Words Taught in Previous Lesson

oh
geese
nothing
other
cover
cheese
ton
shovel

gloves
front
rinse

ton

Phrases

lives on a farm
big grin
up to his tricks
here comes Grandmother

feed the pigs
here and there
slops and stares
ice the cake

put on your gloves
front gate
oh, brother

rinse the geese
lunch and cake
ton of slop

Name

Brother
Grandmother

Turn to page 325 in the activity book.

Have your student practice reading words and phrases that are found in the short story "Oh, Brother!"

New Teaching
(continued)

Teach Vocabulary and Activate Prior Knowledge

Point out the illustration of the ton on the Warm-Up Sheet. "This is a *ton*. A ton is two thousand pounds, so it is very heavy. This word is often used in sentences like *I have a ton of homework*. It means the person has a lot of homework to do."

"Have you ever played a trick on someone? What was the trick? How did people react to it? Has anyone ever played a trick on you?"

"In the next story, the main character likes to play tricks on his grandmother. Let's see what mischief he gets into."

Read "Oh, Brother!"

"Turn to page 127 in your reader and read 'Oh, Brother!' aloud." Discuss your student's ideas for the questions below as you come to them.

After page 130: "How do you think Grandmother feels about Brother's trick?"

After page 133: "What do you think Brother is going to do when he feeds the pigs?"

After page 146: "What do you think Grandmother has in her bucket?"

After reading: "Do you think Grandmother gets angry with Brother for any of his tricks? Do you think that Brother is angry at Grandmother for her trick?"

Explore Multiple Meanings

Guide your student in finding and discussing one or two of the following examples of multiple meanings.

Page 129: What does Grandmother really mean by "put on your gloves"?
Page 138: What does Grandmother really mean by "rinse the geese"?
Page 145: What does Brother really mean by "ice the cake"?

Read-Aloud Time

Read a Story or Poem

Read aloud to your student for twenty minutes.

Track Your Progress

Mark the Progress Chart

Have your student mark Lesson 47 on the Progress Chart.

Lesson 48 ED

Objective

This lesson teaches phonogram ed, the concept of past tense, and words with the past tense ed ending.

You Will Need

- ☐ *Leap into Reading* pages 327-337
- ☐ Phonogram Card 38
- ☐ letter tile ed
- ☐ Word Cards 243-252

Before You Begin

Preview Phonogram ED

Phonogram ed is a suffix used to indicate that something occurred in the past. Today's lesson will introduce all three sounds of ed:

- /ĕd/ as in *wanted*
- /d/ as in *snowed*
- /t/ as in *dropped*

Read the following examples and listen for the /ĕd/, /d/, and /t/sounds.

/ĕd/	**=**	**wanted**	**printed**	**folded**	**tested**	**landed**
/d/	**=**	**snowed**	**smiled**	**dared**	**paled**	**saved**
/t/	**=**	**dropped**	**baked**	**jumped**	**stopped**	**mixed**

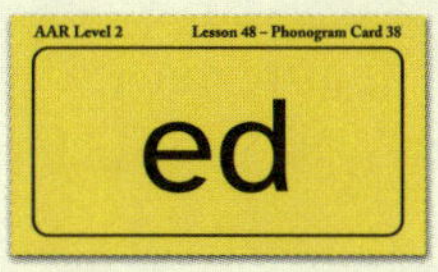

When we practice the Phonogram Card for ed, we say "/ĕd/–/d/–/t/."

The ed tile is stored under the Other Tiles category.

Refer to the Letter Tiles app or Phonogram Sounds app for a demonstration of the ed phonogram sounds.

Native English speakers naturally choose the correct pronunciation for the past tense ending ed, so we will take advantage of this fact during this lesson. We will transfer what the student already knows (in speech) to what she is learning (in reading). Through a series of exercises, the student will learn to identify the base word and then say the word as if it happened in the past.

If you are teaching a nonnative speaker, your student may need additional instruction so she knows whether to pronounce ed as /ĕd/, /d/, or /t/. The sound of the consonant that comes immediately before ed determines the pronunciation of the suffix ed. The following guidelines will help nonnative speakers choose the correct pronunciation for ed.

Before You Begin
(continued)

- When ed is added to words that end in t or d, the ed is pronounced /ĕd/ and is pronounced as a separate syllable, as in *planted*, *handed*, and *trusted.*

- When ed is added to words that end in voiced sounds, the ed is pronounced /d/ and is *not* pronounced as a separate syllable, as in *filled*, *stayed*, and *carved.*

- When ed is added to words that end in unvoiced sounds, the ed is pronounced /t/ and is *not* pronounced as a separate syllable, as in *baked*, *chopped*, and *danced.*

> A *voiced* sound is one in which the vocal cords vibrate. If you put your fingers on your throat, you can feel the vibration in the sounds made by b, d, g, j, l, m, n, ng, r, v, z, th, and the vowels.
>
> *Unvoiced* (or voiceless) sounds include ch, f, h, k, p, s, sh, t, and th.

If your student is a native English speaker, or a nonnative speaker who pronounces past tense words properly, these three guidelines do not need to be learned. The student will automatically say the correct sound when using the simple technique taught in this lesson.

Review

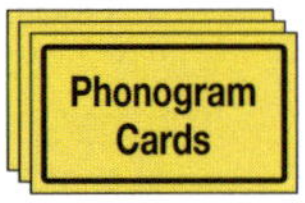

Review the Phonogram Cards that are behind the Review divider in your student's Reading Review Box. Show each card to your student and have him say the sound(s). If necessary, remind your student of the sound(s).

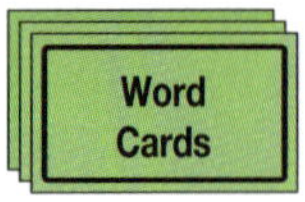

Shuffle and review the Word Cards that are behind the Review divider in your student's Reading Review Box. If your student has difficulty reading a word, build the word with letter tiles and have your student sound it out using the blending procedure shown in Appendix C.

New Teaching

Teach New Phonogram ED

Hold up the ed Phonogram Card.

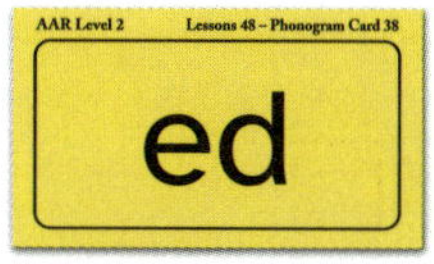

"E-d can say three different sounds: /ĕd/–/d/–/t/. Repeat after me: /ĕd/–/d/–/t/." *Student repeats the sounds.*

Mix in several other Phonogram Cards for mixed review and practice until your student can say the sounds accurately. File the Phonogram Card behind the Review divider in the Reading Review Box.

Move the ed tile into the workspace. ed

Mix in several other letter tiles for mixed review and practice with the new phonogram until your student can say the sounds accurately.

> For extra practice with the new phonogram, try the activity "Color It." For instructions, look for this icon in Appendix L.

Teach the Concept of Past Tense

Build the word *plant*. p l a n t

"Today I will *plant* a garden."

Add ed. p l a n t ed

"Yesterday I *planted* a garden."

"What sound does ed say in *planted*?" */ĕd/.*

Build the word *print*. p r i n t

"Now it's your turn. Finish the sentence: Today I will ______." *Print.*

Add ed. p r i n t ed

New Teaching
(continued)

"Yesterday I ______." *Printed.*

"What sound does ed say in *printed*?" */ĕd/.*

Build the word *spill.* s p i l l

"Today I will ______." *Spill.*

Add ed. s p i l l ed

"Remember that ed can say /ĕd/, /d/, or /t/. Let's find out what it says in this word."

"Finish this sentence: Yesterday I ______." *Spilled.*

> If your student reads *spilled* as /spill–ĕd/, prompt her to finish this sentence without looking at the tiles: *Yesterday, I ______ my milk on the floor.* Your student will naturally say *spilled* correctly. Then remind your student that ed can say /ĕd/, /d/, or /t/, and she should use the sound that makes the most sense.

"When I say that I *spilled* something yesterday, I am talking about something that happened **in the past**. We can say that *spilled* is in the **past tense**."

"What letter tile did I add to the word *spill* to make the word *spilled*?" *Ed.*

Build the word *jump.* j u m p

"Today I will ______." *Jump.*

Add ed. j u m p ed

"Let's find out what sound ed makes in this word."

"Yesterday I ______." *Jumped.*

Point to the ed. What sound does ed say in the word *jumped*?" */t/.*

New Teaching
(continued)

Identify the Base Word

Build the word *folded*. f o l d ed

"Cover the ed tile with your finger and then read the word." *Fold.*

"Now uncover the ed tile and read the word." *Folded.*

Repeat this exercise with the following words until your student understands the concept. If your student says the wrong sound for ed, remind her to use the sound that makes the most sense. Say the word as if the action happened yesterday.

tested	**mixed**	**barked**	**locked**
formed	**bumped**	**twisted**	

Identify the Base Word When the Consonant Is Doubled

> Doubling the consonant before adding a vowel suffix is covered extensively in the *All About Spelling* program. This is an important point for spelling purposes because the student needs to understand the underlying rules in order to achieve the correct spelling.
>
> For reading purposes, though, the student just needs to be aware of the possibility of doubled letters. This is one reason why reading is easier than spelling.

Build the word *stopped*. s t o p p ed

"I will cover the ed tile with my finger." 

"There are two p's, but I can still tell that the base word is *stop*. Today I will *stop*. Yesterday I *stopped*." Uncover the ed tile.

"The p in this word is doubled. That means that there are two p's in a row. The p is doubled so we know that the o is a short o. If the p wasn't doubled, it would look like the o should be long."

Remove the second p. s t o p ed

New Teaching
(continued)

"The reader might try to divide the word like this." s t o p ed

"What would this word say?" *Stō-ped.*

"That isn't the correct pronunciation, so the p is doubled to keep the o short." Replace the p.

Build several of the following words. Have your student cover up the ed tile, identify the base word, and then read the word. If necessary, remind your student to say the word as if the action happened yesterday.

stepped **tapped** **robbed** **planned** **hopped**

Identify the Base Word When the Word Ends in Silent E

Build the word *hike.* h i k e

"When ed is added to a word that ends in Silent E, Silent E is dropped before ed is added."

ed

h i k ↓

e

"If Silent E wasn't dropped, the word would look like this."

h i k e ed

"The reader might think that the e-e belonged together, like a vowel team."

ee

"To prevent this confusion, Silent E is dropped before ed is added."

Build the word *smile.* s m i l e

"Read this word." *Smile.*

"Add ed." Guide your student in dropping Silent E and adding ed.

s m i l ed

Build several of the following words. For each word, have your student read the base word, drop Silent E, add ed, and read the resulting past-tense word.

shape **dance** **like** **stare** **save** **skate**

New Teaching
(continued)

Complete Activity Sheets

"Now it's time to eat some pizza!"

Eat the Pizza

Remove pages 327-328 from the *Leap into Reading* activity book.

Cut out the pizza slices and position them in a circle so they create an entire pizza. Have your student select a slice of pizza and turn it over to read the word aloud. If she reads the word correctly, she may keep the slice of pizza and pretend to eat it. If she reads the word incorrectly, the slice should be returned to the pizza so the student can try the word again later.

Continue until your student has eaten the entire pizza.

"Good job. Now let's sort words that end in ed."

Sound Sorting for Phonogram ED

Remove pages 329-332 from the activity book.

Cut out the word cards, mix them up, and place them in a pile with the words facing up.

Have your student choose a card and read the word aloud. She will then decide whether the word has an /ĕd/ sound (as in *folded*), a /d/ sound (as in *closed*), or a /t/ sound (as in *hiked*) and place the card in the appropriate column. For your reference, the correct columns are indicated on the back of the cards.

Continue until all the cards have been sorted.

> If your student gets confused during this activity, you may wish to have her simply read the words rather than sort them. The important thing is that she can easily read words with past tense endings.

New Teaching
(continued)

Practice Reading Words

Have your student practice reading the words on Word Cards 243-251.

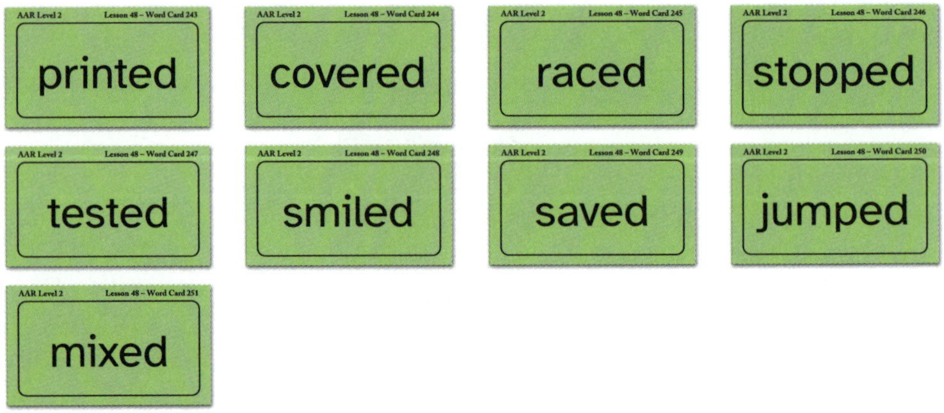

File the Word Cards behind the Review divider in the Reading Review Box.

Teach a Leap word: *they*

Show Word Card 252 to your student.

"This word is *they* as in *They went home*. What sound does the th say in the word *they*?" */th/.*

"The ey says /ā/ in this word. You haven't studied words with ey yet, so this is a Leap Word."

Review this Leap Word several times today and then file it behind the Review divider in the Reading Review Box.

New Teaching
(continued)

Practice Fluency

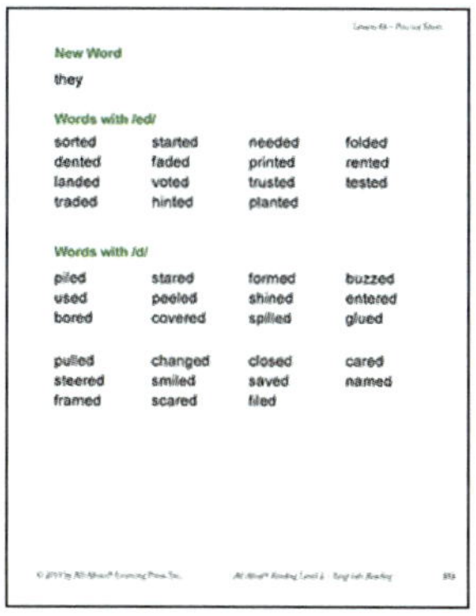

New Word

they

Words with /ed/

sorted	started	needed	folded
dented	faded	printed	rented
landed	voted	trusted	tested
traded	hinted	planted	

Words with /d/

piled	stared	formed	buzzed
used	peeled	shined	entered
bored	covered	spilled	glued
pulled	changed	closed	cared
steered	smiled	saved	named
framed	scared	filed	

Turn to pages 333-337 in the activity book.

Have your student read from the Practice Sheets.

To engage your student in the fluency exercises, try the activity "Fluency Hopscotch." For instructions, look for this icon in Appendix K.

Read-Aloud Time

Read a Story or Poem

Read aloud to your student for twenty minutes.

Track Your Progress

Mark the Progress Chart

Have your student mark Lesson 48 on the Progress Chart.

Lesson 49 Read "Cricket's Picnic"

Objective

In this lesson, students read a rhyming story and practice skimming for information.

You Will Need

- ☐ *Leap into Reading* pages 339-343
- ☐ *Queen Bee* book

Before You Begin

Preview the Purpose of the Activity Sheet

The main character in today's rhyming story, Cricket, interacts with many of his friends. The pre-reading activity is designed to spark your student's interest in the story by introducing him to all the characters and by having him create a woodland scene with Cricket and his friends.

After reading, your student may enjoy having the paper characters act out the story.

Review

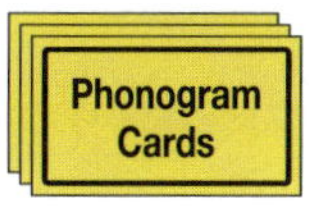

Review the Phonogram Cards that are behind the Review divider in your student's Reading Review Box. Show each card to your student and have him say the sound(s). If necessary, remind your student of the sound(s).

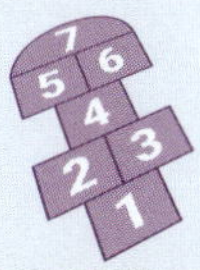

Get your student on his feet for the Phonogram Card review with the game "Phonogram Hopscotch." For instructions, look for this icon in Appendix L.

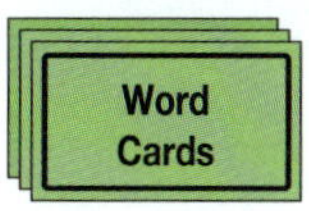

Shuffle and review the Word Cards that are behind the Review divider in your student's Reading Review Box. If your student has difficulty reading a word, build the word with letter tiles and have your student sound it out using the blending procedure shown in Appendix C.

Teach the Words *Taste* and *Lettuce*

Build the word *taste*.

"In this word, Silent E asks the a to say its name. Usually, there is just one consonant between the vowel and Silent E, but sometimes there are two consonants between them. What is this word?" *Taste.*

> Other words that follow this pattern are *haste*, *paste*, *waste*, and *baste*.

Build the word *lettuce*.

"Divide this word into syllables." *Student divides the word.*

"Sound out the first syllable." *Let.*

"In the second syllable, Silent E only has one job. It makes the c soft. What sound will c make?" */s/.*

"Silent E doesn't make the u long in this word. U will say its short sound."

"Sound out the second syllable." */tŭs/.*

"Now push the syllables together and read the word." *Lettuce.*

Complete Activity Sheet

"In our next story, we're going to read about a character named Cricket. But first let's meet Cricket and all his friends."

<u>**Meet the Characters**</u>

Remove pages 339-342 from the *Leap into Reading* activity book.

Cut out the pieces and arrange them on the table with the illustrations facing up.

Have your student select one piece at a time and read the character's name. After the words are read, fold the pieces as indicated and stand them up. Arrange the characters, the tree, the mushrooms, and the sign into a fun woodland scene.

Read the Warm-Up Sheet for "Cricket's Picnic"

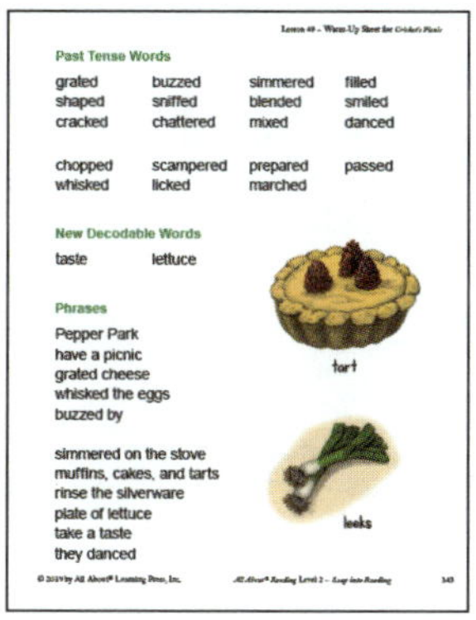
Past Tense Words

grated	buzzed	simmered	filled
shaped	sniffed	blended	smiled
cracked	chattered	mixed	danced
chopped	scampered	prepared	passed
whisked	licked	marched	

New Decodable Words

taste lettuce

Phrases

Pepper Park
have a picnic
grated cheese
whisked the eggs
buzzed by

simmered on the stove
muffins, cakes, and tarts
rinse the silverware
plate of lettuce
take a taste
they danced

Turn to page 343 in the activity book.

Have your student practice reading words and phrases that are found in the rhyming story "Cricket's Picnic."

Many of the words on this Warm-Up Sheet are in the past tense. If necessary, remind your student to locate the base word and then say the word as if the action happened yesterday.

Teach Vocabulary and Activate Prior Knowledge

Point out the illustration of the leeks on the Warm-Up Sheet. "*Leeks* are related to onions, but they taste milder and sweeter than onions do. On the top, a leek has thick, dark green leaves. The bottom part is the part that we eat. It grows underground and is smooth and white. In the next story, leeks are cut up into small pieces, mixed with cheese, and baked into tasty little tarts."

Point out the illustration of the tart. "A *tart* is like a little pie with a crust on the bottom and sides. Some types of tarts have fruit or custard fillings

New Teaching
(continued)

and are eaten as a dessert, like the ones in this drawing. Other types have egg or leek and cheese fillings like in our story, and those are eaten as part of a main meal."

"Have you ever been on a picnic?"

"What are some of your favorite picnic foods?"

"If you were having a picnic today, whom would you invite?"

"In this rhyming story, you'll find out what happens when a cricket throws a picnic for his friends. You'll discover whom he invites and see the foods that he carefully prepares for his guests to enjoy."

Read "Cricket's Picnic"

"Turn to page 151 in your reader and read 'Cricket's Picnic' aloud." Discuss your student's ideas for the question below when you come to it.

After page 159: "Do you think Cricket's face is really blue?"

After reading: Have your student point out several rhyme pairs from the story.

Practice Skimming for Information

"In 'Cricket's Picnic,' Cricket cooks up lots of tasty foods for his friends. Skim through the story and choose which foods you think sound the most delicious. Do you think you'd like the muffins? How about the plum and nutmeg cake? See if you can name three foods from 'Cricket's Picnic' that you would like to try."

Read-Aloud Time

Read a Story or Poem

Read aloud to your student for twenty minutes.

> Read-Aloud Tip!
>
> **Practice Predicting**
>
> Predicting means making a logical guess about what will happen next in a story. Good readers naturally make predictions while they read based on clues from the story and their own experiences, and this improves comprehension.
>
> You can help your student develop this skill by occasionally stopping at exciting points in the story and asking, "What do you think will happen next?" Share your own predictions with your student, too.

Track Your Progress

Mark the Progress Chart

Have your student mark Lesson 49 on the Progress Chart.

That Cricket sure
knows how to throw a party.
I'm drooling over here!
What was your favorite dish
at the picnic? Those tarts
sounded pretty good
to me!

Lesson 50 The Third Sound of A

Objective

In this lesson, students will learn words containing the third sound of a̲.

You Will Need

- ☐ *Leap into Reading* pages 345-352
- ☐ Word Cards 253-262
- ☐ optional: M&Ms, raisins, or chocolate chips

Before You Begin

Review Phonogram A

Your student has learned three sounds for the letter a̲:

- /ă/ as in *apple* (emphasized in Level 1, Lesson 1)
- /ā/ as in *acorn* (emphasized in Level 1, Lesson 44)
- /ah/ as in *father* (emphasized in this lesson)

This lesson will focus on the third sound of a̲. Read the following examples and listen for the /ah/ sound:

father **call** **wash** **salt** **water** **squash**

> Note that a̲ often says its third sound when it is followed by an l̲ (as in *call*) or when it comes after the sound of /w/, as in *water* and *squash*.

There are actually more possible sounds for the letter a̲. Depending on your regional dialect, the a̲ in *all* may sound like the a̲ in *water* and *father*, or it may sound like /aw/ as in *yawn*.

Use the third sound of a̲ taught in this lesson as a starting point, but let your student use the pronunciation that comes most naturally to him. You'll see that as he sounds out the words in this lesson, his tongue will form the words in the way that is natural to him. If your student has a question about the slight differences in sound, let him know that English has many different dialects and the letter a̲ is pronounced with some variation depending on the area of the country or world.

Later in the *All About Reading* series, your student will learn that

- a̲ has a long o̲ sound when it comes between w̲ and r̲, as in *war* and *reward*.
- a̲ has a short i̲ sound in the ending a̲-g̲-e̲ as in *garbage*, *advantage*, and *acreage*.
- like all vowels, a̲ has a schwa sound in unaccented syllables: /ŭh/ as in *tuna* and *amaze*.

Before You Begin
(continued)

a When we use the a letter tile to represent the sound of /ah/, we only say the sound /ah/. To facilitate blending, we don't say all three sounds. If your student doesn't know which sound a says in a word, he should try each sound in sequence until he finds the right one.

Review

Phonogram Cards

Review the Phonogram Cards that are behind the Review divider in your student's Reading Review Box. Show each card to your student and have him say the sound(s). If necessary, remind your student of the sound(s).

Word Cards

Shuffle and review the Word Cards that are behind the Review divider in your student's Reading Review Box. If your student has difficulty reading a word, build the word with letter tiles and have your student sound it out using the blending procedure shown in Appendix C.

New Teaching

Teach Words with the Third Sound of A

Move the a tile into the workspace. a

"Tell me the three sounds of a." */ă/–/ā/–/ah/.*

Build the word *ball.* b a l l

"When a is followed by an l, it often says its third sound, as in the word *ball.*"

"I'm going to change the first part of this word."

c → b a l l

"What does this new word say?" Encourage your student to sound out the new word, *call.*

Continue to change one tile at a time to form the following words. Each time, have your student sound out the new word.

call → fall → mall → wall → tall → stall → small

New Teaching
(continued)

"In all of these words, a says /ah/ when it comes before l."

Build the word *want* and point to the w.

"The letter a can also say /ah/ when it comes after the sound of /w/. What is this word?" *Want.*

Build the word *water.*

"Divide this word into syllables."

Point to the a. "Even though this a is in an Open syllable, it still says its third sound because it comes after /w/. What is this word?" *Water.*

Complete Activity Sheet

"Let's see how many gumballs you can get from the gumball machine."

Get All the Gumballs

Remove pages 345-348 from the *Leap into Reading* activity book.

Cut out the gumball cards. Place the cards in a pile on the gumball machine with the words facing down.

Have your student select a card from the pile and read the word aloud. If he reads the word correctly, he may keep the gumball card. If he does not read it correctly, return it to the bottom of the pile so he may try again later.

Continue until your student has collected all the gumball cards from the machine.

If desired, you can also reward your student with some type of prize—M&Ms, raisins, chocolate chips, or another favorite treat—each time he gets to keep a gumball card.

New Teaching
(continued)

Practice Reading Words

Have your student practice reading the words on Word Cards 253-261.

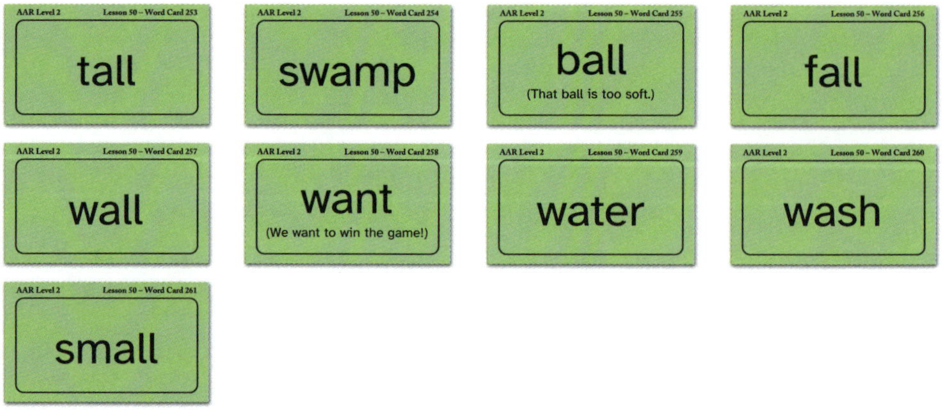

File the Word Cards behind the Review divider in the Reading Review Box.

Teach a Leap Word: *two*

Show Word Card 262 to your student.

"This word is *two* as in *We baked two tarts*. The w is silent, which is why this is a Leap Word. What sound does the letter o make?" */ōō/.*

"Good. That is the third sound of o."

> The word *two* is related in meaning to other words that begin with t-w: *twice, twin, twenty,* and *between.*
>
> Centuries ago, the w became silent in the word *two*, but it is still spelled with a w to show the origin of the word.

Review this Leap Word several times today and then file it behind the Review divider in the Reading Review Box.

New Teaching
(continued)

Practice Fluency

New Words

two	wash	swamp	water
small	tall	wall	fall
want	call	mall	squash
all	hall	ball	

Phrases

two chipmunks
over the wall
call home

the tall man
in the swamp
want some jam

wash with water

squash the bug
a small number
don't fall

all of us
her red ball
in the hall

Turn to pages 349-352 in the activity book.

Have your student read from the Practice Sheets.

To engage your student in the fluency exercises, play the game "Swat the Words." For instructions, look for this icon in Appendix K.

Read-Aloud Time

Read a Story or Poem

Read aloud to your student for twenty minutes.

Track Your Progress

Mark the Progress Chart

Have your student mark Lesson 50 on the Progress Chart.

Ah!
We finally learned the third sound
of A, so now I can read one of my
favorite words:
WATER!

In honor of this occasion, I wrote a little ditty.
I hope you like it!

My pond is full of water
and though it's kind of small,
come hop and splash around with me–
I know we'll have a ball!
Ribbit!

Lesson 51 Read "Life on *The Blue Whale*"

Objective

In this lesson, students learn about synonyms, read a short story, and discuss the concept of realism vs. fantasy.

You Will Need

- ☐ *Leap into Reading* pages 353-355
- ☐ *Queen Bee* book

Before You Begin

Preview Synonyms

In this lesson, your student will complete an activity about *synonyms*, words that are similar in meaning to other words. Besides helping your student broaden his vocabulary, working with synonyms also enriches his language skills by increasing awareness of words and their subtle shades of meaning.

Preview Realism vs. Fantasy

Part of reading comprehension is judging whether the text reflects reality or fantasy. After reading the story, your student will discuss this concept and complete an activity in which he determines whether an action is realistic or pretend.

Review

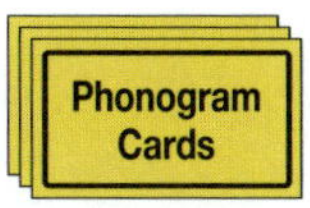

Review the Phonogram Cards that are behind the Review divider in your student's Reading Review Box. Show each card to your student and have him say the sound(s). If necessary, remind your student of the sound(s).

Shuffle and review the Word Cards that are behind the Review divider in your student's Reading Review Box. If your student has difficulty reading a word, build the word with letter tiles and have your student sound it out using the blending procedure shown in Appendix C.

Make Word Card review monstrously fun with the "Feed the Monster" activity. For instructions, look for this icon in Appendix M.

New Teaching

Teach about Synonyms

"Today you are going to learn about a special type of words called *synonyms*. When you have two words that mean the same thing, they are called synonyms. You already know lots of synonyms. Think of a word that means the same as *tiny*." *Possible answers include small, little, petite.*

Fast and Quick

Remove pages 353-354 from the *Leap into Reading* activity book.

Cut out the word cards, mix them up, and set them on the table with the words facing up.

Have your student match up the pairs of words that have roughly the same definition.

Answer Key

weep/cry, wet/damp, large/big, want/crave, zero/nothing
fast/quick, start/begin, ill/sick, job/task, find/locate

Read the Warm-Up Sheet for "Life on *The Blue Whale*"

Words Taught in Previous Lesson

water
all
call
washstand

Phrases

shrimp ship
The Blue Whale
scrubbed the decks

too strong
peeled the spuds
shined the trim

the crab and the starfish
call of the gulls
all the rest
steer the ship

scamper and slide
what happened
big storm swept in
far from the ship

washstand

gull

Turn to page 355 in the activity book.

Have your student practice reading words and phrases that are found in the short story "Life on *The Blue Whale*."

Teach Vocabulary and Activate Prior Knowledge

Point out the washstand on the Warm-Up Sheet. "A *washstand* is a small table. It holds a bowl of water that is used to wash your hands and face. Many washstands have a rack on one side that holds a towel."

New Teaching
(continued)

Point out the illustration of the gull. "*Gulls* are white and gray birds that live in large groups, often near the coastlines of large lakes or oceans."

"The tale you are going to read is about a deckhand on a ship. A *deckhand* is a person who works as a helper on a ship. Sometimes a deckhand will scrub the decks, shine the trim of the boat, or guide the ship."

"One of the deckhand's jobs in the story is to *peel the spuds*. Do you know a synonym for *spuds*?" *Potatoes.*

"The deckhand also *scrubbed the deck*. What is a synonym for *scrubbed*?" *Washed.*

"The deckhand has two visitors on the ship. He calls them *critters*. Do you know another word for *critters*?" *Animals.*

Read "Life on *The Blue Whale*"

"Turn to page 167 in your reader and read 'Life on *The Blue Whale*' aloud."

Teach Realism vs. Fantasy

"Do you think this story really could have happened? Why or why not?"

"Turn to page 172. Read a sentence that describes something that couldn't happen in real life." *Possible answers: [The crab and the starfish] hopped off [the whale] onto the deck of the ship. The crab jumped into a pile of rope. The starfish spun and danced a jig.*

"Why do you think those things couldn't happen?" *Possible answers: Starfish can't spin and dance. A crab is too small to jump that high.*

"This story is fantasy. That means that it isn't real—it is make-believe."

"As I read these activities, tell me if the activity could happen in real life or if it is fantasy." For each fantasy activity, ask your student why it couldn't happen.

"A teenager saves up his money to buy a car." *It could happen.*
"A monkey bakes a banana cream pie." *It's fantasy.*
"The oak tree tells me a story about an eagle." *It's fantasy.*
"My brother stands on his hands in the yard." *It could happen.*

Read-Aloud Time

Read a Story or Poem

Read aloud to your student for twenty minutes.

Track Your Progress

Mark the Progress Chart

Have your student mark Lesson 51 on the Progress Chart.

Lesson 52 OY and OI

Objective

This lesson teaches phonograms oy and oi and words containing those phonograms.

You Will Need

- ☐ *Leap into Reading* pages 357-364
- ☐ Phonogram Cards 39 and 40
- ☐ letter tiles oy and oi
- ☐ Word Cards 263-272

Before You Begin

Preview Phonograms OY and OI

In this lesson, your student will learn two related phonograms: oy and oi. Both phonograms say /oy/.

Phonogram oy is found mainly at the end of words, as in *boy*, but also in the beginning and middle of several words, as in *oyster*. Read the following examples and listen for the /oy/ sound.

toy **ploy** **joy** **oyster** **coy**

Phonogram oi is found only in the beginning or middle of words, as in *oil* and *point*. It isn't found at the end of words because, except for the word *I*, English words don't end in i. Read the following examples and listen for the /oy/ sound.

point **choice** **soil** **join** **voice**

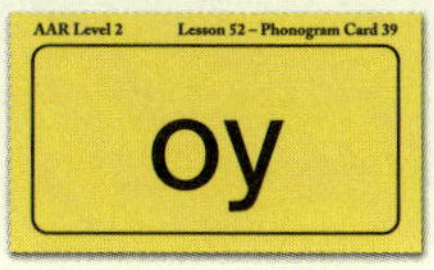

When we practice the Phonogram Card for oy, we say "/oy/, /oy/ that we **may** use at the end of English words."

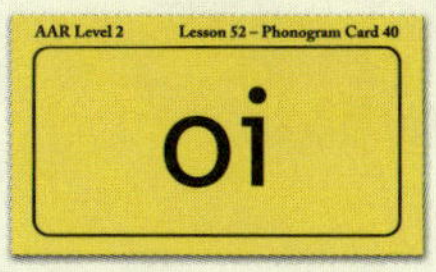

When we practice the Phonogram Card for oi, we say "/oy/, /oy/ that we **may not** use at the end of English words."

When we use the oy and oi letter tiles, we only say the sound /oy/. To facilitate blending, we don't say the second part, "that we may/may not use at the end of English words."

For reading purposes, the student just needs to know that oy and oi both say /oy/. We include the additional phrases "that we **may** use at the end of English words" and "that we **may not** use at the end of English words" on the flashcards so your student won't have to relearn the flashcards for spelling purposes later.

Before You Begin
(continued)

oy oi

The oy and oi tiles are stored under the Vowel Teams category.

Refer to the Letter Tiles app or Phonogram Sounds app for a demonstration of the oy and oi phonogram sounds.

Review

Phonogram Cards

Review the Phonogram Cards that are behind the Review divider in your student's Reading Review Box. Show each card to your student and have him say the sound(s). If necessary, remind your student of the sound(s).

Word Cards

Shuffle and review the Word Cards that are behind the Review divider in your student's Reading Review Box. If your student has difficulty reading a word, build the word with letter tiles and have your student sound it out using the blending procedure shown in Appendix C.

Previous Concepts

Build the following words with letter tiles. Have your student divide the words using the Two Consonant Tiles rule, label with syllable tags, and read.

ginger

Closed Syllable	Bossy R Syllable
g i n	g er

entire

Closed Syllable	Name Game Syllable
e n	t i r e

New Teaching

Teach New Phonograms OY and OI

Hold up the oy Phonogram Card.

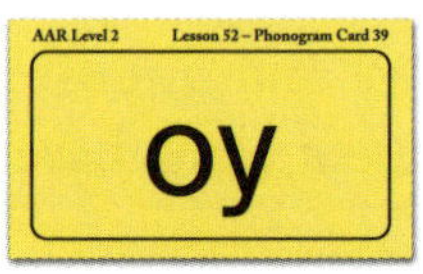

"O-y says /oy/, /oy/ that we **may** use at the end of English words. Repeat

New Teaching
(continued)

after me: /oy/, /oy/ that we **may** use at the end of English words." *Student repeats the sound.*

Hold up the oi Phonogram Card.

"O-i says /oy/, /oy/ that we **may not** use at the end of English words. Repeat after me: /oy/, /oy/ that we **may not** use at the end of English words." *Student repeats the sound.*

Mix in several other flashcards for mixed review and practice until your student can say the sounds of oy and oi accurately. File the Phonogram Cards behind the Review divider in the Reading Review Box.

Move the oy and oi tiles into the workspace. 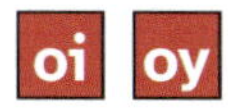

"Both of these tiles say /oy/. When you see these tiles, say just the sound, /oy/. You don't have to say */oy/ that we **may/may not** use at the end of English words* when we are building with tiles, just when we are using the flashcards."

Mix in several other letter tiles for mixed review and practice with the new phonograms until your student can say the sounds accurately.

For extra practice with the new phonograms, try the activity "Jump On It." For instructions, look for this icon in Appendix L.

Blend Sounds with the OI Letter Tile

"All the words you will learn today contain the sound /oy/. First we'll use the oi tile."

Build the word *point*. 

"I'll sound out this first word, and then you'll sound out the next word."

Touch under the p and say */p/.* 

New Teaching
(continued)

Touch under the oi and say */oy/.*

Touch under the n and say */n/.*

Touch under the t and say */t/.*

Now go back to the beginning of the word. Slide your finger under the letters p-oi-n-t and say *point* slowly.

Finally, read the word *point* at a normal pace as we do when we speak.

Using the same procedure for blending, have your student sound out the word *oil.*

Play "Change the Word" with OI

Build the word *join.*

"What is this word?" *Join.*

"I'm going to change the first part of this word."

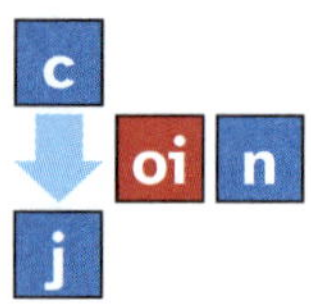

"What does this new word say?" Encourage your student to sound out the new word, *coin.*

New Teaching
(continued)

Continue to change one or two tiles at a time to form the following words. Each time, have your student sound out the new word.

coin → coil → boil → soil → spoil

Build the word *noise*. 

"In this word, the s says /z/ because it is between two vowels. The Silent E keeps the word from looking like a plural. What is this word?" *Noise.*

Blend Sounds with the OY Letter Tile

"Now let's work with the oy tile, which also says /oy/."

Build the word *boy*. 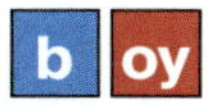

"I'll sound out this first word, and then you'll sound out the next word."

Touch under the b and say */b/.* 

Touch under the oy and say */oy/.* 

Now go back to the beginning of the word. Slide your finger under the letters b-oy and say *boy* slowly.

Finally, read the word *boy* at a normal pace as we do when we speak.

Using the same blending procedure, have your student sound out the word *enjoy*.

New Teaching
(continued)

Play "Change the Word" with OY

Build the word *toy*. 

"I'm going to change the first part of this word."

"What does this new word say?" Encourage your student to sound out the new word, *joy*.

Continue to change tiles to form the following words. Each time, have your student sound out the new word.

joy → soy → coy → ploy

Complete Activity Sheet

"Are you ready to collect some oysters?"

A Bucket of Oysters
Remove pages 357-360 from the *Leap into Reading* activity book.

Cut a slit along the dotted line on the oyster pail. Cut out the oyster cards and arrange them around the pail with the words facing down.

Have your student select a card and read the word aloud. If he reads the word correctly, he may add the oyster card to the pail, pushing it through the slit. If he reads the word incorrectly, return the card to its place so your student can try again later.

Continue until your student has collected all the oysters and placed them in the pail.

New Teaching
(continued)

Practice Reading Words

Have your student practice reading the words on Word Cards 263-271.

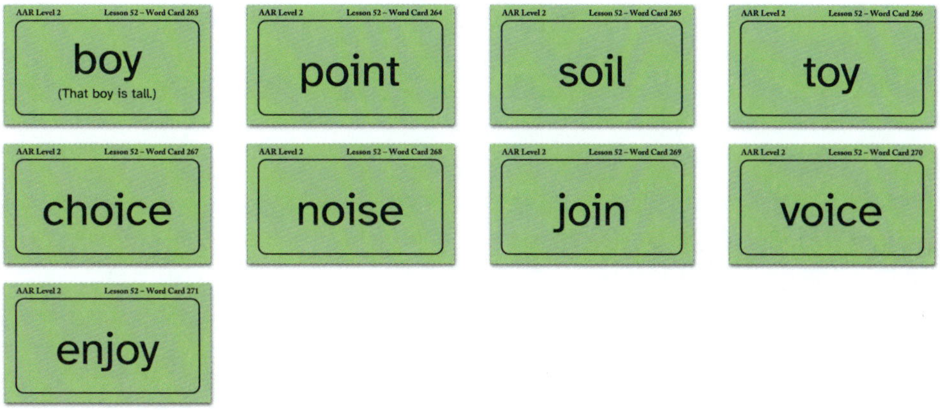

File the Word Cards behind the Review divider in the Reading Review Box.

Teach a Leap Word: *were*

Show Word Card 272 to your student.

"This word is *were* as in *They were late.* Silent E doesn't have a job in the word *were*, so it is a Leap Word."

Review this Leap Word several times today and then file it behind the Review divider in the Reading Review Box.

Practice Fluency

New Words

were boy voice oink
boil oyster spoil moist
toy toilet choice joy

join soil point noise
enjoy coil joint oil
coin

Phrases

join us
enjoy the cake
spoil the fun

point at me
broke the toy
the small boy

oil the hinge
dark soil
were here

a soft voice
one coin
the moist grass

so much noise
not his choice

Turn to pages 361-364 in the activity book.

Have your student read from the Practice Sheets.

Read-Aloud Time

Read a Story or Poem

Read aloud to your student for twenty minutes.

Track Your Progress

Mark the Progress Chart

Have your student mark Lesson 52 on the Progress Chart.

Lesson 53 Read "Wild Rice Harvest"

Objective In this lesson, students read a short story and practice sequencing.

You Will Need

- ☐ *Leap into Reading* pages 365-368
- ☐ *Queen Bee* book

Before You Begin

Preview the Purpose of the Activity Sheet

Today's story is a nonfiction account of how wild rice is harvested. After reading the story, your student will complete a sequencing activity in which she determines the correct order of the steps involved in harvesting.

Such activities help develop not only literacy skills, but also other skills from following instructions (as in a recipe) to scientific inquiry.

Review

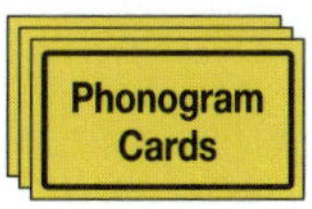

Review the Phonogram Cards that are behind the Review divider in your student's Reading Review Box. Show each card to your student and have him say the sound(s). If necessary, remind your student of the sound(s).

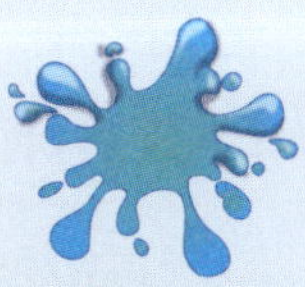

Have fun with today's phonogram review with the "Swat the Phonograms" activity. For instructions, look for this icon in Appendix L.

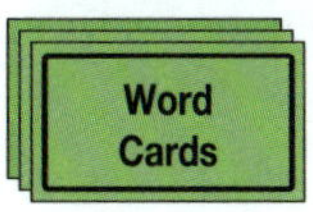

Shuffle and review the Word Cards that are behind the Review divider in your student's Reading Review Box. If your student has difficulty reading a word, build the word with letter tiles and have your student sound it out using the blending procedure shown in Appendix C.

Read the Warm-Up Sheet for "Wild Rice Harvest"

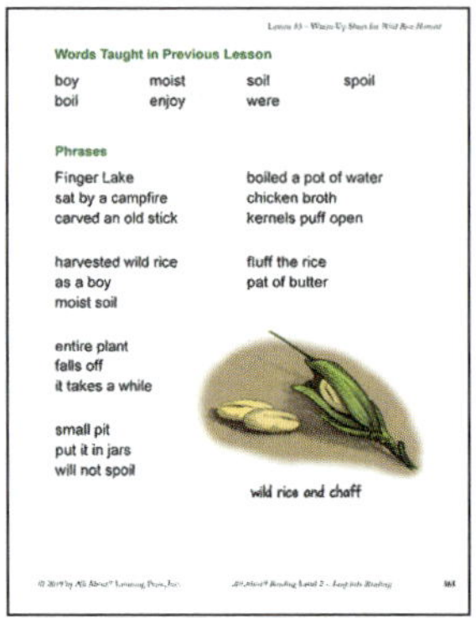

Words Taught in Previous Lesson

boy moist soil spoil
boil enjoy were

Phrases

Finger Lake
sat by a campfire
carved an old stick

harvested wild rice
as a boy
moist soil

entire plant
falls off
it takes a while

small pit
put it in jars
will not spoil

boiled a pot of water
chicken broth
kernels puff open

fluff the rice
pat of butter

wild rice and chaff

Turn to page 365 in the *Leap into Reading* activity book.

Have your student practice reading words and phrases that are found in the short story "Wild Rice Harvest."

Teach Vocabulary and Activate Prior Knowledge

Point out the illustration of wild rice and chaff on the Warm-Up Sheet. "Wild rice is a seed that grows on wild marsh grass. Wild rice is used for cooking, just like white rice."

"The *chaff* is the outer covering of the seed; it protects each seed while it is growing. After the rice is harvested, the chaff is removed, leaving just the edible part of the wild rice. Then the rice is dried so it can be stored for a long time."

"Do you like it when your parents or grandparents tell stories? It can be interesting to hear stories about when adults were children. It's fun to imagine what they must have been like back then! What's the best story your mom or dad or grandparent has ever told you?"

"In our next story, a father tells his children about how he gathered wild rice as a young boy. You can learn how to gather wild rice, too."

Read "Wild Rice Harvest"

"Turn to page 185 in your reader and read 'Wild Rice Harvest' aloud." Discuss your student's ideas for the question below when you come to it.

After page 196: "After reading this recipe, do you think you could cook wild rice by yourself? Why or why not?"

New Teaching
(continued)

Complete Activity Sheet

"Let's see if we can remember what happened in the story you just read."

Harvest the Rice
Remove pages 367-368 from the activity book.

Cut the page into four sections as indicated by the dotted lines. Put the sections in random order and have your student explain how to harvest wild rice by arranging the sections in the appropriate order.

For your reference, the number on the back of each section indicates its placement in the sequence.

Read-Aloud Time

Read a Story or Poem

Read aloud to your student for twenty minutes.

Read-Aloud Tip!

Read a Range of Nonfiction Texts
Reading nonfiction helps kids develop specialized vocabulary as well as background knowledge, which in turn gives kids a wider foundation for all other reading. Here are a few types of informational texts to share with your student:

- Nonfiction picture books and chapter books
- Life-cycle books
- Experiment and activity books
- Special interest books
- Photographic essay books
- Biographies and autobiographies
- Newspapers and magazines
- Browsable books of facts
- How-to guides, cookbooks, field guides, and craft books

Track Your Progress

Mark the Progress Chart

Have your student mark Lesson 53 on the Progress Chart.

Lesson 54 AW and AU

Objective

This lesson teaches phonograms aw and au and words containing those phonograms.

You Will Need

- ☐ *Leap into Reading* pages 369-376
- ☐ Phonogram Cards 41 and 42
- ☐ letter tiles aw and au
- ☐ Word Cards 273-282

Before You Begin

Preview Phonograms AW and AU

In this lesson, your student will work with two related phonograms: aw and au. Both of these phonograms say /aw/.

Phonogram aw is found mainly at the end of words, as in *saw*, but also before the letters l, n, and k in the middle of some words, as in *hawk*. Read the following examples and listen for the /aw/ sound.

law **yawn** **draw** **lawn** **flaw**

Phonogram au is found only in the beginning and middle of words, as in *August* and *haul*. It isn't found at the end of words because, except for the words *you* and *thou*, English words don't end in u. Read the following examples and listen for the /aw/ sound.

maul **August** **haul** **Paul** **pause**

> There are several words in our vocabulary that do end in u, all of which come from other languages. For the full listing, see the "Before You Begin" section in Lesson 44.

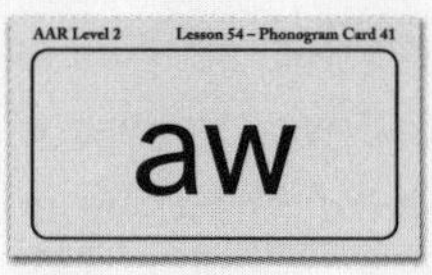

When we practice the Phonogram Card for aw, we say "/aw/, /aw/ that we **may** use at the end of English words."

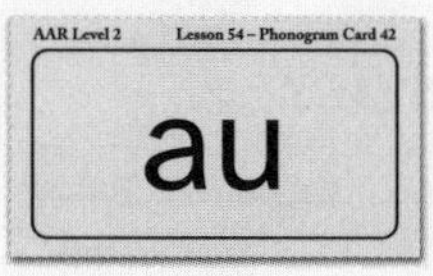

When we practice the Phonogram Card for au, we say "/aw/, /aw/ that we **may not** use at the end of English words."

When we use the aw and au letter tiles, we only say the sound /aw/. To facilitate blending, we don't say the second part, "that we may/may not use at the end of English words."

Before You Begin
(continued)

For reading purposes, the student just needs to know that aw and au both say /aw/. We include the additional phrases "that we **may** use at the end of English words" and "that we **may not** use at the end of English words" on the flashcards so your student won't have to relearn the flashcards for spelling purposes later.

aw au

The aw and au tiles are stored under the Vowel Teams category.

Refer to the Letter Tiles app or Phonogram Sounds app for a demonstration of the aw and au phonogram sounds.

Review

Phonogram Cards

Review the Phonogram Cards that are behind the Review divider in your student's Reading Review Box. Show each card to your student and have him say the sound(s). If necessary, remind your student of the sound(s).

Word Cards

Shuffle and review the Word Cards that are behind the Review divider in your student's Reading Review Box. If your student has difficulty reading a word, build the word with letter tiles and have your student sound it out using the blending procedure shown in Appendix C.

Previous Concepts

Build the following words with letter tiles. Have your student divide the words where necessary, label with syllable tags, and read. *Order* is divided using the Two Consonant Tiles rule.

order

Bossy R Syllable	Bossy R Syllable
or	d er

bike

Name Game Syllable
b i k e

New Teaching

Teach New Phonograms AW and AU

Hold up the aw Phonogram Card.

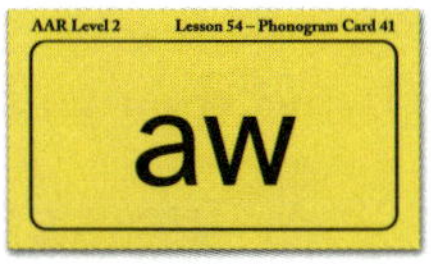

"A-w says /aw/, /aw/ that we **may** use at the end of English words. Repeat after me: /aw/, /aw/ that we **may** use at the end of English words." *Student repeats the sound.*

Hold up the au Phonogram Card.

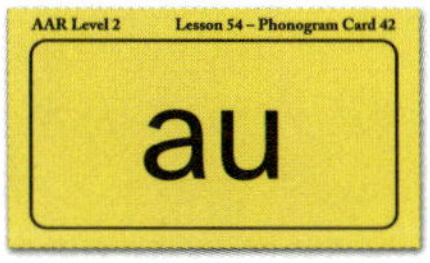

"A-u says /aw/, /aw/ that we **may not** use at the end of English words. Repeat after me: /aw/, /aw/ that we **may not** use at the end of English words." *Student repeats the sound.*

Mix in several other flashcards for mixed review and practice until your student can say the sounds of aw and au accurately. File the Phonogram Cards behind the Review divider in the Reading Review Box.

Move the aw and au tiles into the workspace. 

"Both of these tiles say /aw/. When you see these tiles, say just the sound, /aw/. You don't have to say */aw/ that we **may/may not** use at the end of English words* when we are building with tiles, just when we are using the flashcards."

Mix in several other letter tiles for mixed review and practice with the new phonograms until your student can say the sounds accurately.

For more practice with the new phonograms, play "Phonogram Ball." For instructions, look for this icon in Appendix L.

New Teaching
(continued)

Blend Sounds with the AW Letter Tile

"All the words you will learn today contain the sound /aw/. First we'll use the aw tile."

Build the word *lawn*.

"I'll sound out this first word, and then you'll sound out the next word."

Touch under the l and say */l/*.

Touch under the aw and say */aw/*.

Touch under the n and say */n/*.

Now go back to the beginning of the word. Slide your finger under the letters l-aw-n and say *lawn* slowly.

Finally, read the word *lawn* at a normal pace as we do when we speak.

Using the same procedure for blending, have your student sound out the word *draw*.

New Teaching
(continued)

Play "Change the Word" with AW

Build the word *paw.*

"What is this word?" *Paw.*

"I'm going to change the first part of this word."

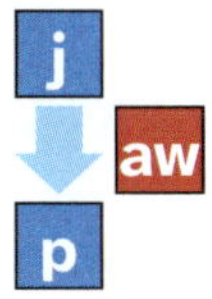

"What does this new word say?" Encourage your student to sound out the new word, *jaw.*

Continue to change one or two tiles at a time to form the following words. Each time, have your student sound out the new word.

jaw → raw → law → claw → thaw* → draw

*Use the th tile for *thaw.*

Blend Sounds with the AU Letter Tile

"Now let's work with the au tile, which also says /aw/."

Build the word *haul.*

"I'll sound out this first word, and then you'll sound out the next word."

Touch under the h and say */h/.*

Touch under the au and say */aw/.*

Touch under the l and say */l/.*

New Teaching
(continued)

Now go back to the beginning of the word. Slide your finger under the letters h-au-l and say *haul* slowly.

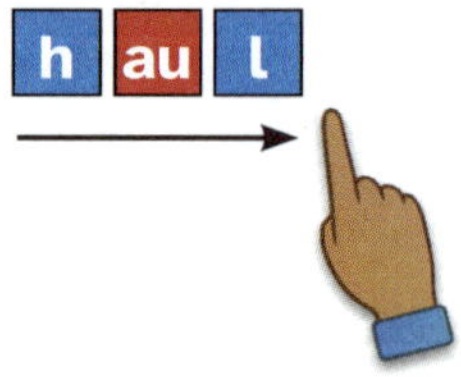

Finally, read the word *haul* at a normal pace as we do when we speak.

Using the same procedure for blending, have your student sound out the word *launch*.

Play "Change the Word" with AU

Build the word *pause*.

"This word is *pause*. What sound does the s say in *pause*?" */z/.*

"Good. The s says /z/ because it is between two vowels."

"Does the e say anything in this word?" *No.*

"Correct. Silent E keeps this word from looking like a plural word."

"I'm going to change the first part of this word."

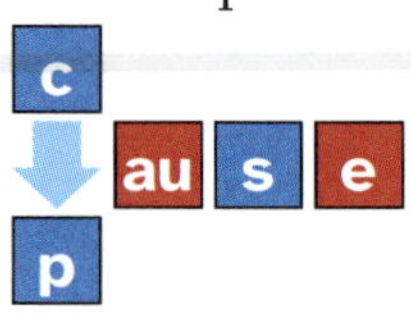

"What does this new word say?" Encourage your student to sound out the new word, *cause*.

"Let's add b-e to the beginning of *cause*." Change the word to *because*.

"Read this word." *Because.*

New Teaching
(continued)

Complete Activity Sheet

"Now we need to help some baby hawks get in the right nest."

Save the Baby Hawks
Remove pages 369-372 from the *Leap into Reading* activity book.

Cut the sheet with the nests in half as indicated. Cut out the egg cards, mix them up, and place them in a pile between the nests with the words facing down.

Have your student select a card from the pile, read the word aloud, and determine whether the word belongs in the aw nest or the au nest. He may then save the baby hawk by placing its egg in the appropriate nest.

Continue until all the baby hawks have been returned to their nests.

Practice Reading Words

Have your student practice reading the words on Word Cards 273-281.

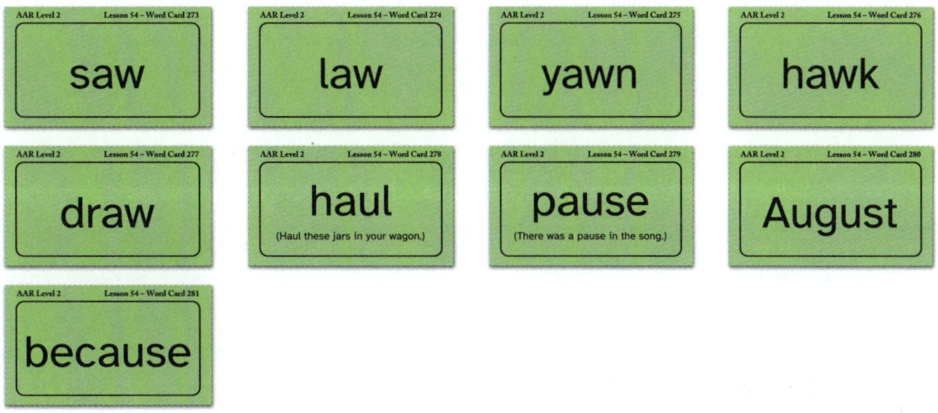

File the Word Cards behind the Review divider in the Reading Review Box.

New Teaching
(continued)

Teach a Leap Word: *aunt*

Show Word Card 282 to your student.

"This word is *aunt* as in *Aunt Meg enjoys oysters.* The au doesn't say /aw/ in this word. We usually pronounce *aunt* like *ant* or /ŏnt/."

Review this Leap Word several times today and then file it behind the Review divider in the Reading Review Box.

Practice Fluency

New Words

aunt	yawn	sauce	claw
raw	fault	crawl	paw
draw	thaw	because	lawn
law	straw	pause	haul
jaw	August	saw	hawk

Phrases

raw beef	bed of straw
not my fault	crawl under it
pause to think	make the sauce
haul the wagon	a huge yawn
broke the law	his Aunt Sue
water the lawn	draw a dog
a sore paw	
thaw the oysters	

Turn to pages 373-376 in the activity book.

Have your student read from the Practice Sheets.

Have some fun with the fluency exercises with a silly sentence activity. For instructions, look for this icon in Appendix K.

Read-Aloud Time

Read a Story or Poem

Read aloud to your student for twenty minutes.

Track Your Progress

Mark the Progress Chart

Have your student mark Lesson 54 on the Progress Chart.

Lesson 55 Read "Rawhide"

Objective

In this lesson, students learn about antonyms, read a short story, and practice reading between the lines.

You Will Need

- ☐ *Leap into Reading* pages 377-379
- ☐ *Queen Bee* book

Before You Begin

Preview Antonyms

In this lesson, your student will complete an activity about *antonyms*, words that are opposite in meaning to other words. Besides helping your student broaden his vocabulary, working with antonyms also helps build other skills like critical thinking, categorizing, and comparing/contrasting.

Preview Reading between the Lines

Sometimes the text doesn't tell the full story. Good readers learn to fill in the details based on their own experiences. We call this "reading between the lines."

After reading the short story, you will ask your student a series of questions that point out that there is a difference between what the words say and what is really meant. By looking at both the text and the illustrations, we are able to guess what the real meaning is. This technique is often used to add humor to a story.

Review

Review the Phonogram Cards that are behind the Review divider in your student's Reading Review Box. Show each card to your student and have him say the sound(s). If necessary, remind your student of the sound(s).

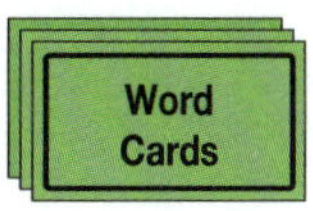

Shuffle and review the Word Cards that are behind the Review divider in your student's Reading Review Box. If your student has difficulty reading a word, build the word with letter tiles and have your student sound it out using the blending procedure shown in Appendix C.

Teach Antonyms

"What is the opposite of *tall*?" *Short.*

"What is the opposite of *hot*?" *Cold.*

"Words that are opposites, like *tall* and *short*, are called *antonyms*. You already know lots of antonyms."

"In this activity, you will match up words that are antonyms."

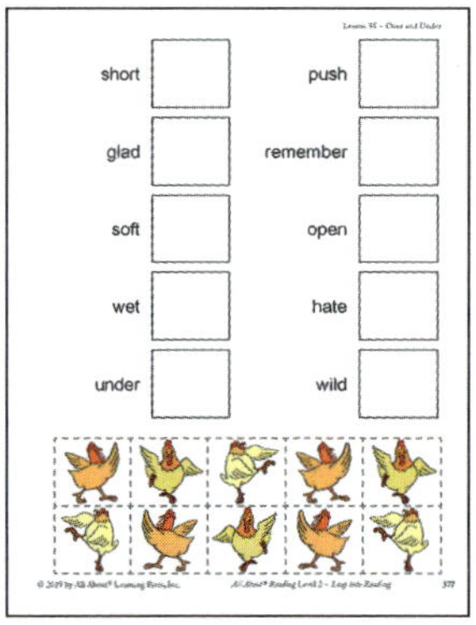

Over and Under

Remove pages 377-378 from the *Leap into Reading* activity book.

Cut out the ten cards at the bottom of the page and mix them up. Set the cards on the table with the chickens facing up. Have your student choose a chicken, read the word on the back, and place the card in the box next to the word that has the opposite meaning.

Continue until all the cards have been placed in the appropriate squares.

Answer Key

short/tall	push/pull
glad/sad	remember/forget
soft/hard	open/closed
wet/dry	hate/love
under/over	wild/tame

Read the Warm-Up Sheet for "Rawhide"

Turn to page 379 in the activity book.

Have your student practice reading words and phrases that are found in the short story "Rawhide."

New Teaching
(continued)

Teach Vocabulary and Activate Prior Knowledge

Point out the sawmill on the Warm-Up Sheet. "Logs are brought to a *sawmill* to be turned into lumber or boards. The bark is removed from the logs and big saws cut the logs into boards. The boards are dried and sanded smooth, and then they are ready to use."

"Our next story is about a dog. As you know, there are all kinds of dogs. There are tiny dogs that make fun pets, there are large dogs that help people, and there are medium-sized dogs that love to run and jump. Do you have a favorite kind of dog?" Discuss dogs and their abilities with your student.

"Some dogs are farm dogs or ranch dogs. They help farmers and ranchers with their daily chores. The dog in this story is a ranch dog who thinks he is the boss of the place. He creates a lot of commotion when his owners are away for the day. Let's read 'Rawhide' to see how much trouble he can stir up."

Read "Rawhide"

"Turn to page 199 in your reader and read 'Rawhide' aloud."

Read between the Lines

Draw attention to Rawhide's exaggerations by asking the following questions.

Turn to page 203. "Rawhide says that he's chasing a 'large rat,' but the illustration shows a very small mouse. Do you think Rawhide is imagining the mouse to be bigger than it is?"

Turn to page 207. "Rawhide thinks the ranch hand is stealing the eggs. But what is the ranch hand really doing?" *Collecting the eggs for the family.*

Turn to page 209. "Rawhide thinks he has saved the children from a huge snake. What is he really carrying?" *A garden hose.*

"Rawhide seems to exaggerate a lot. He adds a few made-up details, like a big rat and a huge snake. Why do you think he does that?" *Possible answers: He wants to feel important. He really thinks he's helping the family.*

Read-Aloud Time

Read a Story or Poem

Read aloud to your student for twenty minutes.

Track Your Progress

Mark the Progress Chart

Have your student mark Lesson 55 on the Progress Chart.

Oh, boy, antonyms are just as fun as synonyms. I got out my banjo and wrote you a little "opposites" song. Feel free to croak along!

Antonyms are opposites,
and that's true, right or wrong.
Hot and cold, black and white,
really short or long.
I love all the opposites,
whether cat or dog.
And YOU'LL love them or my name isn't
Webfoot, Awesome Frog!

Lesson 56 OW and OU

Objective

This lesson teaches phonograms ow and ou and words containing those phonograms.

You Will Need

- ☐ *Leap into Reading* pages 381-389
- ☐ Phonogram Cards 43 and 44
- ☐ letter tiles ow and ou
- ☐ Word Cards 283-292

Before You Begin

Preview Phonograms OW and OU

In this lesson, your student will work with two related phonograms: ow and ou. Both phonograms can say /ow/, which is the focus of this lesson, and both have additional sounds as well.

Phonogram ow has two sounds:

- /ow/ as in *cow* (emphasized in this lesson)
- /ō/ as in *low* (emphasized in Level 3, Lesson 4)

Phonogram ou has four sounds:

- /ow/ as in *mouse* (emphasized in this lesson)
- /ō/ as in *soul* (emphasized in Level 4, Lesson 16)
- /o͞o/ as in *soup* (emphasized in Level 4, Lesson 18)
- /ŭ/ as in *touch* (emphasized in Level 4, Lesson 20)

The sound of /ow/ spelled ow is typically found at the end of words, as in *plow*, and before the letters l, n, and d in the middle of words, as in *brown*. Read the following examples and listen for the /ow/ sound.

town **brow** **flower** **down** **now**

Phonogram ou is found only in the middle of words, as in *mouse*. It isn't found at the end of words because, except for the words *you* and *thou*, English words don't end in u. Read the following examples and listen for the /ow/ sound.

house **found** **cloud** **mouth** **out**

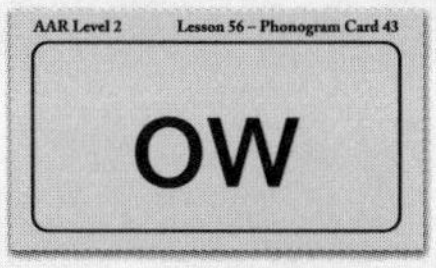

When we practice the Phonogram Card for ow, we say "/ow/–/ō/."

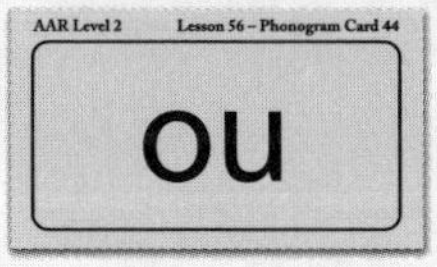

When we practice the Phonogram Card for ou, we say "/ow/–/ō/–/o͞o/–/ŭ/."

Before You Begin
(continued)

When we use the ow and ou letter tiles to represent the sound of /ow/, we only say the sound /ow/. To facilitate blending, we don't say all the sounds.

The ow and ou tiles are stored under the Vowel Teams category.

Refer to the Letter Tiles app or Phonogram Sounds app for a demonstration of the ow and ou phonogram sounds.

Review

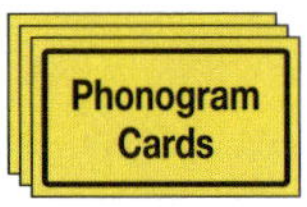

Review the Phonogram Cards that are behind the Review divider in your student's Reading Review Box. Show each card to your student and have him say the sound(s). If necessary, remind your student of the sound(s).

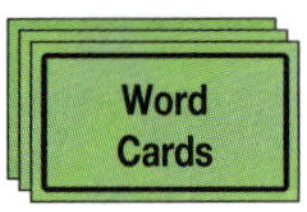

Shuffle and review the Word Cards that are behind the Review divider in your student's Reading Review Box. If your student has difficulty reading a word, build the word with letter tiles and have your student sound it out using the blending procedure shown in Appendix C.

Build the following words with letter tiles. Have your student divide the words where necessary, label with syllable tags, and read. *Recent* is divided using the One Consonant Tile rule.

New Teaching

Teach New Phonograms OW and OU

Hold up the ow Phonogram Card.

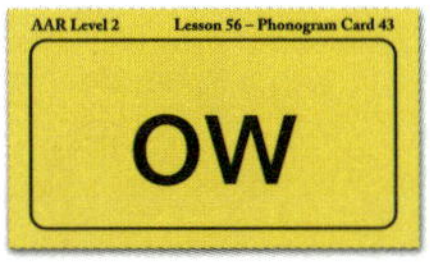

"O-w says /ow/–/ō/. Repeat after me: /ow/–/ō/." *Student repeats the sounds.*

Hold up the ou Phonogram Card.

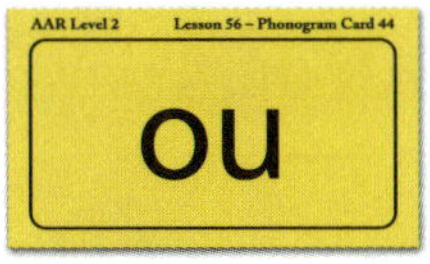

"O-u says /ow/–/ō/–/o͞o/–/ŭ/. Repeat after me: /ow/–/ō/–/o͞o/–/ŭ/."
Student repeats the sounds.

Mix in several other flashcards for mixed review and practice until your student can say the sounds of ow and ou accurately. File the Phonogram Cards behind the Review divider in the Reading Review Box.

Move the ow and ou tiles into the workspace. 

"Both of these tiles can say /ow/. All the words you will learn today contain the sound /ow/."

Mix in several other letter tiles for mixed review and practice with the new phonograms until your student can say the sounds accurately.

For extra practice with the new phonograms, play the game "Phonogram Bingo." For instructions, look for this icon in Appendix L.

Blend Sounds with the OW Letter Tile

"First let's use the ow tile to build words."

Build the word *cow.* 

New Teaching
(continued)

"I'll sound out this first word, and then you'll sound out the next word."

Touch under the c and say */k/.*

Touch under the ow and say */ow/.*

Now go back to the beginning of the word. Slide your finger under the letters c-ow and say *cow* slowly.

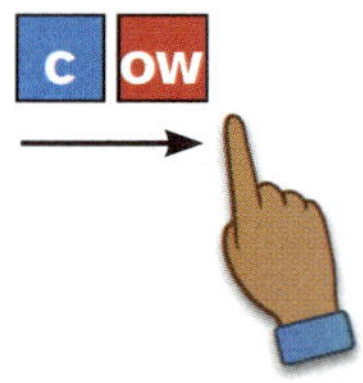

Finally, read the word *cow* at a normal pace as we do when we speak.

Using the same procedure for blending, have your student sound out the word *owl.*

Play "Change the Word" with OW

Build the word *down.*

"What is this word?" *Down.*

"I'm going to change the first part of this word."

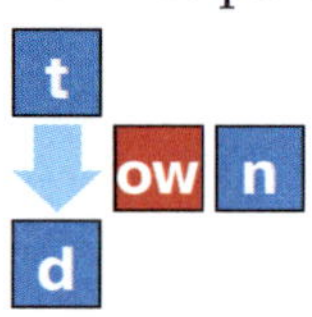

"What does this new word say?" Encourage your student to sound out the new word, *town.*

Continue to change one or two tiles at a time to form the following words. Each time, have your student sound out the new word.

town → clown → crown → crowd → brown → frown

New Teaching
(continued)

Blend Sounds with the OU Letter Tile

"Now let's work with the ou tile, which can also say /ow/."

Build the word *mouth*.

"I'll sound out this first word, and then you'll sound out the next word."

Touch under the m and say */m/.*

Touch under the ou and say */ow/.*

Touch under the th and say */th/.*

Now go back to the beginning of the word. Slide your finger under the letters m-ou-th and say *mouth* slowly.

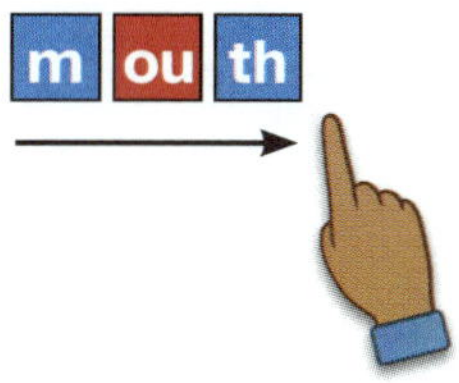

Finally, read the word *mouth* at a normal pace as we do when we speak.

Using the same procedure for blending, have your student sound out the word *found.*

Leave the word *found* in the workspace.

New Teaching
(continued)

Play "Change the Word" with OU

"I'm going to change the first part of this word."

"What does this new word say?" Encourage your student to sound out the new word, *pound.*

Continue to change one tile at a time to form the following words. Each time, have your student sound out the new word.

pound → sound → round → ground

shout* → out → ouch* → couch*

*Use the sh tile for *shout*. Use the ch tile for *ouch* and *couch*.

Build the word *house.* 

"In this word, Silent E keeps the word from looking like a plural. What is this word?" *House.*

Change the word to *mouse.* 

"Read this word." *Mouse.*

Complete Activity Sheet

"Now let's help this cowboy round up his cows."

Help a Cowboy

Remove pages 381-384 from the *Leap into Reading* activity book.

Cut out the cow cards and mix them up. Spread the cards on the table to the right of the corral sheet with the words facing down.

Have your student select a card and guide the cow through the gate. Before the cow can enter the corral, your student must stop and turn the card over to read the word aloud. If he reads the word correctly, the cow continues through the gate

New Teaching
(continued)

and into the corral. If he reads the word incorrectly, the cow escapes back to the open range.

Continue until the roundup is complete and the cows are safe in their corral. Then have your student count the cows in the corral.

Practice Reading Words

Have your student practice reading the words on Word Cards 283-290.

File the Word Cards behind the Review divider in the Reading Review Box.

Teach Two Leap Words: *any* and *many*

Show Word Card 291 to your student.

"This word is *any* as in *Are there any fish in the pond?* The a doesn't say the sound we expect it to. The y says /ē/, which is the fourth sound of y. You haven't studied words with this sound yet, so this is a Leap Word."

Show Word Card 292 to your student.

"This word is *many* as in *We have many books. Many* rhymes with *any*, and it is also a Leap Word."

Review these Leap Words several times today and then file them behind the Review divider in the Reading Review Box.

New Teaching
(continued)

Practice Fluency

New Words

any	frown	count	cowboy
mouth	shout	owl	without
cow	outside	sound	many
out	clown	proud	now
howl	cloud	power	ouch
town	round	south	flower
found	our	shower	loud
crowd	down	pound	flour
brown	crown	plow	how
growl	ground	gown	powder
anything			

Turn to pages 385-389 in the activity book.

Have your student read from the Practice Sheets.

To engage your student in the fluency exercises, let him illustrate a selection of words. For instructions, look for this icon in Appendix K.

Read-Aloud Time

Read a Story or Poem

Read aloud to your student for twenty minutes.

Track Your Progress

Mark the Progress Chart

Have your student mark Lesson 56 on the Progress Chart.

Lesson 57 Read "Queen Bee"

Objective

In this lesson, students learn about homophones and read a short story.

You Will Need

- ☐ *Leap into Reading* pages 391-395
- ☐ *Queen Bee* book

Before You Begin

Preview Homophones

Before reading today's story, your student will complete an activity sheet about homophones. Homophones are words that sound alike but are spelled differently, such as *be* and *bee* or *flower* and *flour.*

Review

Phonogram Cards

Review the Phonogram Cards that are behind the Review divider in your student's Reading Review Box. Show each card to your student and have him say the sound(s). If necessary, remind your student of the sound(s).

Word Cards

Shuffle and review the Word Cards that are behind the Review divider in your student's Reading Review Box. If your student has difficulty reading a word, build the word with letter tiles and have your student sound it out using the blending procedure shown in Appendix C.

New Teaching

Teach the Word *Sadness*

Build the word *sad.* s a d

"Read this word." *Sad.*

"I'm going to add n-e-s-s." s a d n e s s

"Now what word is this?" *Sadness.*

New Teaching
(continued)

Teach Homophones

"Listen to this sentence and tell me how many times I say the word *ate/eight*: *I ate eight sandwiches.* How many times did I say the word *ate/eight*?" *Two times.*

"Right. Have you ever noticed that some words sound the same but have different meanings? I can go to a *sale* to buy things, or I can *sail* in a boat. *Sale* and *sail* sound exactly the same, but they have two different meanings and spellings."

"Here's another example: *I saw a <u>bear</u> in the woods. The baby took off her diaper and was completely <u>bare</u>.* *Bear* and *bare* sound alike."

"Words like *bear* and *bare* are homophones. That means that they sound alike but are spelled differently. You know lots of homophones. In this next activity, you will match up homophones with the correct picture.

<u>Be a Bee</u>

Remove page 391 from the *Leap into Reading* activity book.

Cut out the words at the bottom of the page and divide them into four piles of homophone pairs. Point out the first illustration on the page (the paws) and show your student the pair of homophones for *pause/paws.*

Ask your student to select the word that correctly identifies the illustration and place the card in the space underneath the illustration. Continue with the illustrations of the bee, ant, and flower.

Four of the words will be matched with illustrations and four words will be left over.

Read the Warm-Up Sheet for "Queen Bee"

Words Taught in Previous Lessons

outside	wildflowers	brown	sound
flowers	down	found	now
crown	south	ground	frowns
out	hello	crowd	campground
without	loud	owl	any

New Decodable Word

sadness

Phrases

outside her hive
spring has sprung
any more

flowers are the best
cover the ground

without a sound
owls are the best
the owl yawned
at a campground

Names

Queen Bee
Princess Dragonfly

throne

Turn to pages 393-394 in the activity book.

Have your student practice reading words and phrases that are found in the short story "Queen Bee."

New Teaching
(continued)

Teach Vocabulary and Activate Prior Knowledge

Point out the throne on the Warm-Up Sheet. "A *throne* is a special chair used by a royal ruler such as a king or a queen. Thrones are usually very fancy, made of carved wood and decorated with gold and beautiful velvet cushions. Only the person of royalty is allowed to sit in the chair."

"Our next story is about a queen, but she's not the type of queen that you are probably thinking of. She is a queen *bee*."

"In a beehive, thousands of bees live and work together. Most of the female bees are called worker bees and all the male bees are called drones. There is one very special bee in each beehive, and she is the most important bee of all: the queen bee. The queen bee lays all the eggs in the hive."

"In our next story, a queen bee suddenly decides that she doesn't want to be the queen any longer."

Read "Queen Bee"

"Turn to page 217 in your reader and read 'Queen Bee' aloud." Discuss your student's ideas for the question below when you come to it.

After page 220: "What is Queen Bee's main reason for wanting to leave the hive?"

Practice Skimming and Discuss the Story

"At the beginning of the story, Queen Bee feels unhappy with her life in the hive. At what point in the story does Queen Bee become content and happy?" Encourage your student to skim through the story again, if necessary.

"Queen Bee learns an important lesson from her friends in the forest. Do you think Queen Bee will be happy from now on?"

"The characters in the story say what they think is 'best,' and their answers include fire, trees, wildflowers, owls, and bees. Now it's your turn to answer the question: You've seen many things from south to west, what do *you* think is the best thing in nature?"

Read-Aloud Time

Read a Story or Poem

Read aloud to your student for twenty minutes.

> Read-Aloud Tip!
>
> **Make Connections to Real Life**
>
> Children love to see themselves reflected in the books they read. You can facilitate this by encouraging your student to make connections between his life and the life of the characters. Perhaps he feels the same way as one of the characters or has had a similar experience. Readers who connect with literature in this way are more engaged since they feel more in touch with the people and events in the world of the story. As a result, they are more likely to remember what they have read.

Track Your Progress

Mark the Progress Chart

Have your student mark Lesson 57 on the Progress Chart.

Present Your Student with the Certificate of Achievement

CONGRATULATIONS!
You did it!
I am one proud froggy,
and you should be too!
Thank you for reading with me.
I know you'll use your new knowledge
to reach new heights of frogginess.
ONWARD
to the next pond!

3

Appendices

APPENDIX A

Scope and Sequence of Level 2

Your Student Will:	Lesson
Review concepts taught in Level 1 and learn about Open and Closed syllable types	1
Read words with consonant blends at the beginning and end	2
Read a short story and use pantomime to act out actions	3
Read words with /ī/ spelled y	4
Read a short story and practice meaningful expression	5
Review and learn the Compound Words and Two Consonant Tiles syllable division rules	6
Learn about unaccented syllables, read a short story, and analyze important details in the text	7
Read words with three-letter blends	8
Read a short story and practice skimming for information	9
Learn Part 1 of the One Consonant Tile syllable division rule	10
Read a short story and learn about the use of speech bubbles for dialogue	11
Learn Part 2 of the One Consonant Tile syllable division rule	12
Read a short story, learn about abbreviations, and answer comprehension questions	13
Learn the first job of Silent E and read words with the VCE pattern	14
Learn the Name Game syllable type and read more words with Silent E	15
Read a short story and discuss character motivation	16
Learn the two sounds of long u and the sound of s between two vowels	17
Read a short story and compare and contrast characters	18
Learn phonogram wh and read words beginning with wh	19
Read a short story, learn about text features, identify the main character, and discuss the characters	20
Read words that combine consonant blends with the Name Game pattern and learn about heteronyms	21
Read a short story and practice sequencing	22
Read plural Silent E words	23
Read a short story and learn about possessives and onomatopoeia	24
Learn phonogram ee and the Vowel Team syllable type and read words with ee	25
Read a short story and discuss the main conflict	26
Learn to form and read contractions	27
Read a poem and complete a Venn diagram	28

Your Student Will:	Lesson
Read words with long i or o before two consonants	29
Read a short story and create hints for a guessing game	30
Learn phonogram er as in *her* and the Bossy R syllable type and read words with er	31
Read a short story and compare settings	32
Learn phonogram ar, decode three-syllable words, and read words with ar	33
Read a short story and learn about the five senses in literature	34
Learn phonogram or and read words with or	35
Read a short story and complete a concept map	36
Learn the third sound of u and read words with the sound of /o͝o/	37
Read a short story and learn about alliteration	38
Learn the second job of Silent E and read words with soft c	39
Learn that Silent E can have two jobs in the same word and read more words with Silent E	40
Read a short story and imagine an alternate ending	41
Read words with soft g	42
Read a poem, learn about rhyme and stanzas, and relate the poem to life	43
Learn the third job of Silent E and read more words with Silent E	44
Read a short story and make inferences from words and illustrations	45
Learn the fourth job of Silent E and read words with /ŭ/, the fourth sound of o	46
Learn about words with multiple meanings, read a short story, and make predictions	47
Learn phonogram ed and the concept of past tense	48
Read a rhyming story and practice skimming for information	49
Learn the third sound of a and read words with the sound of /ah/	50
Read a short story, learn about synonyms, and discuss the concept of realism vs. fantasy	51
Learn phonograms oy and oi and read words with the sound of /oy/	52
Read a short story and practice sequencing	53
Learn phonograms aw and au and read words with the sound of /aw/	54
Read a short story, learn about antonyms, and practice reading between the lines	55
Learn phonograms ow and ou and read words with the sound of /ow/	56
Read a short story and learn more about homophones	57

APPENDIX B
Phonograms Taught in Levels 1-4

Phonograms are letters or letter combinations that represent a single sound. For example, the letter b represents the sound /b/ as in *bat*. The letter combination sh represents the sound /sh/ as in *ship*.

Card #	Phonogram	Sound	For the Teacher's Use Only (example of word containing the phonogram)				Lesson/ Level
Phonograms Taught in Level 1							
1	m	/m/	moon				Level 1
2	s	/s/–/z/	sun	has			
3	p	/p/	pig				
4	a	/ă/–/ā/–/ah/	apple	acorn	father		
5	n	/n/	nest				
6	t	/t/	tent				
7	b	/b/	bat				
8	j	/j/	jam				
9	g	/g/–/j/	goose	gem			
10	d	/d/	deer				
11	c	/k/–/s/	cow	city			
12	y	/y/–/ĭ/–/ī/–/ē/	yarn	gym	my	happy	
13	h	/h/	hat				
14	k	/k/	kite				
15	r	/r/	rake				
16	i	/ĭ/–/ī/–/ē/	itchy	ivy	radio		
17	v	/v/	vase				
18	f	/f/	fish				
19	z	/z/	zipper				
20	o	/ŏ/–/ō/–/o͞o/–/ŭ/	otter	open	to	oven	
21	l	/l/	leaf				
22	w	/w/	wave				
23	u	/ŭ/–/ū/–/o͝o/	udder	unit	put		
24	e	/ĕ/–/ē/	echo	even			
25	qu	/kw/	queen				
26	x	/ks/	ax				

Card #	Phonogram	Sound	For the Teacher's Use Only (example of word containing the phonogram)	Lesson/ Level
27	th	/th/–/~~th~~/	three then	Level 1
28	sh	/sh/	ship	
29	ch	/ch/–/k/–/sh/	child school chef	
30	ck	/k/, two-letter /k/	duck	
31	ng	/ng/	king	
32	nk	/ngk/	thank	
		Phonograms Taught in Level 2		
33	wh	/hw/	while	19
34	ee	/ē/, double e	feed	25
35	er	/er/ as in *her*	her	31
36	ar	/ar/	car	33
37	or	/or/–/er/ as in *work*	corn work	35
38	ed	/ĕd/–/d/–/t/	wanted snowed dropped	48
39	oy	/oy/ that we **may** use at the end of English words	toy	52
40	oi	/oy/ that we may **not** use at the end of English words	oil	52
41	aw	/aw/ that we **may** use at the end of English words	saw	54
42	au	/aw/ that we may **not** use at the end of English words	haul	54
43	ow	/ow/–/ō/	cow low	56
44	ou	/ow/–/ō/–/o͞o/–/ŭ/	mouse soul soup touch	56
		Phonograms Taught in Level 3		Level 3
45	ai	/ā/, two-letter /ā/ that we may **not** use at the end of English words	rain	
46	ay	/ā/, two-letter /ā/ that we **may** use at the end of English words	day	

Card #	Phonogram	Sound	For the Teacher's Use Only (example of word containing the phonogram)	Lesson/ Level
47	oa	/ō/, two-letter /ō/ that we may **not** use at the end of English words	boat	Level 3
48	ir	/er/ as in *first*	first	
49	ur	/er/ as in *nurse*	nurse	
50	oo	/o͞o/–/o͝o/–/ō/	food book floor	
51	ea	/ē/–/ĕ/–/ā/	leaf bread great	
52	igh	/ī/, three-letter /ī/	light	
53	tch	/ch/, three-letter /ch/	watch	
54	dge	/j/, three-letter /j/	badge	
55	ew	/o͞o/–/ū/	grew few	
56	wr	/r/, two-letter /r/ used **only** at the beginning of a word	write	
57	kn	/n/, two-letter /n/ used **only** at the beginning of a word	know	
58	eigh	/ā/, four-letter /ā/	eight	
59	oe	/ō/, two-letter /ō/ that we **may** use at the end of English words	toe	
60	ti	/sh/, tall-letter /sh/	nation	
Phonograms Taught in Level 4				Level 4
61	ey	/ē/–/ā/	key they	
62	ear	/er/ as in *early*	early	
63	ui	/o͞o/	fruit	
64	ie	/ē/–/ī/	field pie	
65	ph	/f/, two-letter /f/	phone	
66	gu	/g/, two-letter /g/	guide	
67	gn	/n/, two-letter /n/ used at the beginning or end of a word	gnat	
68	augh	/aw/, four-letter /aw/	daughter	
69	ei	/ā/–/ē/	vein ceiling	

Card #	Phonogram	Sound	For the Teacher's Use Only (example of word containing the phonogram)	Lesson/ Level
70	ough	/ō/–/o͞o/–/ŭff/– /ŏff/–/aw/–/ow/	though through rough cough thought bough	Level 4
71	si	/sh/–/zh/	mission vision	
72	mb	/m/, two-letter /m/	lamb	
73	our	/er/ as in *journey*	journey	
74	ci	/sh/, short-letter /sh/	special	
75	rh	/r/, two-letter /r/ used in Greek words	rhyme	

APPENDIX C
Blending Procedure

Blending one-syllable words

1. Build the word with letter tiles. 

2. Touch under one letter at a time and say the sound of each letter.

3. Go back to the beginning of the word and blend the first two sounds together.

4. Start over at the beginning of the word. Slide your finger under the letters and blend all three sounds together.

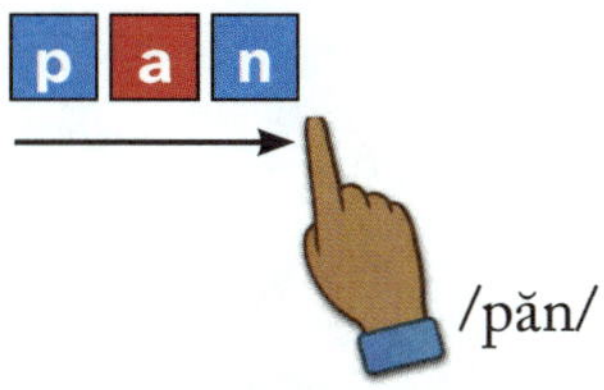

> **Tip!**
>
> Starting over at the beginning of the word is optional. Some students need the extra support provided by this step, while others do not.
>
> Whenever you feel that your student is ready, blend all the letters without this additional step.

5. Finally, say the word at a normal pace as we do when we speak.

> **Tip!**
>
> **"Touch the Vowel" Technique**
> Many errors in sounding out words are related to the vowel. If your student says the wrong vowel sound, ask him to touch the vowel and say the vowel sound first. After he says the correct sound for the vowel, he should go back and sound out the word from the beginning.

Blending multisyllable words

1. Build the word with letter tiles. 

2. Divide the word into syllables using the appropriate syllable division rules.

3. Label the syllable types.

4. Decode one syllable at a time, following the same procedure you would use for a one-syllable word.

5. Start at the beginning of the word again. Slide your finger under each syllable, saying the sound of the syllables.

6. Finally, say the word at a normal pace as we do when we speak.

APPENDIX D

The Six Syllable Types

Closed

A **Closed syllable** ends in a consonant. The vowel has a short vowel sound, as in the word *bat*. On the syllable tag, the closed door represents a closed syllable because the consonant "closes in" the vowel.

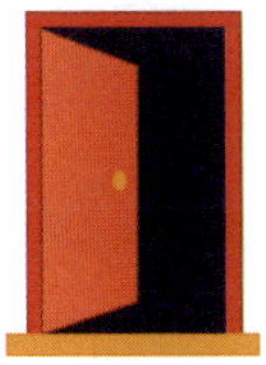

Open

An **Open syllable** ends in a vowel. The vowel has a long vowel sound, as in the first syllable of *acorn*. On the syllable tag, the open door represents an open syllable. In an open syllable, there is nothing after the vowel. The vowel is "open."

Name Game

A **Name Game**, or VCE, syllable is typically found at the end of a word. The final e is silent and makes the previous vowel long, as in the word *name*. On the syllable tag, the vowel and Silent E are at a party. Silent E asks the vowel what its name is, and the vowel says its name.

Vowel Team

A **Vowel Team** syllable has two vowels next to each other that together say a new sound, as in the word *south*. On the syllable tag, the team of horses represents a Vowel Team syllable. Just as a team of horses works together, vowel teams work together to make one sound.

Bossy R

A **Bossy R** syllable contains a vowel followed by the letter r. The r controls the vowel and changes the way it is pronounced, as in the words *her*, *car*, and *firm*. On the syllable tag, the Bossy R syllable is represented by a bossy-looking r letter tile.

Pickle

A **Pickle** syllable contains three letters: consonant + l + e. Examples include the second syllable in the words *handle*, *puzzle*, and *middle*. The second syllable in the word *pickle* is a memorable example of this syllable type.

APPENDIX E
Syllable Division Rules

The first three syllable division rules are taught in Level 2. Remember to keep multiletter phonograms together when dividing words.

Division Rule	Other Words	First Taught In
Compound Words Rule Divide compound words into smaller words. d u s t m o p	anthill, suntan, dishcloth, cobweb	Level 2, Lesson 6
Two Consonant Tiles Rule Point to the vowels. If there are two consonant tiles between them, we usually divide between the consonants. n a p k i n	insect, contest, invent, muffin, upset	Level 2, Lesson 6
One Consonant Tile Rule **Part 1:** Point to the vowels. If there is one consonant tile between them, we usually divide before the consonant. b r o k e n **Part 2:** If that doesn't make a real word, move the consonant tile to the first syllable. r o b i n p o ck e t	**Part 1:** belong, hotel, hero, protect, basic **Part 2:** cabin, habit, seven, blanket, rocket	**Part 1:** Level 2, Lesson 10 **Part 2:** Level 2, Lesson 12
Two Vowel Tiles Rule When two vowel tiles are together, divide between them. d i e t	poet, meow, duet, create	Level 3, Lesson 2

Division Rule	Other Words	First Taught In
Pickle Syllables Rule When a word ends in a Pickle syllable, count back three letters from the end and divide. s t a p l e	pickle, sample, middle, candle, uncle	Level 3, Lesson 8
Three Consonant Tiles Rule **Part 1:** Point to the vowels. If there are three consonant tiles between them, we usually divide after the first consonant. ch i l d r e n **Part 2:** If that doesn't make a real word, divide after the second consonant. p u m p k i n	**Part 1:** monster, hundred, pilgrim, explode **Part 2:** sandwich	Level 3, Lesson 12
Suffixes Rule **Consonant suffixes** form their own syllables, with the exception of suffix *s*. g r a c e ful b ea k s **Vowel suffixes** usually form their own syllables, although they often grab the preceding consonant. s w i m m er w a v ing	**Consonant suffixes:** careful, quickly, sadness, movement **Vowel suffixes:** colder, jumping, biggest, sandy	Level 3, Lessons 13 and 15
Prefixes Rule Divide after a prefix. pre p l a n	mistake, nonsense, overdue, recharge	Level 3, Lesson 35

APPENDIX F
Jobs of Silent E

When you see e at the end of a word, it is usually a Silent E. But just because we don't pronounce the e doesn't mean it isn't doing a job.

★ The starred jobs are very common. The jobs without stars are not nearly as common.

Job	Explanation	First Taught In	Other Words
1 ★	Silent E can make the vowel before it long. g a m e Silent E does this job in 50% of words ending in e.	Level 2, Lesson 14	made, joke, cute, smile, white
2 ★	Silent E can make c and g soft. f e n c e ch ar g e	Level 2, Lessons 39 and 42	dance, prince, spruce, hinge, orange, large
3 ★	Silent E keeps u and v from being the last letter in a word. c l u e g i v e English words don't end in i, j, u, or v.	Level 2, Lesson 44	have, glue, argue, live, nerve
4 ★	Silent E shows that the word is not plural. r i n s r i n s e	Level 2, Lesson 46	dense, lapse, close, tease, house, nurse
5 ★	Silent E adds a vowel to a Pickle syllable. a p p l e Every syllable needs a vowel.	Level 3, Lesson 8	title, table, chuckle, candle, jungle, maple
6	Silent E makes th say its second sound, /th/. t ee th e b a th e	Level 3, Lesson 25	clothe, breathe, wreathe, loathe
7	Silent E clarifies the meaning of the word. b y b y e aw aw e	Level 3, Lesson 41	ew/ewe, ow/owe, or/ore

- Silent E can be added to Rule Breakers, such as *come, are, where, shoe, were,* and *one*. In these words, the reason for Silent E isn't obvious.
- Silent E can do two jobs in a word. For example, in the word *race*, Silent E makes the a long and makes the c soft. Other examples of two jobs include *hive, mice, trace, page,* and *cage*.

APPENDIX G
Ways to Spell Long Vowel Sounds

Method	Examples	First Taught In
Put a vowel at the end of a syllable. A vowel can be long when it is placed at the end of a syllable. In the word *we*, for example, the vowel e̲ is at the end of the syllable, and it says /ē/.	i tem pa per no ble pre vent	Level 1, Lesson 52
Add Silent E to the end of the word. Silent E can make the preceding vowel long.	note whole spine compete	Level 2, Lesson 14
Use a vowel team. A long vowel sound can be made using a vowel team. Vowel teams are two vowels that work together to make one sound.	pie feet boat main	Level 2, Lesson 25
Put i̲ or o̲ before two consonants. Vowels i̲ and o̲ can be long before two consonants.	roll mind hold child	Level 2, Lesson 29

APPENDIX H
How to Handle the Schwa Sound

What Is the Schwa Sound?

The schwa sound is the most common vowel sound in English and occurs in unaccented syllables. It is represented by an upside-down e symbol (ə), which you've probably seen when looking up words in the dictionary.

When speaking, you use the schwa sound without even being aware of it. Say these words aloud and listen to the sound the underlined vowels make:

a ➔ pleasant
e ➔ problem
i ➔ stencil
o ➔ parrot

In each of these words, the underlined vowel in the unaccented syllable makes a quick and muffled /uh/ sound instead of the clear sound taught on the Phonogram Cards. Now go back and read these same words with a clear vowel sound. The pronunciation seems unnatural, doesn't it?

The Challenge for Students

If you pronounce the word *button* with a short o sound in the second syllable, as in /bŭt–tŏn/, you'll sound like a robot and listeners may have a hard time understanding you. Since many vowels in speech don't have a clear vowel sound, we have to be prepared to make slight adjustments and use the schwa sound in order to "say it like a word."

If your student has difficulty sounding out a word that contains the schwa sound, use an activity called "Say It Like a Word," which helps the student get used to the idea that we often don't use pure vowel sounds when we read. Note that you don't need to introduce the term *schwa*, as that would be confusing to most students.

"Say It Like a Word" Activity

This activity may have to be repeated several times a day for many days in a row, so don't be discouraged if your student doesn't "get it" right away.

1. Choose a word that is in your student's oral vocabulary, such as *problem*. Say the word to your student as if you were a robot, without using the schwa sound: /prŏb–lĕm/.

2. Have your student "say it like a word" by repeating the word in normal speech.

Once your student is proficient at repeating the words using the schwa sound, you can remind him to use this activity as he reads to help decode unfamiliar words. Soon you'll be able to remind your student to "say it like a word" and he'll correct himself.

APPENDIX I
How to Assemble Word Flippers

Word Flippers are a fun way for your student to practice fluency. Follow these steps to assemble and use them in your lessons.

1. Remove the appropriate pages from the activity book. Cut apart the pages on the dotted lines.

2. Put the larger pieces of paper on the bottom. Stack the smaller pieces on top. Note that some Word Flippers will be stacked on the left side and some on the right side.

3. Staple the Word Flipper along the left or right side, as indicated.

4. Have your student turn the pages and read the words that are formed.

APPENDIX J
List of Comprehension Activities

Pre- and post-reading comprehension activities are included in every story-related lesson in Level 2. Depending on your student's needs and interests, you may choose to use some of these additional activities.

Pre-Reading Discussions and Activities

- Before your student reads, skim the story and note possible **vocabulary** words your student may not know. Introduce them briefly before your student reads the story.
- Activate **prior knowledge** by asking one or two questions related to the story. For example, a question for "The Grump" might be *Have you ever watched a caterpillar make a cocoon?* Follow the questions with a brief discussion of your student's experiences.
- Show the title page. Based on the title and any illustration that appears there, discuss what the story might be about.
- Make **predictions** about the story by asking story-specific questions. For example, questions for "Matt the Musk Ox" might include *What do you think might happen if a musk ox met a dog by a lake? Do you think they would be friends?*
- Discuss the **setting** of the story. If the story is set in a new or unusual place, use a globe or map to introduce the place to your student.
- Relate the story to your student's own experiences. Questions you might ask include *Have you ever helped a friend solve a problem? Have you ever built anything from scratch?* Questions may also be story-specific: *What are some reasons you might not want a skunk to move into your garage? What would you do if it happened?*
- Introduce any **literary devices** used in the story, such as onomatopoeia, alliteration, and rhyme. Have your student keep his eyes open for these devices while reading the story.

Post-Reading Discussions and Activities

- Discuss the **main character** of the story. Who is the main character in this story? What is the character's problem? How does he feel about it? What does he do about it? How does he feel by the end of the story? How has he changed?
- Discuss the main **conflict** of the story. What problem does the main character face? What does the character do to solve the conflict? Does the character's solution work? What would you have done if you were the character?

- Practice meaningful expression. When reading **dialogue**, demonstrate for your student how you can change your tone of voice to reflect how the character is feeling. For example, if the character is frustrated, you could read "I'm at my wits' end!" in a frustrated voice. Then let the student give it a try.

- Skim through the story and ask **comprehension questions** that require more than a yes or no answer. Types of questions you might ask include *Why do you think the character said that? Does the character look upset or happy? What does your face look like when you're upset? Why do you think the character did that? What happened after the character left home?*

- Have your student **skim the story** for information about a question you ask. For example, a question for "Storm in the North" might be *Which animals were sleeping during the big storm?*

- Relate the story to your student's own experiences. Questions you might ask include *What would you do if you were this character? How would you solve the problem? What are some things you could do to raise money (or help a friend, or join a spy club, and so on)?*

- Connect the story to other literature the student has read. Talk about similarities in **theme**, conflict, setting, or character between stories.

- Imagine an **alternate ending** for the story. For example, questions for "Open Rink" might include *What would have happened if Chick and her friends hadn't won the hockey game? How would that have changed the outcome of the story?*

- Practice **story sequencing**. Choose three action sentences from the story and write them on separate slips of paper. Have your student read the sentences and place them in the correct order as they happened in the story.

- Talk about **similarities and differences** between characters or settings in the story. For setting, the student could also compare the story setting to his own location.

- Discuss how authors often use the **five senses** of sight, hearing, touch, smell, and taste in their writing. Encourage your student to go back through the story and point out places that appeal to any of the senses.

- Talk about **realism** and **fantasy**. Which parts of the story could have happened? Which parts could not have happened? Why?

APPENDIX K

Tips and Activities for Using the Practice Sheets

Fluency is the ability to read smoothly, accurately, and with expression, and the Practice Sheets are an important part of developing your student's fluency. But students don't always find the Practice Sheets as exciting as the other hands-on activities in the lessons.

If working on Practice Sheets becomes a chore for you and your student, try some of the following games and creative activities to make them fun again.

Be sure to photocopy the Practice Sheets before playing games that require the pages to be cut into strips or single words.

Games and Activities

Feed the monster. Cut out the monster on page 407. Cut the Practice Sheets into strips. Have your student feed the strips to the monster as he reads them. For a fun alternative, go to blog.allaboutlearningpress.com/feed-the-puppy-alphabet-game to download our Feed the Puppy printable.

Number the rows of words and sentences on the Practice Sheet from 1 to 6, repeating those numbers as necessary. Have the student roll a die and read the words or sentences in the row of the number he rolled. For example, if he rolls a 2, he must read the words in row 2.

Read with a buddy. Take turns reading lines with your student, or let her read with a favorite stuffed animal or toy.

Use sticker dots. Break up the assignment and reduce your student's frustration by creating a "starting dot" and a "stopping dot."

Play hide and seek with words and sentences. Cut up the Practice Sheets and hide the pieces around the room. When the student finds a piece, he must read it before searching for the next piece.

Use an online word search puzzle maker to create your own word search puzzle using your student's fluency words. Have the student read the words as she finds them.

Choose a letter and have your student search for and read only words that begin with that particular letter.

Play Swat the Words. Cut out the splat graphic on page 409. Attach it to an object to use as a swatter, such as a new flyswatter, a plastic ruler, or even just your student's hand. Cut out words from the Practice Sheet and lay them on the table. Have your student find and swat each word as you read it out loud. Then switch—you swat while your student reads.

Break up the Practice Sheet by covering it with a piece of paper. Slide the paper down to uncover one line or section at a time.

Make progress more concrete. Allow your student to track progress using colored highlighters or fun stickers.

Play Fluency Hopscotch. Write fluency words in each square of a hopscotch grid. Gather a different marker for each student, such as a beanbag, stone, or bottle cap. Follow the standard rules, but when the student stops to pick up his marker, he reads the word(s).

Play Fluency Snowball Fight. Cut up the Practice Sheets into strips and tape them to the wall. Have your student read the fluency words. After each strip is read correctly, have him stand back and throw a snowball at it! Use Ping-Pong balls, Nerf balls, styrofoam balls, or even crumpled paper for snowballs.

Art and Creative Play

Make a word road. Cut the rows of words into long strips. Place the strips on a long table or on the floor to make a road. Have your student drive a matchbox car over the words as he reads them.

Illustrate the words. Select a few words and have your student draw a picture for each one. She may then make a collage of the words and pictures.

Silly sentences. Have your student read a word and then make up a silly sentence using the word.

Have fun with emotions! Cut out the emojis on page 411. Put the faces in a hat. Cut out the words and sentences from the Practice Sheet and put those in another hat. Have your student pick a word/sentence from one hat, pick a face from the other hat, and then ham it up by reading the word with the selected emotion.

Snacks and Rewards

Eat your words! Motivate your student to read each row of the Practice Sheet by putting a chocolate chip, marshmallow, M&M, popcorn, granola, fruit, or other favorite treat at the end of a section or row. At the end of the practice session, snuggle up with a story and munch on the rest of the snack.

Set up a points system in the corner of your white board or on a separate chart and give your student a small prize when she reaches 100 points. For example, you might give your student one point for every correct word she can read in five minutes. You might combine the points system with Phonogram Card and Word Card review as well so your student has more chances to rack up points. There are many point variations, so use what works best for you.

Positive Words

Fluent reading is hard work for your student! Catch him working hard and give him a few words of encouragement. Try positive words like these:

"Very good! You are a quick learner!"
"Hey, you got that the first time!"
"You are doing great!"
"That was a tough one, and you got it!"
"You remembered that from yesterday—great!"
"I can tell that you tried hard to figure that out."

> Many of the tips and activities in Appendices K, L, and M can be mixed and matched to review Practice Sheets, Phonogram Cards, or Word Cards. **Tip!**

Feed the Monster

Instructions: Print the monster and cut a slit in its mouth. Cut your Practice Sheet into strips. Have your student read each strip aloud and "feed" it to the monster as it is completed.

Swat the Words

Instructions: Cut out the splat graphic and attach it to an object to use as a swatter. Cut out words from the Practice Sheet and lay them on the table. Have your student find and swat each word as you read it out loud.

Fun with Emotions

Instructions: Cut out the emojis and place them in a hat. Cut out the words and sentences from the Practice Sheet and put those in another hat. Have your student pick a word/sentence from one hat, pick a face from the other hat, and then ham it up by reading the word with the selected emotion.

Activities for Reviewing Phonograms

Games and Activities

Play Fun with Phonograms. Go to info.allaboutlearningpress.com/fun-with-phonograms to download five free folder games to use for reviewing Phonogram Cards.

Play Swat the Phonograms. Cut out the splat graphic on page 409. Attach it to an object to use as a swatter, such as a new flyswatter, a plastic ruler, or even just your student's hand. Cut out words from the Practice Sheet and lay them on the table. Have your student find and swat each phonogram as you say the sounds. Then switch—you swat while your student says the sounds.

Play Phonogram Bingo. Download our Phonogram Bingo cards at blog.allaboutlearning press.com/phonogram-bingo, or make your own bingo cards with a selection of review phonograms.

Play Phonogram Go Fish. Choose ten to fifteen phonograms to practice. Use index cards to make up two identical sets of cards. Play according to the regular rules.

Play Phonogram Snowball Fight. Write a selection of review phonograms on index cards and tape them to the wall. As you call out phonograms, have your student locate the phonogram on the wall, say the sound(s), and throw a snowball at it. Use Ping-Pong balls, Nerf balls, styrofoam balls, or even crumpled paper for snowballs.

Jump on it! Write a selection of review phonograms on index cards and spread them around the floor. Have your student locate and jump to the correct phonogram as you call out the sound(s).

Play Phonogram Hopscotch. Write a different phonogram in each square of a hopscotch grid. Gather a different marker for each student, such as a beanbag, stone, or bottle cap. Follow the standard rules, but when the student stops to pick up his marker, he says the sound(s) of the phonogram in that square.

Play Phonogram Ball. Use a marker to write phonograms on a large beach ball. Have the student throw the ball in the air, catch it, and then say the sound(s) of the phonograms closest to his thumbs.

Art and Creative Play

Stamp it. If you have letter stamps, use them to reinforce the phonogram of the day. After teaching a phonogram, use the stamps to stamp the phonogram on the back of your student's hand. Refer to it throughout the day, asking what the phonogram is, what sound(s) it makes, and so on.

Color it. Look for coloring book pages with big spaces and write review phonograms in those spaces. Have the student say the sound(s) of each phonogram. If she says the sound(s) correctly, she may color that space. Continue until the picture is complete.

Build a Phonogram Card city. Create a city in your living room by arranging the Phonogram Cards face up on the floor and furniture so that every Phonogram Card is a building. Have your student drive around the city, saying the sound(s) of the phonograms as he arrives at each building. If he says the sound(s) correctly, turn that card face down. The game continues until all the cards have been turned face down.

Make a salt tray. Fill a baking pan, jelly roll pan, or other shallow container with salt or sand. Have your student write phonograms in the salt tray with the pointer finger of the dominant hand. Gently shake the salt tray to "erase" phonograms. For added fun, experiment with different colors and scents. Go to blog.allaboutlearningpress.com/salt-trays for recipes.

Create a race track. Line up the Phonogram Cards to form a "track." Place a toy car on the first card. Have your student say the sound(s) of the Phonogram Card. If he says it correctly, he can drive his car to the next Phonogram Card, and so on until he arrives at the finish line.

Snacks and Rewards

Play Phonogram Cup Hunt. Choose five to seven review phonograms, write them on mailing labels, and attach the labels to plastic cups. Under one of the cups, place a small wrapped treat, like a few raisins or chocolate chips in plastic wrap, and then have your student close her eyes as you mix up the cups. Have your student open her eyes, choose a cup, say the sound(s) of the phonogram on the cup, and lift the cup. Continue playing until she finds the treat.

Play Snack Track. Use the Phonogram Cards to make a snack track on your floor. Place a small snack next to each card. Starting at the beginning of the track, have your student hop forward one space and say the sound(s) of the phonogram. If he says the sound(s) correctly, he gets to eat the snack and advance to the next card. If incorrect, he must move back two spaces and try again.

APPENDIX M
Activities for Reviewing Word Cards

Games and Activities

Play Swat the Words. Cut out the splat graphic on page 409. Attach it to an object to use as a swatter, such as a new flyswatter, a plastic ruler, or even just your student's hand. Choose a selection of Word Cards and lay them on the table. Have your student find and swat each word as you read it out loud. Then switch—you swat while your student reads.

Have your student type a selection of words on the computer. This activity is especially good for kids who struggle with handwriting.

Play Word Card Slapjack. Designate one word as the "jack" and then deal out a stack of cards to two players. Play as you would Slapjack, slapping the "jack" as it comes up. Play several times, changing the "jack" card each time. To make it more challenging, have the student say the word every time he lays down a card.

Guess the Word. Lay down two Word Cards at a time and have your student read one of the cards. You then "guess" which one she read. Be sure to guess wrong now and then! Switch sides and let your student guess which word you read.

Use favorite family board games for Word Card review. Pull out games like Sorry! or Candy Land and have each player read a word before his or her turn.

Play Word Card Concentration. Choose ten to fifteen review words. Use index cards to make two identical sets of cards, and then play according to the regular rules.

Play Fun with Word Cards. Go to info.allaboutlearningpress.com/fun-with-phonograms to download five free folder games. Instead of Phonogram Cards, use Word Cards for review.

Play Bingo. Download our Phonogram Bingo cards at blog.allaboutlearningpress.com/phonogram-bingo, but use Word Cards instead of phonograms. Or make your own bingo cards with a selection of review words.

Play Go Fish. Choose ten to fifteen Word Cards to practice. Use index cards to make up two identical sets of cards. Play according to the regular rules.

Art and Creative Play

Tell a story. Lay out a selection of review words and have your student make up a silly story using all the words. It's okay if it doesn't make sense; in fact, it probably won't!

Illustrate the words. Select a few words and have your student draw a picture for each one. She may then make a collage of the words and pictures.

Color it. Look for coloring book pages with big spaces and write review words in those spaces. Have the student read each word. If read correctly, she may color that space. Continue until the picture is complete.

Create a racetrack. Line up the Word Cards to form a "track." Place a toy car on the first card. Have your student read the Word Card. If he reads it correctly, he can drive his car to the next Word Card, and so on until he arrives at the finish line.

Glue the Feed the Monster graphic from page 407 to an empty cereal box and cut a hole where the mouth is. Have your student read the Word Cards and feed them to the monster. You might also use the monster box as an alternative storage place for the mastered cards. Or go to blog.allaboutlearningpress.com/feed-the-puppy-alphabet-game to download our Feed the Puppy printable.

Create a colorful word cloud. Choose a selection of review words and have your student write each one several times, each time using a different color marker. Create the cloud on a light-colored piece of construction paper. Encourage your student to vary the direction and size of each word.

Snacks and Rewards

Snack stacks. Select fifteen review words and place them in five piles of three in front of your student. Place some chocolate chips, marshmallows, M&Ms, popcorn, granola, fruit, or other favorite treat behind each stack of cards. Have your student choose a stack and read the words. If she reads them correctly, she may enjoy the snack from that stack. Continue until all the words have been read correctly, and all the snacks eaten!

Play Yucky Snacks. Select fifteen review words and have your student use them to make up "Silly Recipes for Yucky Snacks." For example, the recipe might be to add three cups of *grass*, mix in a tablespoon of *rat*, and garnish with some *bells*. Don't forget to have your student name her creation at the end—and then go make a *real* snack to celebrate.

APPENDIX N
If Your Student Struggles with the Stories

Do any of these situations sound familiar?

- Your student has trouble reading an entire story in one sitting.
- Your student sees how many pages a story is and feels discouraged before he begins.
- Your student has a decoding special need.

If so, it's important to be proactive and tackle the problem head-on so you can maintain your student's motivation to read. Here are some suggestions.

- **Review.** Spend more time reviewing with the flashcards, activities, and Practice Sheets before reading the story. The more familiar the student is with the words, the easier it will be to read the story.

- **Set a timer.** Have your student read until the timer goes off. Choose the length of time according to your student's ability. You may need to start with a short time, such as three minutes, and then gradually build up to ten minutes.

- **Divide the story into two or three parts.** Have your student read just one section in a sitting. Bookmark the page. At the next reading session, have your student listen as you reread the part he has already read, and then have him continue reading on his own.

- **Reread.** Rereading stories from previous lessons will help your student gain fluency.

- **Try buddy reading.** Split up the reading duties by reading with your student. Alternate pages by reading a page yourself and then having your student read the next. For even more practice, you might read the story three times by buddy reading twice, switching the pages you each read, and having your student read the story on his own the third time.

  Younger students may enjoy buddy reading with Ziggy the Zebra puppet or another favorite puppet or stuffed animal.

- **Practice blending to eliminate word guessing.** Sometimes students struggle because they guess at words rather than try to decode them. The best solution for word guessing is to use the blending (or decoding) procedure in Appendix C.

- **Check for vision problems.** Be alert to vision problems that may be interfering with your student's ability to read fluently. Some signs to watch for include:

  - frequent eye rubbing, blinking, or squinting
  - short attention span
  - avoiding reading and other close activities
  - frequent headaches
  - covering one eye
  - tilting the head to one side
  - holding reading materials close to the face
  - an eye turning in or out
  - seeing double
  - losing place when reading
  - difficulty remembering what he or she read

APPENDIX O

Magnet Board Setup at the End of Level 2

In Level 2, your student learns twelve new phonograms. If you are using a magnetic white board instead of the Letter Tiles app, you will add the letter tiles to your board as they are taught and as indicated in the lessons.

At the end of Level 2, your white board will look like the illustration below. This is also how your white board will be set up when you begin Level 3.

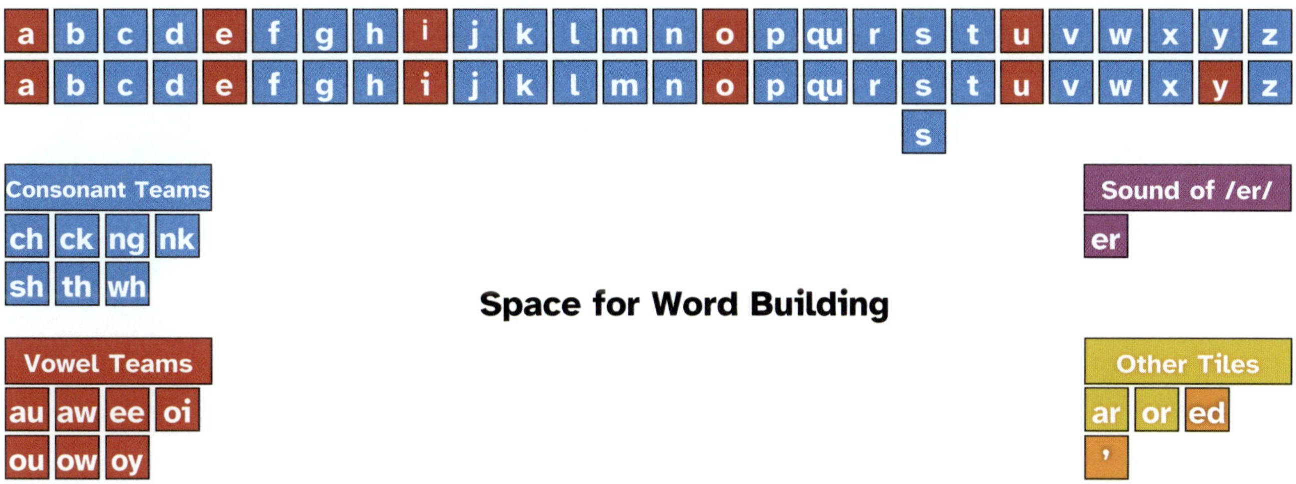

In future levels, more letter tiles will be added to the board, organized under the following category:

Sound of /sh/

APPENDIX P

Leap Words Taught in Level 2

Leap Words are high-frequency words that either don't follow the normal rules or contain phonograms that your student hasn't practiced yet. Your student will be "leaping ahead" to learn these words as sight words. They are indicated on the Word Cards by the leaping frog.

There are thirty-two Leap Words in Level 2.

Leap Word	Lesson	Why Taught as a Leap Word	True Rule Breaker?
you	2	The ou phonogram has not been taught yet.	No
are	2	The ar phonogram and Silent E have not been taught yet.	No
from	4	The o says /ŭ/, which has not been taught yet.	No
your	4	The letters o-u-r work together to say /or/, which has not been taught yet.	No
have	6	Includes Silent E, which has not been taught yet.	No
her	8	The er phonogram has not been taught yet.	No
some, something, come	19	The o says its fourth sound, /ŭ/. The Silent E doesn't make the o say its name.	Yes
what	19	The a doesn't say the sound we expect it to.	Yes
pony	23	The letter y often says /ē/ at the end of two-syllable words, which has not been taught yet.	No
sandwich	23	This word follows a syllable division rule that has not been taught yet.	No
been	25	In many regions, the ee doesn't say the sound we expect it to.	Yes

Leap Word	Lesson	Why Taught as a Leap Word	True Rule Breaker?
who	29	Wh says /h/ instead of /hw/ as we expect it to. The o says the third sound of o, /o͞o/.	Yes
move	29	The o says /o͞o/ instead of /ō/.	Yes
done, none	31	These words contain the fourth sound of o, which has not been taught yet.	No
one	31	The o says /wŭ/, which is unusual.	Yes
warm	33	In many regions, the ar doesn't say the sound we expect it to.	Yes
Mr., Mrs.	33	Abbreviations of ***mister*** and ***missus.***	No
too	33	The two o's say /o͞o/, which has not been taught yet.	No
where, there	37	The letters e-r-e don't say the sound we expect them to.	Yes
pumpkin	42	This word follows a syllable division rule that has not been taught yet.	No
oh	46	The h is silent.	Yes
they	48	This word contains ey, which has not been taught yet.	No
two	50	The w is silent and the o says its third sound, which has not been taught yet.	Yes
were	52	Silent E doesn't have a job in this word.	Yes
aunt	54	In some regions, the au doesn't say the sound we expect it to.	Yes
any, many	56	The a doesn't say the sound we expect it to, and the y says the fourth sound of y, which has not been taught yet.	Yes

APPENDIX Q

Words Taught in Level 2

The number listed corresponds with the lesson in which the word is first introduced.

A

absent ... 6
ace ... 40
acorn ... 35
admit ... 6
after ... 31
age ... 42
all ... 50
amber ... 31
any ... 56
anything ... 56
are ... 2
aren't ... 27
argue ... 44
arm ... 33
armrest ... 33
art ... 33
asked ... 48
aster ... 31
ate ... 14
audit ... 54
August ... 54
aunt ... 54
auto ... 54

B

backbone ... 21
backfire ... 21
backslide ... 21
backstage ... 42
bacon ... 37
bake ... 15
baked ... 48
ball ... 50
ballpoint ... 52
bankroll ... 29
bantam ... 7
banter ... 31
barber ... 33
bare ... 15
barge ... 42
bark ... 33
barked ... 48
barn ... 33
barnyard ... 33
base ... 15
baseball ... 50
basket ... 6
bawk ... 54
bawl ... 54
became ... 15
because ... 54
bedpost ... 29
bedroll ... 29
bedtime ... 15
bee ... 25
beef ... 25
beeline ... 25
been ... 25
beep ... 25
beet ... 25
before ... 15
began ... 10
begin ... 10
begun ... 10
behind ... 29
belong ... 10
berth ... 31
beside ... 15
better ... 31
bike ... 15
bikes ... 23
billfold ... 29
bind ... 29
bite ... 14
bites ... 23
blade ... 21
blame ... 21
bland ... 2
blanket ... 12
blare ... 21
blast ... 2
blaze ... 21
bleed ... 25
blend ... 2
blimp ... 2
blind ... 29
blister ... 31
blockbuster ... 31
blond ... 2
blue ... 44
bluebell ... 44
bluefish ... 44
blueprint ... 44
blunder ... 31
blunt ... 2
boil ... 52
bold ... 29
bolt ... 29
bone ... 15
bones ... 23
bonnet ... 6
bonus ... 10
bore ... 15
bored ... 48
born ... 35
both ... 29
bound ... 56
boy ... 52
brace ... 40
brake ... 21
brakes ... 23
branch ... 2
brand ... 2
brave ... 21
brawl ... 54
brawn ... 54
breeze ... 25
Brent ... 2
bribe ... 21
bride ... 21
brine ... 21
brisk ... 2
broil ... 52
broke ... 21
broken ... 10
brother ... 46
brow ... 56
brown ... 56
brunt ... 2
brute ... 21
bucket ... 12
bulge ... 42
bull ... 37
bulldog ... 37
bullfrog ... 37
bumped ... 48
bush ... 37
butter ... 31
butterfly ... 31
buttermilk ... 31
button ... 37
buzzed ... 48
by ... 4
bylaw ... 54
bypass ... 4

C

cabin ... 12
cactus ... 6
cage ... 42
cake ... 15
cakes ... 23
call ... 50
came ... 15
campfire ... 15
campground ... 56
campsite ... 15
can't ... 27
cane ... 14
canteen ... 25
cape ... 15
car ... 33
card ... 33
cardstock ... 33
care ... 15
cared ... 48
carefree ... 25
cares ... 23
caretaker ... 31
carp ... 33
carpet ... 33
carport ... 35
cart ... 33
carve ... 44
case ... 15
cause ... 54
cave ... 15
caw ... 54
cell ... 39
cement ... 39
cent ... 39
center ... 39
champ ... 24
chance ... 39
change ... 42
changed ... 48
charge ... 42
charm ... 33
chart ... 33
chase ... 15
checkmate ... 21
cheek ... 25
cheer ... 25
cheerless ... 25
cheese ... 46
chicken ... 7
chide ... 15
child ... 29
chime ... 15
chipmunk ... 6
chive ... 15
choice ... 52
choke ... 15
chore ... 15
chores ... 23
chose ... 17
cider ... 39
cinder ... 39
clamp ... 2
clapped ... 48
Clare ... 24
clasp ... 2
claw ... 54
cleft ... 2
clench ... 2
clerk ... 31
clockwise ... 17
clone ... 21
close ... 21

liked 48
likes 23
likewise 21
limestone 21
limit 12
line 15
live (long i) 15
live (short i) 44
liver 31
locate 21
locked 48
lone 15
lore 15
loud 56
loudmouth 56
love 46
lumber 31
lunge 42

M

made 14
magnet 6
make 15
makes 23
makeshift 21
male 15
mall 50
mane 15
mankind 29
many 56
March 33
mare 15
margin 42
mark 33
marked 48
marvel 33
mascot 6
master 31
maze 15
meek 25
meet 25
member 31
method 12
mice 40
Mike 15
mild 29
mile 15
miles 23
milkweed 25
mince 39
mind 29
mine 15
minus 10
mitten 6
mixed 48
modern 31
modest 12
moist 52
mold 29
molt 29
moment 10
more 15
moreover 31
morning 35
most 29
motel 10
mothball 50
mother 46
mouth 56
move 29
Mr. 33
Mrs. 33
muffin 6
mule 17
Mum 20
muse 17
mustang 6
mute 17
my 4
myself 4

N

name 15
named 48
names 23
namesake 21
napkin 6
Nate 16
need 25
needed 48
nerve 44
never 31
nice 40
nine 15
noise 52
none 31
nor 35
north 35
nose 17
note 14
notepad 15
notes 23
nothing 46
noun 56
now 56
number 31
nutcracker 31
nutmeg 6

O

object 6
o'clock 27
oh 46
oil 52
oink 52
old 29
omit 10
one 31
open 10
or 35
orange 42
orbit 35
order 35
ostrich 9
other 46
ouch 56
ounce 56
our 56
out 56
outbid 56
outcast 56
outfit 56
outfox 56
outlaw 56
outnumber 56
outpost 56
outrage 56
outrun 56
outshine 56
outside 56
outsider 56
outsmart 56
over 31
owl 56
oxen 12
oyster 52

P

pace 40
page 42
pale 14
pancake 15
paper 31
paperback 31
paperclip 31
park 33
part 33
passed 48
patent 12
pattern 31
pause 54
pave 15
paw 54
pawn 54
peek 25
peeled 48
peep 25
peer 25
pencil 39
pepper 31
perhaps 31
perk 31
permit 31
person 37
Pete 14
picnic 6
pike 15
pile 15
piled 48
piles 23
pine 14
pines 23
pinpoint 52
pipe 15
pipeline 21
piper 31
pipes 23
place 40
plane 21
planes 23
planet 12
plant 2
planted 48
planter 31
plastic 6
plate 21
plates 23
plow 56
ploy 52
plume 21
plump 2
plunge 42
ply 4
pocket 12
point 52
poise 52
poke 15
pole 15
poles 23
polite 21
poll 29
pony 23
popcorn 35
popover 31
porch 35
pork 35
port 35
porthole 35
pose 17
post 29
postcard 33
postman 29
potent 10
pothole 21
pouch 56
pounce 56
pound 56
pout 56
powder 56
power 56
prance 39
preen 25
prepare 21
pretend 10
prevent 10
price 40
pride 21
prime 21
primp 2
prince 39
princess 39
print 2
printed 48
prize 21
prizes 23
problem 6
produce 39
prone 21
proper 31
prose 21
protect 10
proud 56

prune 21
pry 4
publish 6
pull 37
pulled 48
pullover 31
pumpkin 42
puppet 6
pure 17
push 37
put 37

Q

quake 15
queen 25
quite 14
quote 15

R

rabbit 6
race 40
raced 48
radish 12
rage 42
ragtime 21
ragweed 25
rake 15
raked 48
range 42
rare 15
rate 14
raw 54
rawhide 54
recent 39
reed 25
reef 25
refund 10
rejoice 52
relax 10
relive 44
remember 33
rented 48
request 10
rescue 44
revenge 42
revert 31
rice 40
ride 14
rides 23
rigid 42
ringmaster 31
ringside 21
rinse 46
ripe 14
ripen 10
rise 17
river 31
riverside 31
robber 31
robe 14
robin 12
robot 10
rocket 12
rode 14
rodent 10
roll 29
rope 15
ropes 23
rose 17
round 56
roundup 56
rubber 31
rubdown 56
Ruben 32
rude 17
rule 17
ruler 31
rules 23
rushed 48

S

sadness 57
safe 15
sage 42
sake 15
sale 15
sales 23
same 14
sandpaper 31
sandstone 21
sandstorm 35
sandwich 23
sauce 54
saucepan 54
save 15
saved 48
saw 54
sawdust 54
sawmill 54
scale 21
scalp 2
scamp 2
scamper 31
scant 2
scar 33
scare 21
scared 48
scares 23
scone 21
scope 21
score 21
scorn 35
scout 56
scowl 56
scram 8
scrap 8
scrape 21
screen 25
scrimp 8
script 8
scroll 29
scrub 8
secret 32
see 25
seed 25
seek 25
seem 25
seen 25
seep 25
seesaw 54
selfish 18
server 31
seven 12
seventeen 25
shade 15
shake 15
shaken 10
shakes 23
shame 15
shape 15
share 15
shark 33
sharp 33
shave 15
shawl 54
she'll 27
she's 27
sheen 25
sheep 25
sheer 25
sheet 25
shelter 31
shimmer 31
shine 14
shined 48
shines 23
shipmate 15
shipyard 33
shiver 31
shore 15
shorn 35
short 35
shortcake 35
shorthand 35
shortstop 35
shout 56
shove 46
shovel 46
shower 56
shrimp 2
shy 4
side 15
sidekick 21
sidelong 21
sides 23
sidestep 21
sidetrack 21
silent 10
silver 31
silverware 31
simmer 31
since 39
singe 42
siren 10
sister 31
site 15
sixteen 25
size 15
skate 21
sky 4
skylark 33
skyline 21
slant 2
slate 21
slave 21
sleep 25
sleet 25
slept 2
slice 40
slide 21
slides 23
slime 21
sliver 31
slope 21
slump 2
sly 4
small 50
smart 33
smile 21
smiled 48
smiles 23
smoke 21
smokestack 21
snake 21
snare 21
sneer 25
snore 21
snort 35
snout 56
softball 50
software 21
soil 52
sold 29
solve 44
some 19
something 19
somewhere 37
son 46
sore 15
sort 35
sorted 48
sound 56
soundtrack 56
south 56
southwest 56
space 40
spaceship 40
spade 21
spare 21
spark 33
speed 25
spellbound 56
spend 2
spent 2
spice 40
spider 31
spike 21
spilled 48
spine 21
spite 21
splash 8
splat 8

splint 8
split 8
spoil 52
spoke 21
spoken 10
sport 35
sportsman 35
sprang 8
sprawl 54
spree 25
sprig 8
spring 8
springtime 21
sprint 8
sprite 21
sprout 56
spruce 39
sprung 8
spry 8
spy 4
spyglass 4
square 21
squash 50
squawk 54
stage 42
stagehand 42
stake 21
stale 21
stall 50
stamp 2
stance 39
stand 2
standby 4
standpoint 52
star 33
stare 21
stared 48
stares 23
starfish 33
stark 33
start 33
started 48
starve 44
state 21
states 23
stateside 21
steed 25
steel 25
steep 25
steer 25
steered 48
stepladder 31
stepped 48
stockyard 33
stoke 21
stole 21
stomp 2
stone 21
stones 23
stopped 48
store 21
storekeeper 31
stores 23
stork 35
storm 35
stout 56
stove 21
stovepipe 21
strand 8
strap 8
straw 54
street 25
stress 8
strict 8
stride 21
strife 21
strike 21
strikeout 56
string 8
strip 8
stripe 21
stripes 23
strive 21
stroke 21
stroll 29
strong 8
struck 8
strum 8
strung 8
strut 8
student 10
stump 2
stunt 2
subject 6
sublime 21
sudden 6
Sue 44
summer 31
sundown 56
sunflower 56
sunrise 17
super 31
superman 31
supermarket 33
superstar 33
supper 31
support 35
suspect 6
swamp 50
sweep 25
sweet 25
swept 2
swift 2
swine 21

T

take 15
tale 15
talent 12
tales 23
tall 50
tame 15
Tang 20
tape 14
taped 48
tapped 48
tar 33
tarp 33
tart 33
taste 49
taunt 54
taut 54
teem 25
teen 25
teenage 42
teeth 25
telltale 21
temper 31
tender 31
term 31
tested 48
that's 27
thaw 54
there 37
these 17
they 48
thorn 35
those 17
three 25
thrift 2
thrive 21
throne 21
thunder 31
tide 15
tiger 31
tile 15
tiles 23
time 14
times 23
timeworn 35
timid 12
tire 15
tires 23
toil 52
toilet 52
told 29
toll 29
ton 46
tone 15
too 33
topsoil 52
tore 15
torn 35
town 56
township 56
townsman 56
toy 52
trace 40
trade 21
traded 48
trademark 33
trance 39
tree 25
trend 2
tribe 21
tricked 48
trike 21
trite 21
troll 29
tromp 2
trout 56
trove 21
truce 39
true 44
trump 2
trumpet 6
trust 2
trusted 48
try 4
tryout 56
tube 17
tune 17
tweed 25
tweet 25
twelve 44
twice 40
twine 21
twinge 42
twist 2
two 50

U

under 31
underarm 33
underbid 31
undercut 31
underdog 31
underline 31
underside 31
understand 31
understate 31
undertake 31
undertone 31
underwater 50
unit 10
unseen 25
until 6
update 15
upgrade 21
uphold 29
upkeep 25
upset 6
upstate 21
use 17
used 48

V

vacant 10
value 44
valve 44
vanish 12
vault 54
venue 44
verb 31
vice 40
vine 15
vines 23
visit 12
voice 52
void 52
vole 15
volt 29

– NOTES –

- NOTES -